THE IRISH DI

Fergal Tobin is a freelance writer and historian. Now retired, his career was in publishing and he was president of the Federation of European Publishers in Brussels from 2010 to 2012. Under the pen name Richard Killeen he is the author of several acclaimed works of Irish history, including *Ireland in Brick and Stone: The Island's History in Its* Buildings, *The Historic Atlas of Dublin* and *The Concise History of Modern Ireland*.

THE IRISH DIFFERENCE

The Story of Ireland's 400-Year
Journey to Independence

Fergal Tobin

Atlantic Books
London

First published in hardback in Great Britain in 2022 by Atlantic Books,
an imprint of Atlantic Books Ltd.

This paperback edition published in Great Britain in 2023 by Atlantic Books.

10 9 8 7 6 5 4 3

A CIP catalogue record for this book is available from the British Library.

Paperback ISBN: 978-1-83895-263-1
E-book ISBN: 978-1-83895-262-4

Printed in Great Britain by Clays Ltd, Elcograf S.p.A.

Atlantic Books
An imprint of Atlantic Books Ltd
Ormond House
26–27 Boswell Street
London WC1N 3JZ

This book is for Leo, Alex, DJ and Hugo: welcome, lads

CONTENTS

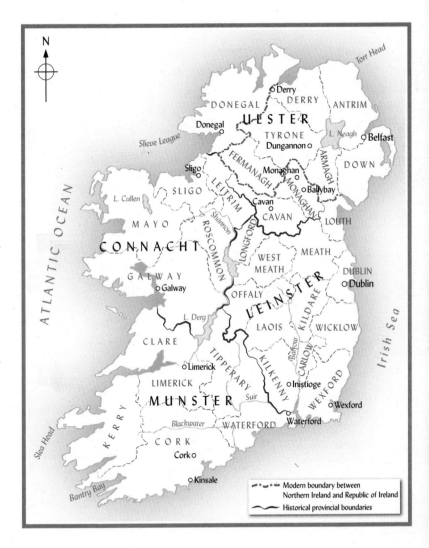

PREFACE

LIKE A LOT of books, this started out as something else. I was fascinated by the considerable number of travellers who visited Ireland, for one reason or another, in the sixty years before the catastrophic Great Famine of 1845–52. I thought that, in aggregate, their reports might yield a portrait of an utterly vanished world: pre-Famine, pre-industrial, pre-urban for the most part, and teeming with people. English travellers' accounts of Irish backwardness and poverty could too easily be dismissed as the cultural condescension of metropolitans for provincials, especially when the English had centuries of previous form in that regard. It was harder to play that card when French and German visitors were furnishing corroborating evidence. But they were also spotting things that the English tended to miss or minimize, such as the extraordinary bond of loyalty that subsisted between Catholic clergy and laity.

It might have made an interesting study of a pre-modern world, now otherwise lost to us and beyond imaginative recovery. But then, it suddenly ran into a new course for reasons that I can't quite recapture. But there is no doubt that Brexit was a proximate cause of change. Once the UK voted by plebiscite to leave the European Union, it was clear that no matter how the thing played out – and it played out nearly as badly as the worst pessimist might have supposed – it meant nothing but trouble for Ireland.

Yet the English – for it was they who carried the vote – never gave a moment's thought to Ireland. That was true from the top down. People in Ireland were perplexed by this. We simply *had* to be a crucial factor in the inevitably protracted negotiations with Brussels, but it was abundantly clear that the English knew nothing about our strategic position, or how it must inevitably affect the EU's negotiating strategy; indeed, they seemed to know nothing much about us at all.

This was amplified, if not actually confirmed, by a number of people I know in the tourism and hospitality business who reported on the astonishing ignorance of Ireland exhibited by some English visitors. My initial reaction was to say, well, what does even the average well-educated Paddy, let alone hoi polloi, know about Wales or Scotland? Could even a humanities graduate, with a good first-class degree, talk about either country's history or society coherently and extempore for more than five minutes without drying up? On the same basis, why should the English be expected to know all about us?

The relationship between England and Ireland is, of course, hugely asymmetrical and skewed towards the bigger island. English power, both hard and soft, has been a constant presence in Irish life for centuries. We have been less visible to them. But that seemed inadequate to explain how the British political and diplomatic elite could be so utterly indifferent to the Irish dimension when a child could see that that very dimension was bound to be in play. This is especially so in the context of the hard Brexit that eventuated, with the UK departing the single market and the customs union

– something that even Nigel Farage considered too extreme a
possibility at one stage.

The fact that the dyspeptic, ill-educated and alienated provincials who constituted a significant, perhaps decisive, element of
the pro-Brexit vote in England were ignorant of Ireland was
neither here nor there. Knowing nothing about Ireland is no
crime, any more than Irish ignorance of Wales and Scotland is.
It's just that, in the English case, this ignorance is bought at a
price. Ireland has a well-developed habit of making a nuisance
of itself in British affairs. Your average Brit need not be alert
to this. But the fabled British elite, with centuries of political
stability, a parliamentary system admired and copied all over
the world (including in Ireland) and a tradition of skilled and
sedulous diplomacy behind it, should have known better.

So this book is first of all addressed to a British, or more
precisely an English, readership. It aims to explain the degree of
Irish difference, such as carried us out of the United Kingdom a
century ago and latterly made us such a stone in the Brexit shoe.
But it also places more emphasis on British imperatives and
motives than many Irish writers do. We may be different, but
we are still cousins. Irish people need to reflect on the historical
and strategic imperatives that drive British indifference towards
Ireland: they are not just being bad-minded. So a little mutual
knowledge and understanding will cut both ways. That is the
primary purpose of this book.

When I write Ireland, I generally mean geographically
nationalist Ireland. That is roughly coterminous with the territory of the modern Republic of Ireland. I am well aware – who
could not be? – of the large nationalist minority, perhaps soon
to be a demographic majority, in Northern Ireland. There is

already a monumental library of history and analysis available on Northern Ireland: I don't think that I have anything useful to add to it. My primary focus therefore is on that large chunk of the island, roughly 83 per cent of its total land area, that has left the United Kingdom altogether. I started by asking myself: why are we the only part of the British Isles that has not made some sort of viable accommodation with the other parts? I realize that other accommodations, the Scottish one in particular, are strained and may not hold. But historically, the Scottish union, even if it is now ailing, has been remarkably successful and durable. Why are we *so* different? It is an inversion of the normal default setting for Irish thought, for we take the separate nature of independent Ireland as the natural order of things. What if it's not, as appeared to be the case for centuries? By inverting the question, the route to an answer or two may take in some scenic byways.

THERE ARE A few technical terms, or more properly shorthands, scattered through the text. It is as well to explain them now.

Old English The descendants of the Normans who first arrived here in 1169. Their 'tribal' difference from the Gaelic population, who had been in undisturbed possession of the land for more than a millennium except for the relatively minor and recent Viking presence, was always acknowledged. But a degree of accommodation between the two tribes softened these boundaries in medieval times. What was far more important was that both Gaels and Hiberno-Normans remained Catholic at the time of the Reformation. So the Old English, as they came to be called, were persons of Hiberno-Norman descent whose emotional ties to the distant English monarch were stronger than those of the Gaelic lords, but not so strong as to detach them from their confessional allegiance to the Pope. It was their Catholicism, not their tribal ethnicity, that was crucial.

New English A very different kind of beast. These were Elizabethan and Stuart adventurers and conquistadores bent on a civilizing mission and possessed of a ruthless hunger for land. They were the backbone of the Dublin Castle colonial administration from the mid-sixteenth century onward. Their land holdings were principally in Leinster and Munster. They were ignorant of Ulster until after the defeat of Hugh O'Neill's great rebellion in 1603 and may be thought of separately from the Anglo-Scottish planters who settled Ulster after the lands of the defeated Gaelic chieftains – O'Neill's allies – had been declared forfeit to the crown. The New English were solidly, indeed stridently, Protestant: they encompassed most tendencies in early Anglicanism, although inclining towards Puritanism. Unlike the Ulster settlers, they had no significant number of Presbyterians.

Creoles This is the term I sometimes use for a later group of settlers. The Old English date from the twelfth century, the New English from the sixteenth. This group, a further influx of English, came to occupy most of the lands east of the Shannon and outside Ulster from the mid-seventeenth century onwards. After his final and complete conquest of Ireland in the early 1650s, Cromwell confiscated almost all existing Catholic land titles in these areas, settling those Catholic landowners not reduced to trade or emigration on the poorer land in Connacht, although ensuring that coastal areas were settled on loyal Protestants, lest hostile navies come calling. In short, these Cromwellian settlers who replaced the dispossessed Catholics were the basis of the fabled Anglo-Irish ascendancy. In 1640, Catholics owned most of the land of Ireland outside Ulster; by 1703, that number had fallen to 14 per cent and would fall further in the course of the following century. The term creole requires some explanation. Anglo-Irish has always been a maddening term, satisfying very few. Were they English or Irish, or what, some kind of hybrid?

Rather than looking for a European analogue, I have reached for a South American one. The ascendancy behaved more like the light-skinned Spanish and Portuguese conquistadores who established themselves all over that continent, while remaining quite distinct and aloof from the natives. In South America, differentiation was by pigmentation; in Ireland, by religious confession. In both cases, possession of land was crucial. The difference was that in the various South American countries, the white creoles established colonial nation states that endured – usually at the material expense of indigenous people. The Irish creoles attempted a version of this in the eighteenth century – generally known as Grattan's Parliament. It did not endure. Instead, the Irish difference found a new voice, in the social group that bore a likeness to the South American indigenes: Catholics.

I realize that not everyone will agree with this term creole – some may even find it offensive – but I think that it gives an explanatory glimpse of how the ascendancy actually functioned: dominant but never integrated into the wider fabric of the country they now owned on leasehold from London; often admired but seldom loved. In this, they were quite distinct from the medieval Old English. It all fell apart for them at the end of the nineteenth century. The lighter-skinned descendants of the Spaniards and Portuguese in South America have had a longer innings and are still the dominant minority on that continent.

THIS BOOK IS a work of explanation and interpretation. I have therefore kept source references to a minimum. It is the product of many years as a publisher, not least a publisher of Irish history. It cheerfully plunders the work of many whom I have published and others whom I have not, but whose work it has been a pleasure to read. It has germinated in libraries, pubs and restaurants and in the course of conversations with people – academics, journalists and some deeply learned friends – who know more about the subject than I ever will. I am extremely grateful to them all.

It has been a pleasure to work with the team at Atlantic Books. Will Atkinson commissioned this book and gave me every encouragement, especially valuable at times when I doubted myself. How times change: for many years I used to do what Will is doing now and often wondered if it did any good. It does. James Nightingale is a scrupulous editor whose many structural suggestions for change – moving material to more appropriate locations, for example, or dumping it altogether – has made this a better book. Tamsin Shelton copy-edited the text and saved me from much embarrassment, as well as ensuring consistency of presentation throughout the text. Copy-editors are the indispensable, and often unsung, heroes and heroines of publishing.

INTRODUCTION

L ET'S TALK ABOUT the British Isles. It's a term that Irish nationalists profess to dislike, as representing an imperial sense of propriety over the little archipelago at the edge of North-west Europe. But it has the merit of brevity, a quality that has not always commended itself to Irish nationalist gasbags.

For half a millennium, these islands and their constituent tribes have subsisted next door to each other in a manner that, over time, suggested some movement towards political union. It was an uneven, stop-start business and it worked better in some places than in others. Wales has been subordinated to the English crown since 1282, having been occupied and overrun by Normans and Flemings in the previous century, without ever losing a distinct sense of its cultural difference. Scotland retained its ancient regnal separation until the union of crowns in 1603, followed by a full political union in 1707, caused largely by the bankruptcy of the kingdom of Scots.

Still, the bigger island has hung together through thick and thin, despite internal divisions of language, religion, law, culture and disposition that might have broken up a less resilient polity. And, for a long time, it seemed that something similar might have been said about the smaller island to the west. Ireland was always a more awkward fit in the London-centric mini-imperium but no one imagined – other than dreamers and loonies – that it might detach itself altogether from the mother ship, until the moment came for rupture. Then, quite suddenly, in the fall-out from World War I and the Easter Rising, the dreamers and loonies were proved to be the very essence of common sense and practical reasoning; and the solid, temporizing men of affairs were left with their arses out of the window.

So, what was it – is it – about Paddy that makes him that different? Different enough, I mean, to sever historical ties of centuries with such sudden violence and unapologetic efficiency. Why can't we just bloody well fit in? Wherein lies the Irish difference, a difference sufficient to have caused a rupture of that nature?

The answer is in no sense obvious because just as the precarious unity of Great Britain occludes regional and national differences that might yet break it up, Ireland's political separation conceals a cultural accretion to the bigger island – or, more particularly, to the dominant English element of it – that is adhesive. I mean, fish and chips, double-decker buses and Manchester United: that sort of thing.

I was in a pub one night a few years ago in rural Co. Wexford – a county that was the epicentre of the 1798 rebellion against English rule, an event still celebrated with pride in popular recollection – and every eye in the place was fixed on the various screens, all of which were showing the same thing. It was a game in the English Premier League between Liverpool and Newcastle United. There were lads in there wearing replica jerseys and referring to their teams as 'we' and 'us', as if this were Wexford playing Kilkenny in the hurling. Liverpool you could half-understand, given the long historical connection across the

Irish Sea (why don't the English moan about *that* proprietorial claim?), but Newcastle-upon-Tyne, for God's sake, as distant as the moons of Saturn.

In trying to measure the difference, you cannot forget or ignore the common culture that holds the British Isles in a kind of unity. Anyone travelling here, even from the near abroad of North-west continental Europe – say from the Benelux, Germany and France – let alone from the Latin south, would immediately register that common culture. It is palpable in its similarities, which in turn could be readily contrasted with what they had left behind at home. Suburban housing patterns alone would mark the difference as the plane descends anywhere in the Isles. British and Irish suburbs look quite like each other, less like continental suburbs. This little archipelago looks different – and its difference is distributed across both islands, which are more like each other than anywhere else.

So there is a common culture. Grand. It's there in language and literature and football and food and suburban housing patterns and double-decker buses and replica football shirts and a regrettable tendency to honk up surplus beer on the pavement after closing time. Except that it doesn't find any higher institutional or political expression.

Most of Ireland is a sovereign state, politically independent of the United Kingdom and an enthusiastic member of the European Union, a body from which an ageing, irritable element of the Englishry has managed to extract the entire UK.* For the

---

* Except for Northern Ireland, which remains in alignment with the EU customs regulations, in an act of cheerful Tory treachery which sold the province, or rather its irreconcilable unionist majority, down the river.

best part of a millennium, the whole island of Ireland had some sort of a relationship with England; at the start of the twentieth century the feeling was that that relationship was going to be re-set to give Ireland some devolved autonomy in domestic matters – home rule, it was called – but no one imagined that the Great Rupture was on the cards. Yet that's what happened.

So, for all the common culture of the Isles, when it came to the sticking place, the Irish difference proved decisive. It is, therefore, worth exploring wherein this difference consists. What is it about the Irish that the Scots and the Welsh lack? Or should that question be inverted?

THE TRADITIONAL NATIONALIST analysis sees the root of Ireland's woes in the English presence in the island, which goes back to the first arrival of the Normans in the late twelfth century. Thus, the 800 years of slavery narrative, which sustains and comforts the perpetually affronted. It is, of course, unhistorical rubbish, but emotionally potent rubbish. (A pantomime is always going to fill a theatre faster than *Hamlet*.) Ireland's difficulty begins not with a success – the arrival of the Normans – but with a failure. What failed in most of Ireland was the Reformation, and that failure sowed dragon's teeth.

The reasons for the failure of the Reformation in most of Ireland are not the subject of this book, although they give a glimpse of other causes whose effects, over time, marked the difference of Ireland. The great ecclesiastical historian Diarmaid MacCulloch has touched on one: the failure to evangelize in the Irish language, the common vernacular of the majority. Crucial to the enterprise of conversion was the translation of the Bible into the vernacular. But the earliest Irish-language version of the New Testament did not appear until 1603, almost a century after Luther. The Old Testament was not translated until the 1680s. The contrast with Wales is instructive: as early as 1563, the process began at Westminster with the passing of an Act for the Translation of the Bible into Welsh.

This meant that Ireland was a latecomer to the print revolution, as to so many other things, because the Bible was *the* text. Gutenberg invented printing by moveable type in Mainz in 1454; yet the historian Maurice Craig, in his classic *Dublin 1660–1860*, states that 'anything printed in Ireland before 1700 can be classed as "rare"'. Contrast this with the continental core: the first Italian press was established in 1465. The first printed books in Paris and Venice appeared in 1470, less than twenty years after Gutenberg's breakthrough. By 1480, more than a hundred towns and cities had printing presses, the most easterly being Krakow, the most southerly Naples.

By 1500, it is estimated that there were already seventy million volumes in circulation – the so-called *incunabula* – and the number of towns with presses had risen to more than two hundred. In the course of the sixteenth century, more than a hundred and thirty thousand new books were published in France, Germany, Italy, England and the Netherlands. But in Ireland, two centuries later, books were still 'rare'. By the mid-eighteenth century, books in the French language alone were being printed in major cities outside France, from London to Dresden and Geneva. Ireland was coming from a long way back.

The Australian historian Geoffrey Blainey, writing of his own country, entitled one of his books *The Tyranny of Distance*, something that even the modern traveller to Oz can appreciate. But the tyranny of distance affected Ireland, too. Until the discovery of the Americas, it was the island at the end of the world, Europe's cul-de-sac. In school, we were taught that of course the Romans never came to Ireland. This was said with pride, as if it marked our insular purity and inviolate status. It was never suggested that the Romans just couldn't be bothered, any more than they could be bothered to go much farther north than Hadrian's Wall.*

I mean, why would you bother with places like these, so remote from the centre of a civilization rooted in the Mediterranean? *We* don't lust to live in Greenland or the Faroe Islands for the same reason.

Of course, Rome fell. It took about three centuries for Europe to recover. Then two things happened, both of which still left Ireland a long way from the heart of things. First, the spiritual authority of the papacy remained in Rome (with occasional excursions to Avignon in Provence). Second, political power now moved north of the Alps, out of Italy, and began to solidify on either side of the Rhine.

Ireland was not merely distant from this civilizational heartland: it was of little interest to it. (I am deliberately ignoring the fabled Irish Christian missionaries who re-evangelized parts of the continent at the end of the Dark Ages: it was

---

* Whereas they could be very much bothered to go to Cornwall, where there was tin to be mined, which when alloyed with lead produced useful compounds such as pewter. Lead mines have been discovered all over Roman Britain, even as far north as Alston Moor, practically on the Scottish border. Lead was crucial for the Roman economy and society, not always with long-term benefits, as in lead piping which caused poisoning. There was tin and lead to be mined all over Roman Britain. But there was nothing to be had in Ireland: had there been, you may be sure that they would have known of it and hastened there.

magnificent traffic, but one-way traffic.) The only intruders who had disturbed the island's long isolation had come from the other direction: the Vikings. They did much good, not least by forming towns – unknown in Gaelic Ireland – and introducing seaborne commerce. But their presence was not in any sense definitive. They were a damned nuisance or a handy ginger group, depending on how you regarded them, but they did not change the basic dynamic of Gaelic society. For that, the island had to await the Normans in the late twelfth century.

The proximate reason for their arrival in 1169 was a dynastic dispute among Gaelic warlords, one of whom sought military assistance from Normans already well established in Britain. The Normans themselves were Frenchified Vikings who had established themselves on the lower reaches of the Seine and paid homage to the King of France. Their arrival was traditionally taught as the first English invasion of Ireland. It was not: they weren't English at all, being mainly Normans – swaggering conquerors in England itself and now sovereign there – with some Flemings. Between the lot of them, they did not speak a word of English. Best day Ireland ever saw, the day they arrived.

A good question is why their sovereign, Henry II, didn't just invade Ireland anyway. After all, he was an empire builder; through conquest and marriage, he controlled vast territories, England itself, of course, and the entire western half of France. Indeed, he exercised control over more territory in France than did the French king. This endlessly restless man, bursting with energy, none the less couldn't be bothered with Ireland. Why? For the same reason as the Romans before him and every English or British government after him: he couldn't work up the interest. For England/Britain, foreign begins at Calais, not at the back door. Only when the back door is a threat or a nuisance does it pay attention.

The place just wasn't important enough. Only when his Norman-Flemish military adventurers threatened to establish a separate kingdom in the east of Ireland did Henry feel the need to take things in hand and remind them of where their ultimate loyalty must lie. So he came over and bullied them and the Gaelic kings into submission. This was the fateful moment that inserted the English crown into Irish affairs.

Ireland did not see another English king until the wretched John Lackland came first as a child, then as king in 1210, laying the early foundations for English royal power in Dublin. Richard II arrived twice, to little effect, in the 1390s. After that, we had to wait until James II and William III fought things out in the 1690s at Derry, Aughrim and the Boyne. In fact, no English king arrived on a wholly peaceful mission until George IV in 1821 – and he was as pissed as a butcher's boy most of the time he was here and a martyr to the runs (these twain being not unconnected).

Ireland's unimportance was compounded by the tyranny of distance. Ireland was an enormous distance from the centre of royal power, just as the Highlands and Islands were remote from Edinburgh and effectively remained independent of the kingdom of Scots until the sixteenth century. Land travel was a nightmare: things were not too bad once you were on board ship – although they could be bad enough, as generations of travellers testified – but the overland part of projecting English royal power – centred then as now on London and the south – in Ireland was an enormous challenge. As late as 1690, nearly a hundred years after O'Neill's rebellion, William of Orange brought an army to Ireland. It mustered at Hounslow Heath, just west of London, with cavalry going ahead to clear the road to Chester. There followed 3,000 ox-carts stretching back a whole 29 kilometres carrying the supplies alone. At Chester, 300 ships made sail for Belfast Lough.

The cost of raising troops, equipping them, feeding them, paying them and transporting them to Ireland to fight in alien conditions was incredibly expensive and only worth considering out of the most compelling strategic necessity. Elizabeth I's eventual success against Hugh O'Neill's rebellion in the 1590s almost broke the English Treasury, as earlier incomplete military efforts had always threatened to do. Ireland just wasn't worth it. It was awkward to get to – the tyranny of distance again – and not worth the expense when you finally landed.

Then, as with so many other things, all changed with the Reformation. Suddenly, that unignorable strategic necessity presented itself. England had lost its medieval empire in France, with even the last redoubt, Calais, falling to the French in 1558.*

France and its southern neighbour Spain were Catholic, England Protestant. Spain had a sense of mission, which found expression in the Armada and also in the assistance given to the Gaelic lords in the latter stages of the Elizabethan wars in Ireland. For, as we saw, Ireland had not embraced Reform and thus presented a potential back door for England's Catholic enemies. Strategic imperatives – terrible necessity – meant that

---

* Every British schoolchild can – or could – rattle off the English victories in the Hundred Years War, Crécy, Agincourt and Sluys, while remaining perfectly ignorant of the two decisive French victories, at Formigny and Castillon. The Anglo-Welsh archers had been superseded by a new French fancy, artillery.

Ireland had to be conquered, even at the cost of almost emptying the Treasury.

After a nine-year war (1594–1603) that Ireland's Gaelic lords under O'Neill very nearly won, Elizabeth's army eventually secured victory in the first few years of the seventeenth century. But it had been a desperately close-run thing. Cromwell finished off the job fifty years later.

THERE ARE OTHER themes that contribute to the Irish exception: colonial condescension and cultural cringe; a poorly developed agriculture; antique church customs surviving into relatively modern times before finally being suppressed by the ferocious ultramontanism of the post-Famine settlement.* Most of all, the destruction first of the old Gaelic aristocracy at the beginning of the seventeenth century and later the defeat of the Old English** lords and burghers in the Williamite wars at the end of the same century. That robbed Ireland of its only two sources of native social leadership. The Anglo-Irish ascendancy creoles were no substitute. There remained for centuries a social leadership vacuum, which has only been filled by the slow and halting development of an Irish middle class in the twentieth century. There are other, minor themes, and the purpose of this book is to explore them all further, the better to try to understand the Irish difference.

The Irish difference is unique but it has echoes everywhere. Europe is an immense patchwork of subcultures, dialects and

---

* Ultramontanism (meaning 'beyond the mountains' [the Alps]) identified those Catholics who supported direct papal authority.
** As explained in the Preface, the Old English were descendants of the twelfth-century Normans who rejected the Reformation.

regional particularisms. There is no reason other than the vagaries of political and military history why Bavaria and Catalonia are not independent states. The same may be said of Scotland, which was independent for the best part of a millennium and may yet be again – although there, the further subdivision between the Lallans-speaking Lowlands and the Gaelic-speaking Highlands formed another line of exception. There are nations and regions – highly differentiated from their metropoles – which are not separate states: Wales and the Alto Adige.

And then there is Belgium, where religion used to matter and no longer does but language marks a particularly virulent line of internal division. The territory now called Belgium was a remnant of the Holy Roman Empire which had passed from the Spanish to the Austrian branch of the Habsburgs. It was (like little Luxembourg adjacent) a scrap of the *ancien régime* left over in the tidy-up that followed the Revolutionary and Napoleonic wars. But the Spaniards had earlier saved it for Catholicism, just as they had lost the Calvinist Netherlands to the north.

So Belgian unity, such as it is, rests principally on its embrace of Catholicism and rejection of Reform – sounds familiar? – but that unity is in turn fractured along the horizontal line of language division that runs through the middle of the country, Flemish to the north and French to the south. They really don't like each other.

So, Europe is full of little Irelands. The Irish exception is not so very exceptional. But it's there. Let's take a closer look.

PART ONE

—>€—

CAUSES AND
CONSEQUENCES

ONE

—⊰ ⊱—

FAITH AND FATHERLAND

T HE MOST OBVIOUS place to begin with is religion, from which no discussion of anything Irish can escape for long. It can be exasperating, especially for liberal post-religious people, who are disproportionately represented among opinion-formers: journalists, academics and the social gratin of the urban elite. Oh, you know, those tiresome sectarian quarrels, such as subsist in Ulster, are just so – so *archaic*. Well, yes, but only if you know no history and are incurious about the world.

Otherwise, you'll note that well within living memory crimes against humanity and something not far short of genocide returned to the European continent. Yugoslavia, patched together after the collapse of the Habsburgs and the Ottomans following World War I and run with an iron fist by Tito following World War II, fell apart with the collapse of communism in the late 1980s. It descended into a vile civil war, whose principal markers were sectarian: Catholic Croats against Orthodox Serbs and all against the Bosnian Muslims.

The world's two most unstable powder-kegs are the Middle East and the Indian subcontinent. In the case of the latter, the unity of British India was shattered by religious conflict, as Muslims carved out their own state of Pakistan (part of which became Bangladesh in due time) leaving Hindus as a dominant majority in India proper. For decades, India was formally secular in its politics but the hyper-nationalists now in power use religion unapologetically as their principal marker of difference and their standard of allegiance.

Border disputes between India and Pakistan, both nuclear powers, are frightening. In his memoir *Reporter*, the renowned American journalist Seymour Hersh quotes a senior US foreign policy official as saying that a threatened Indian invasion of Kashmir – the disputed border province – was 'the most dangerous nuclear situation that we have ever faced… It may be as close as we've come to a nuclear exchange. It was far more frightening than the Cuban missile crisis.'

It is hardly necessary to rehearse the mess in the Middle East. It's not just Jew against Muslim, although it's that as well. The founders of Israel were, for the greater part, secular Jews, many of them non-observant. But successive waves of immigrants have brought in deeply religious Jews and they are over-represented among the new settlements on the occupied West Bank. Whereas the founders of Israel relied on the Balfour Declaration and land acquired by proper legal purchase – the latter, of course, hotly disputed by Arabs – the newer, religious Jews claim their warrant to the land from a covenant made with their god three thousand years ago. And we know, without fully comprehending, the fissiparous tendencies within Islam which have been such a trigger for the mayhem in Lebanon, Syria, Yemen and Iraq.

Confessional allegiance tore Latin Europe apart at the time of the Reformation. At the Bavarian town of Augsburg in 1555, a formula was agreed that kept the peace between Protestant and Catholic for two generations. The Latin formula which summarized the agreement was *cuius regio, eius religio*, which effectively meant that the king or ruler of any territory could choose between the old church or Reform and his decision was binding on his people. Persons for whom this created a crisis of conscience were allowed a period of grace to remove to another territory whose ruler had made a choice more congenial to them.

This rickety formula worked for almost seventy years but when it fell apart the result was the Thirty Years War, the most destructive conflict in Europe prior to World War I. It retarded the development of Germany for two centuries. Estimates of fatalities are problematic; Peter Wilson, the leading anglophone historian of the war, suggests a population loss within the Holy Roman Empire (which included most of modern Germany) of 15 to 20 per cent. As he points out, even the lower figure is sufficient to make the Thirty Years War the most destructive conflict in all of European history. By comparison, population losses in the Soviet Union, which bore the brunt of casualties in World War II, were 12 per cent.

Religion was *the* ideological question of the era, as keenly felt as the rivalry between capitalism and communism in the twentieth century. The Swedish warrior-king Gustavus Adolphus summed it up: 'This is a fight between God and the Devil.' And in this fight, Ireland proved to be the great exception. It did not follow the Augsburg formula. The English crown had embraced the Reformation and Protestantism became a key marker of English – and later British – identity, especially in contrast to menacing continental Catholic powers – first Spain, then France.

Ireland, which had been a lordship of the English crown since 1172, was declared a sister kingdom in 1541. And yet, in most of the island, the Reformation failed. Diarmaid MacCulloch sets the context: 'In Elizabethan Ireland... the Protestant Reformation became fatally identified with Westminster's exploitation of the island and made little effort to express itself in the Gaelic language then spoken by the majority of the population. Ireland became the only country in Reformation Europe where, over a century, a monarchy with a consistent religious agenda failed to impose it on its subjects.'

The only country in Europe! Our theme is Irish exceptionalism and here it is laid bare in respect of the supreme question of the age. For this was not just dissent on an insular but on a continental scale. It is tempting to see all of subsequent Irish history as a footnote to the failure of the Reformation. That's far too schematic: history is a series of accidents and contingencies. We know only what happened – and then that imperfectly – and cannot even imagine what might have happened had Ireland, like England, Scotland and Wales, embraced some form of Protestantism.

INEVITABLY, RELIGION WILL weave its way through this book. Of all the things that made the Irish difference and that eventually detached most of Ireland from the British state, it is foremost. Before the Reformation, there were cultural tensions between the Old English and the Gaelic lords. But these were frontier warlord tensions. They were not so urgent as to prevent inter-marriage between the two groups; the gaelicization of the Old English to a degree that offended English sensibilities; or military alliances – usually short-term, opportunistic and provisional – between the two. In aggregate, it amounted to a reasonably coherent provincial warlord culture, with a top-dressing of urbanity in small port towns like Dublin and Waterford.

What never happened in pre-Reformation Ireland was an open revolt against the crown. The crown was vastly far away, below the horizon in London, as uninterested in Ireland as Ireland was in it. The modern idea of a centralized royal (or republican) sovereignty, projecting its power into remote places, did not exist in Ireland any more than it did in most of France until after the Revolution. This was an antique world which we can only apprehend through a glass very darkly.

There was no need to rebel against the crown, because the crown didn't matter. It did not trouble the Gaelic lords of Ely O'Carroll in the Irish midlands any more than they troubled it. What troubled the Ely O'Carrolls was the nearness and potency of the Kildare FitzGeralds, just next door. The fact that the house of Kildare acted as some sort of point man for this faraway crown was neither here nor there as far as the Ely O'Carrolls were concerned. We all have our eccentricities.

The problem was those old school-day twins, the Renaissance and Reformation. They marched together – and the effect was transformative. The story is well known and requires only the briefest summary here. Henry VIII's understandably desperate desire for a male heir eventually caused him to cast aside his wife, Catherine of Aragon, in favour of the younger (and hopefully more fertile) Anne Boleyn. In doing so he managed to alienate the Pope and the Holy Roman Emperor Charles V, Catherine's nephew. The Pope might have nodded Henry's divorce through, in the cynical way of the papacy, but at the material time he was effectively a prisoner of the emperor, who naturally wanted to protect his aunt.

All this got caught up in the early Reformation, the great theological fissure in the Latin Christian church begun in 1517 when Martin Luther proposed doctrines that were offensive to the papacy. By the time the dust had settled in England, Henry had secured his divorce, broken with Rome and declared himself sovereign in church affairs; he had encouraged Protestantism without fully embracing it himself. In asserting sovereignty in church affairs, he also embraced the fashionable new concept of Renaissance kingship, which entailed a more powerful central state and the submission of over-mighty provincial magnates – something that would have dire consequences for the Kildare FitzGeralds, as we shall see later.

The encroachment of royal authority upon traditional semi-independent magnate power in the provinces was resented, and not just in Ireland. But it took a fatal twist in Ireland by becoming mixed up with the religious question. Basically, the Irish magnates didn't want Henry VIII all over them, nor did they want the Reformation. So resentment towards the importunities of the king became enmeshed with loyalty to Rome. When the revolt of Silken Thomas, 10th earl of Kildare (p. 43ff, chapter 2), broke out in 1534, it was thought by the Kildares to be just a traditional reminder that the king should do as his predecessors had done for the most part – keep his distance and let the Kildares get on with doing what they did best, namely running Ireland while nominally acknowledging the king's lordship – happily occluded below the far horizon.

Too bad for the Kildares, the world had changed. Lenin's remark that there are decades where nothing happens and there are weeks where decades happen might almost have applied. By asserting an aggressive new royal dispensation, Henry turned what might otherwise have been an exercise in magnate muscle-flexing into a revolt against the crown. He was asserting a centralizing policy which meant that resistance perforce became rebellion. It was a fundamental change to the rules of the game. Henry was alert to it; the Kildares were not, or at least not yet.

Fatally, Silken Thomas now rather desperately – seeing that these strange new rules were in play – appealed to anti-Reformation sentiment. He tried to contact recusants in England and Wales, denounced the new Lutheran theology and appealed (without success) to the Pope and the emperor. Here, right at the start of the entire Reformation saga – less than twenty years after Luther first announced his novel theology – a bit of local Irish bother inflates into an unprecedented rebellion against royal authority *both in church and state*. That junction of faith and fatherland, first made in the 1530s, proved incredibly durable. Every subsequent difficulty between the two islands bore this watermark.

From here on, rebellions came thick and fast. The other branch of the FitzGeralds, the earls of Desmond in central and west Munster, rose in the 1570s. The Ulster Gaelic lords followed suit in the 1590s, as we'll see in greater detail later. The recusant Old English maintained a strained relationship with an English crown that was, by the end of the sixteenth century, decisively Protestant. The Ulster rebellion of 1641, directed at the recently planted Protestant colony, was openly sectarian, something that burned itself into the collective memory of Ulster Protestants ever after. Cromwell was hardly a religious neutral. He dispossessed nearly all Catholic landowners in Leinster and Munster and established new settlers – all reliably Protestant – who mutated in time into the fabled ascendancy.

Religion was the immoveable object resistant to all dynamic forces. Even in the 1790s, when under the influence of the Enlightenment and the French Revolution, a new kind of non-sectarian nationalism was proposed, it ended in tears. There was a major rebellion in the south-east, mainly in Co. Wexford, ostensibly in the name of this newly minted secularism, which collapsed into a number of horrible sectarian massacres. In effect, it became a Catholic rebellion. A less vigorous regional revolt broke out simultaneously in east Ulster: it turned out to be a wholly Presbyterian affair, reflecting the grievances of that literate and talented bourgeois community against Anglican social and political pre-eminence. Even here, religious confession was a marker of revolt.

A more enduring tradition in Ulster had begun three years earlier. In 1795, the Orange Order had been founded. It is, of course, still with us. Far from being literate and bourgeois, it was the latest iteration of lower-class rural sectarian solidarity. There had been a number of rough, rural secret societies antecedent among poor Protestants, in particular the charmingly named Peep o' Day Boys. The Orange might be considered a consolidating exercise for such groups.

Enlightenment non-sectarianism became a theoretical minor key in nineteenth-century Irish republicanism. In practice, nationalism of every kind was overwhelmingly a Catholic project. It is true that it attracted some enlightened Protestant support throughout the century, although in ever-diminishing numbers. It is notable that the leaders of the Easter Rising of 1916 contained not a single Protestant, unlike various eruptions in the preceding century. In Ulster, the doings of 1798 had disabused most Protestants of any residual Enlightenment liberalities. As the nineteenth century went on, that community found the Orange Order and a reactionary evangelical theology ever more congenial, the better to maintain deep water between themselves and the Catholics. The liberal Presbyterian tradition, a residue of 1798, atrophied.

THE ENLIGHTENMENT ITERATION of Irish nationalism was given its most famous formula by Theobald Wolfe Tone (1763–98) who wished 'to unite the whole people of Ireland, to abolish the memory of all past dissentions and to substitute the common name of Irishman in place of the denominations of Protestant, Catholic and Dissenter'. It was a noble ambition, but it barely survived the fires of the Wexford rebellion in 1798; thirty years later, when Daniel O'Connell mobilized the mass movement that began modern Irish nationalism, it was on an openly Catholic agenda. That has remained the major key in the nationalist symphony until very recently. But the minor key was never quite silenced. That non-sectarian dream of a secular Irish identity remained an important part of the republican and separatist element in the nationalist tradition. The mainstream was unapologetically Catholic – even under the leadership of such a conspicuous Protestant as Parnell, who was canny enough to make the requisite accommodations with Mother

Church, knowing very well which side the nationalist bread was buttered on – but rather like the quiet, still voice of conscience, the non-sectarian ideal troubled the nationalist soul.

It did not trouble it sufficiently to stop the independent state that finally emerged from the historical process from being a hyper-Catholic, introverted backwater for forty years, and happy to be so. But it was there, all the same, nagging away quietly. It is one reason that, for all the excesses of the new Catholic state, it never became a mirror image of the brazenly sectarian arrangement north of the border. It ultimately had the means to slough off the influence of the church – which had seemed overwhelming at the midpoint of the twentieth century – and assume a more secular direction. Reform in Northern Ireland, on the other hand, was imposed from without, usually against howls of anguished protest from Protestants, the *echt volk* being extruded *extra muros* by 'liberal' metropolitan bullies.

The seventeenth-century Plantation of Ulster was the nearest example of a successful British colonizing exercise in Ireland, in that it established a tenacious and rooted Anglo-Scots community on the land, all reliably and implacably Protestant. That conquest endured, unlike all other previous plantation schemes in Ireland, which were marginal at best. There was nothing marginal about Protestant Ulster. If the English could somehow have managed something similar in the whole island and turned the entire place Protestant, a lot of subsequent trouble might have been avoided. But what would that have entailed? Well, something like genocide for a start: Edmund Spenser's prescription – Philip Sidney's, too. Rather like early twentieth-century intellectuals recoiling from the heaving democratic masses, Yeats's 'filthy modern tide', they could contemplate the extermination of the Hibernian *Untermenschen* without a qualm. But such an enterprise, even had it been thought desirable, was beyond the reach of the crown. It was never seriously contemplated.

Even in Ulster, a large minority of Catholics survived the plantation. In the rest of the island, the failure of Reform became the key marker of difference. Great Britain, as it became after the Scottish Act of Union in 1707, was a self-consciously Protestant state, in an age where religion mattered and religious difference was keenly felt. That immediately placed most of Ireland outside the larger British ambit, as O'Connell so decisively demonstrated in the 1820s. The whole history of Ireland in the nineteenth century – and much of what follows in this book – is a series of adjustments by the British state to accommodate and appease the Irish difference. This expressed itself in amendments to property law; in the compromising of the Union settlement by the disestablishment of the Anglican Church of Ireland; and in doomed attempts to provide 'good government' at a time when the clamour was for self-government.

By the same token, the Irish Catholic community was distancing itself from metropolitan manners and mores, declining to abide by the proper usages of parliament; by fashioning its own sports and recreations; by trying to recover the lost elements of the Gaelic cultural past, especially the Irish language. It is true that, as we shall see, in this latter endeavour there was a distinguished Protestant presence. But even then, it was largely unrepresentative of its own confessional community, and became more so as the nationalist programme waxed in strength.

But always in nationalism there was that old nag. Theirs may have been a largely Catholic enterprise, but the ghost of Wolfe

Tone never quite left them alone. Mainstream nationalism was unembarrassed for the most part by its dominant Catholicism. That left Tone and the non-sectarian residue largely to the more radical, Fenian and anti-clerical minority tradition. In pre-partition Ireland, the Fenians could command support from an impressively broad cross-section of society: Yeats, for instance, was almost certainly a Fenian for a while. But they always regarded themselves, quite correctly, as an elite vanguard, which may of course have been part of what made them attractive to Yeats. Their attitude to democracy and representative politics ranged from outright hostility to reluctant tactical accommodation. The Easter Rising of 1916 – the Fenian apotheosis – may have come to be regarded by all nationalists as Year Zero but it had nothing to do with democracy. It was a conspiratorial triumph, although retrospectively validated at the ballot box.

—❧❦—

TWO

IT'S A LONG WAY
TO TIPPERARY

EVER SINCE ENGLAND was first a kingdom, in Anglo-Saxon times, before 1066 and all that, the south was the part that mattered. The Anglo-Saxon kingdoms that succeeded Roman England were most heavily concentrated in the south-east, in Kent, Sussex and Wessex (their core being roughly modern Hampshire, but over time pushing west and north towards Devon and the Bristol Channel). There were other Anglo-Saxon kingdoms to the north and east of England but they were less populous and had fewer urban settlements than the south-east. Moreover, they in turn were overrun by invading Danes who established the Danelaw, which, at its greatest extent, ran north from the Thames Estuary through the heart of England, very roughly staying to the east of the current M1 motorway, up to the borders of Northumberland and across to the Lake District.

In Anglo-Saxon England, the two most consequential royal centres were successively Winchester and then – decisively

– London (or, more precisely, Westminster). This was the part of the island with the best land; in time, a vigorous sheep-rearing economy developed there and English wool – later exported in enormous quantities to the cloth towns of Flanders – formed the basis of many fortunes. This trade established the importance of the English Channel as the highway to market.

Goods outwards invite goods inwards. The principal import into Anglo-Saxon England was spiritual, with the arrival of St Augustine to Canterbury – safely in Kent – in 597, there to establish a form of Roman orthodoxy. It faced a rival Christianity based in the Scottish islands and the north-east of England. Originally of Irish provenance, it differed liturgically and devotionally from the Roman norm, now planted gingerly in Canterbury. The key dispute turned on how the date of Easter is calculated, a matter that was eventually settled at the Synod of Whitby in 664 in favour of Canterbury.[*]

So the south had established both a temporal and a spiritual ascendancy. Then, as the various Anglo-Saxon and Anglo-Danish kingdoms gradually coalesced, something visibly like a kingdom of England had emerged by 900. By 954, the principal mercantile and ecclesiastical centre in the north, York, was consolidated to the embryonic English state, pushed ever more to the north from Wessex by the exertions of Alfred the Great's successors.

Once the Normans came, the pattern was reinforced. The south was now even more important than ever because the kingdom of England was joined by the Conqueror in a personal

---

[*] To this day, different varieties of Christianity worldwide celebrate Christmas and Easter on different dates.

union with his Duchy of Normandy. And Normandy was just across the Channel. Later came the Plantagenets. Henry II married Eleanor of Aquitaine, whose dowry brought him control of most of western France, so that he was a much more consequential dynast in France, in terms of direct power, than the King of France whose writ barely ran beyond the Île-de-France.

These French acquisitions and the dynastic claims to the French throne that accompanied them caused what seemed like endless trouble. The eventual upshot was the Hundred Years War, which the French won, thus consolidating their kingdom as a formidable presence on the European continent – and, later, as the pre-eminent one for about two hundred years – and ending England's long continental adventures.

Well, almost. Trade and military imperatives alone had taught the rulers of England one key strategic lesson: control of the Channel – either directly through residual possessions as at Calais or through friendly proxies *in situ* – was a vital English interest. In particular they watched the mouths of the Rhine and of the Scheldt below Antwerp. These were strategic ports at the end of great navigable rivers that were potential mustering points for any invasion force looking towards England.

The rulers of England were watching the door: the front door. For the most part, they were able to maintain indirect control and influence along that coast, so near to the vulnerable southeastern English heartland. This explains why Queen Mary was so upset at the loss of Calais, the last little residue of England in France – a medieval Gibraltar. 'When I am dead and opened, they will find Calais written on my heart.' This is where the Armada was defeated, and where Napoleon mustered an army at Boulogne before abandoning his invasion plans. Nor is it an accident that, in 1940, the Battle of Britain was fought and won in the skies overhead. Here was the potential soft underbelly of the English kingdom. To be fair, this is a point that can too easily be exaggerated: the Spanish Armada may have had dog's luck but they still found their task beyond them; both Napoleon and Hitler concluded that an invasion of England was too risky, and when, in 1944, the Allies managed it going the other way on D-Day, it was regarded in almost miraculous terms. It even drew praise from Stalin, not one much given to dispensing same.

Still, for most of English history, it was from over there – across the Channel – that the clear and present danger was likely to come. As Churchill put it simply: 'that's where the weather comes from', and evidence from Julius Caesar to Göring could be adduced in support of it. It made every sense to watch the front door.

But what about the back door: Ireland?

THERE ARE NO cathedrals in Ireland. We have churches that we call cathedrals but they are not the real thing. By cathedrals I mean those huge, imposing, intimidating structures that reflected the majesty of the Christian God in overwhelming form, behemoths in stone. In Ireland, we have none of that: what we do have are a few bonsai imitations, and not many of those. The larger churches that might fairly be called cathedrals are without exception restored nineteenth-century confections, like St Patrick's and Christ Church in Dublin, or nineteenth-century Gothic Revival originals, of which St Finn Barre's in Cork is a pre-eminent example.

But there is little, either from the Romanesque era or the Gothic, of any consequence. These were the successive styles of ecclesiastical architecture that dominated Western Europe as it began its long recovery from the Dark Ages. Romanesque began its evolution as early as the sixth century – long before there were towns in Ireland – but its fully mature style is generally dated to the middle of the eleventh century, around the time the Normans were invading England. From this period date such impressive examples of Romanesque as the cathedrals at Angoulême (founded in 1017 and modified in later centuries) and distant Durham (founded in 1093 but taking so long to build that it also contains many features of the Gothic style that succeeded Romanesque).

Gothic, of course, we all know: Chartres, Salisbury, Notre Dame. Again, it is the sheer scale and bravura of these cathedrals that hold the eye and the imagination. That is what is absent in Ireland. The principal monumental buildings put up by the Normans after their arrival in the late twelfth century were massive castles at places like Limerick, Trim and Carrickfergus. These were the impregnable fortresses of conquistadores, letting the natives know who their new bosses were.* They were not hymns to Christ in stone. Ireland was too much a frontier, warlord society for that kind of indulgence.

None the less, continental styles are not entirely absent, just more feebly represented. Unsurprisingly, the best evidence we have is architectural survivals because of their physical durability. A mixture of traditional building techniques inflected with

---

* The Normans in Wales built even more formidable castles, and for the same reason.

continental influences gives us the insular style referred to as Hiberno-Romanesque. Good examples of this are Cormac's Chapel (1127–34) on the Rock of Cashel and the west door of Clonfert cathedral (1179) in Co. Galway. But the 'cathedral' at Clonfert is about the size of a decent English parish church. And it is its littleness – and the exiguous nature of its ornamentation – that are characteristic.

It is all a variation on the tyranny of distance. The influence of contemporary English and German craftsmen has been noted by scholars at both sites but the pulse beats weakly in the remote west. And it beats small. Nothing was ever attempted in Ireland on the monumental scale of the great English cathedrals, or those on the continent. The richer, core lands of the post-Carolingian west were able to produce the kinds of economic surpluses that Ireland was incapable of; without such largesse, it's hard to imagine how such vast construction enterprises could have been contemplated.

The secular built environment also lagged behind England and Europe. The first undefended domestic dwelling in Ireland that we know of is at Carrick-on-Suir, Co. Tipperary. It dates from as late as 1569; it was built for Thomas Butler, 10th earl of Ormond and head of the Butler family, one of the three great magnate families of Hiberno-Norman times. Up to then – and well into the next century – the standard form of domestic architecture was the tower house, designed for defence in what was a marchland where warfare was the norm rather than the exception.

The Butler manor house in Carrick was making a statement in stone that this was now a land of peace. But it was an outlier: undefended manor houses are rare in Ireland before 1700. Even in 1569, it was in comparative European terms a late arrival. By then, England was full of undefended manor houses, most of them unsurprisingly in the south. Hatfield Old Palace (not to be confused with the later and current Hatfield House adjacent) dates from 1497, almost a century before Carrick. Avebury Manor in Wiltshire, Garsington Manor outside Oxford and Grimshaw Hall near Birmingham – to name but a few – were all earlier than or near contemporary with the Butler house, and there were dozens of others in a similar category. In France, the utterly spectacular Château de Chambord was finished twenty years before Carrick was started.

As with manor houses, so with towns. Medieval Ireland did not have a vigorous urban life. Of course, there were towns. Settlements of one sort or another had existed since Viking times and even before that the bigger monasteries might have been regarded as proto-towns, in that they were centres of wealth and learning. But they provided little in the way of commercial life, although some places held annual fairs where basic forms of exchange could take place. In general, however, urban development was a product of invasion. First, the Vikings as noted; then came the Normans with the idea of the chartered town.

A chartered town was one granted rights to trade and to self-government; the ultimate source and guarantor for the grant was the crown. The idea of the charter system was descended from the Romans, whose empire had been a necklace of chartered urban settlements. That was why, in post-Roman Europe, the Christian church was organized on a diocesan basis – with each diocese centred on a town – while in Gaelic Ireland ecclesiastical organization was based on monasteries, for want of towns.

Irish towns were principally a product of colonization, first that of the Vikings and Normans and, after the Reformation, that of the New English arrivals: Elizabethan chancers and adventurers on the make. It was a process not dissimilar to that along the Baltic shore where German colonists pushed east into Slav lands to establish trading networks of which the Hanseatic League was the most famous. Hansa towns such as Danzig (Gdansk) and Riga were German-speaking islands in an ocean of Slavs. Ireland was not unlike that, in that urban development was driven, more than anything else, by external influences.

SO IRELAND IS at once near and remote. Irish people are conscious of the substantial presence of the larger island adjacent. Sure it's only across the way and we speak the same language and eat similar food, and go doolally for the Premiership. Like most people everywhere, we suppose our patch of earth to be the centre of creation – just like people in the Home Counties, in fact.

However, it's to the Home Counties that we need to turn, because if you are measuring distance you should be doing so from Charing Cross. That alters the picture. At the front door, Brussels is 341 kilometres from London; Amsterdam 358 kilometres; Calais, a mere 187 kilometres. At the back door, Dublin is 463 kilometres away, which in the front-door direction would carry you most of the way to Cologne. Or consider the Nine Years War (1594–1603), the Irish rebellion against the English crown that most nearly succeeded. Its leader was Hugh O'Neill, earl of Tyrone. Dungannon, the modern town standing at the very heart of O'Neill's territory, is nearly as far from London as is Frankfurt-am-Main. Dublin is further away from London than is Paris.

All these distances are as the crow flies and no one, then or now, has ever travelled by crow. To these neat straight-line comparisons must be added the immense difficulties attending any form of travel or movement in pre-modern times. At the end of the sixteenth century, when O'Neill's rebellion against Queen Elizabeth presented the English crown with an existential challenge unlike any other, what is now Co. Tyrone might as well have been on the moon.

Seen from London – or even from Dublin, snug inside the Pale* – Gaelic Ulster was a *terra incognita* away below the horizon. It was a faraway country of which they knew little. One simple proof of this lies in contemporary maps, which start to appear in the second half of the sixteenth century. They include maps by the Flemish engraver Pieter van den Keere; Abraham Ortelius from Brabant – whose work is less accurate than that of van den Keere despite Ortelius's reputation as the father of Flemish cartography; and Giovanni Batista Boazzio, an Italian whose map influenced Ortelius. All three maps have this in common: they show the southern half of the island, roughly everything south of the Dublin–Galway line, to a recognizable degree of accuracy. They show, for instance, the four peninsulas of the remote south-west to a high degree of precision, considering the non-existence of modern surveying techniques.

But in all three maps, the northern half of Ireland is a mess, and the mess gets messier the farther north you look. The north-western and north coasts are largely little more than sketched-in guesswork, with one or two features such as the

---

* The English Pale was an area near Dublin where the English king's writ ran through his governors. This distinguished it from warlord marchlands – Old English and Gaelic alike – which were regarded as 'lands of war'.

deep estuarial indentation of Lough Foyle below Derry rendered in a manner that tells that the cartographers knew of them and roughly of their location but nothing more. All three knew that Lough Erne in south-west Ulster was a decent body of water. They also knew that there was another lake inland – in Hugh O'Neill's heartland – which they had heard was significant. So they showed it, more or less in the right place. They showed it much smaller than Lough Erne, when in reality it is twice as big. Not only is Lough Neagh bigger, it is the biggest fresh-water lake in the British Isles. They also dotted it with islands, just like Lough Erne, whereas in fact Lough Neagh has hardly any islands at all.

In extenuation, it's worth noting that map-making was a hazardous and sometimes lethal business. Forty years after Boazzio and the others, in 1609 after the defeat of O'Neill and the flight of the Gaelic earls to the continent, a plantation cartographer, Thomas Bartlett, was decapitated in Tyrconnell (Co. Donegal) because, as the attorney-general explained, the inhabitants 'would not have their country discovered'.

Boazzio and the others exaggerated the size of Lough Erne because there was an English presence on the borders of south-west Ulster. The town of Sligo, just across the provincial border in Connacht, had been founded by the Normans but – uniquely among Irish towns of such provenance – it passed into Gaelic hands and flourished in medieval times under a family who styled themselves O'Connor Sligo. It commanded one of the easiest crossings into Ulster, whose southern boundary was for the greater part impenetrable, being protected by low hills (drumlins) and a network of lakes and bogs. But its strategic position was as obvious to aggressive Elizabethan governors as it had been to the Normans and the O'Connor Sligos. By the 1580s, the governor of Connacht was Sir Richard Bingham, a bellicose man who imposed himself on the province and tried to project his power across the provincial boundary into Ulster. This ended badly for him, for he succeeded only in agitating the local Gaelic chieftains, who were then among the first to rebel against this English expansion. Sligo itself fell to the rebels in 1595.

But the point was that north-west Connacht and bits of south-west Ulster adjacent were *terra cognita*. So our three cartographers would have naturally known far more about nearby Lough Erne than they possibly could have known about faraway Lough Neagh, beneath the far horizon. And there was more to it than that. Within a few years, the military clashes on the southern margins of Ulster escalated. England was faced with a major rebellion in these parts that threatened to expel all English influence at least from the northern half of the island. It was necessary to send armies to bring the rebels to heel. This was done with the greatest reluctance, for the perils of the enterprise were well recognized: the whole business of raising a sufficient army and supplying it; then sailing it across the Irish Sea and marching it into Ulster.

Where they were lost. They had no accurate maps, while the Gaelic chieftains and their men knew every stone in the place. The battles that were won – and they were impressive – were mostly defensive ambush battles. So for the moment Elizabeth's lads were floundering in the bogs.

Hugh O'Neill (1550–1616) was The O'Neill, chief of his clan – the most powerful in Ulster – and simultaneously 2nd earl of Tyrone under English law. This intriguing illustration of how Ireland was half in and half out of the English world is exemplary. A policy had been put in place earlier in the sixteenth century called surrender and regrant. This meant that Gaelic chieftains surrendered their traditional titles and were granted in return new titles that were good in English law. The idea was that the old Gaelic order, seen as archaic and backward, would yield in time to the new, English arrangement. That did not happen. Instead, what developed was a confused, hybrid world. Centuries of Gaelic usage could not just be legislated away without military muscle to back it – and that was notably absent. Rather like Germany east of the Elbe, the conquest was colonial and incomplete.

It meant that for someone like Hugh O'Neill, the contest to be chief of his people was effectively fought in Irish law, not in English. Not only were the O'Neill lands the richest in Ulster and the title of ancient lineage, Ulster itself had no English presence in its heartlands and only a series of vulnerable and exposed fortifications along its southern margin. So what mattered was being The O'Neill. After much intrigue and many murders, he eventually attained the title in 1593, having been earl of Tyrone since 1587.

Until 1593, he had been outwardly loyal to the crown. He had been educated, effectively fostered, among the New English of the Pale. Ever after, he maintained cordial relations with his foster-family. None the less, the reality he faced in his central Ulster fastness, now that his rule there was uncontested, was that of constant English pressure on his southern provincial border. The crown had a significant, if often precarious, presence in all the three other provinces. So why not in Ulster?

The result of all this was that O'Neill, after some displays of loyalty bordering on the reckless, changed sides. He went into open rebellion against the crown. What followed was what is commonly called the Nine Years War. O'Neill was to prove himself a military and political leader of the highest quality. He organized an army capable of fighting and winning in the open field – something the English thought impossible for him to do – although defensive ambush battles were obviously preferred, given the Irish familiarity with the ground.

Moreover, he stitched together a political alliance of chieftains and warlords all over Ireland, a political confederation which fought with him and against the English. This was in no sense a proto-nation or the shadow of a national army. It was, none the less, unprecedented in its ambition and its reach – not to mention its successes – although its fragility contributed significantly to O'Neill's final defeat. But first, he and his confederates swept all before them. It culminated at the Battle of the Yellow Ford, again on the southern marches of Ulster, where in 1598 O'Neill destroyed a large English force under the command of Sir Henry Bagenal, a man cordially detested by O'Neill. Bagenal died, along with about four thousand of his men.

In the meantime, O'Neill had received undertakings of Spanish support. That was new. Previous Irish rebels might have invoked the Pope in vain, but now Philip II of Spain promised material help to the Irish. Quite what Philip was thinking is a matter for speculation because when it came to the sticking place Philip proved a vacillating friend. A naval flotilla promised in support in 1596 never materialized; it mustered but then Philip suddenly redeployed it to attack Brest, at which point, the king lost interest. To be fair to Philip, for all the fabled wealth flowing to his coffers from Peru – or, on some readings, because of his misuse of it – he had been forced into a default on his public debts, what we would now call a sovereign default, in 1595. Now his coffers were empty again. Ireland was probably not the first thing on his mind.

O'Neill had appealed to the old twins of faith and fatherland, denouncing Protestantism, while still failing to win the Old English of the Pale and provincial towns – still conspicuously Catholic – to his cause. This, too, was to prove a factor in his eventual defeat.

For the moment, however, in the wake of the Yellow Ford, he looked like an irresistible force. The road to Dublin lay open and there was outright panic in the capital. Why O'Neill did not march south is a question that can never be answered, rather as the one that asks why Hannibal did not march on Rome after his victory at Cannae. It is noteworthy that, for all his successes, O'Neill did not take a single town of significance in the course of the war. He might have concluded that if he couldn't take the small town of Newry, on the margin of his own lands, how could he take the capital?

O'Neill eventually got his longed-for Spanish help in the autumn of 1601, although it proved too little, too late and in the wrong place. A small force of 1,700 men[*] landed on the south coast, at Kinsale in Co. Cork, which they occupied and where they were promptly besieged by the new English commander, Charles Blount, Lord Mountjoy, who had already demonstrated

---

[*] The expedition, which had sailed from Lisbon, had originally comprised thirty-three ships and 4,500 men; most were scattered at sea in a storm and failed to make it to Ireland. Spanish Armadas never had much luck in northern waters.

his mettle by taking the war into Ulster to destructive effect. For the first time in the war, O'Neill and his allies had felt the pressure in their hitherto impregnable back yard. Mountjoy had starved Ulster, burning crops and laying waste as he went, fighting in winter so that the Gaelic troops did not have the shelter of woods in leaf.

It was an ugly business and not easy, fighting a war like this in unknown country. But its successes were such that it put O'Neill on the back foot for the first time in seven years and prompted his appeal to Spain, as he came to realize that he could no longer rely wholly on his own resources. This is what brought the Spanish expedition to Kinsale. But Kinsale is about as far from Ulster as you can get and still be in Ireland. O'Neill and his allies were now obliged to march the length of the island in midwinter, lured out of their Ulster fastness. Once they reached Kinsale, they in their turn besieged Mountjoy, who was now sandwiched between the Spaniards and O'Neill's army. The English army was wracked with illness and men were dying, so Mountjoy hesitated to assault the Spaniards head on. Moreover, an English naval fleet arrived off Kinsale, giving them control of the outer harbour, and the ability to bombard the Spaniards in the town, while also cutting off any hope of Spanish resupply.

The Spaniards were trapped. They lacked the resources to break out and attack Mountjoy head on; contrariwise their small force felt vulnerable in a town surrounded by hills and bluffs and strategically exposed on both the landward and the seaward sides. They needed the Irish to do something to break this game of cat and mouse. If somehow the English could deliver artillery to Mountjoy, that would be the end for the

Spaniards. But one thing was clear to all sides: the entire war would be settled at Kinsale. Mountjoy admitted as much: the winner would take all.

The Spaniards and O'Neill hatched a plan whereby he would move into open country, occupy one of the hills surrounding Kinsale and co-ordinate an attack upon the English with a Spanish breakout from the town. It all went wrong. O'Neill's new position was spotted by Mountjoy's lookouts. The English moved to engage the Irish immediately before the Spaniards could arrive. O'Neill pulled back to a ford some distance to the west and it was there that the Battle of Kinsale was fought. Mountjoy won hands down. It was effectively the end of the Nine Years War; what remained was just mopping up.

The English had got there eventually. But even when they had won, they themselves admitted that the campaign in Ulster had forced the issue and that Ulster had been utterly unknown to them. No less a person than the lord deputy, Sir Arthur Chichester – the founder of modern Belfast – admitted that the Ulster lands eventually conquered had been as remote and in-accessible to the English as 'the kingdom of China'. They won in the end because they found in Lord Mountjoy a commander of ruthless strategy and unbending will. Mountjoy was a brute, but he was an effective brute. The contrast with his failed predecessors is instructive. Mountjoy went for the jugular, risks and all, and got his reward.

Nothing except terrible necessity would have induced any English monarch to take on a fight such as this. Previously, deals and accommodations would have been made with uppity provincial magnates. And lo and behold, this is exactly what happened at the end of the war. The surrender terms were extremely generous to O'Neill, considering the degree of trouble he had made for the crown, not least financial. It was as if London, having attained its Irish victory by the skin of its teeth, now wanted shot of the damn place – and fast. There was little point in imposing a Carthaginian peace. All this was much to the disgust of the colonial English administration in Dublin, which considered that O'Neill had got away with it and which wanted nothing less than a Carthaginian peace.

The terrible necessity that had forced England to commit such massive resources to the Irish campaign was the new European configuration in the wake of the Reformation wars. Protestant England was now faced by its traditional enemy, France, and the greatest power of the age, Spain – which was very near, holding control of Flanders and the Low Countries. Both Spain and France were conspicuously Catholic. It was less than ten years after the Armada. For the English crown, this was no small matter. The mere thought of Spanish power being projected in support of Irish rebels brought the dangers of the front door to the back door. That was something which simply could not be ignored or appeased.

AT THIS POINT, we need to wind back a couple of generations, for there was nothing inevitable about O'Neill's rebellion. Trouble had been brewing for some time, or at least a series of unrelated developments conspired in aggregate to bring trouble to the door. First, England lost the Hundred Years War and was finally extruded from the European continent in the 1450s – except for the temporary carbuncle at Calais. This meant, among other things, that it was no longer faced with possible battles on two fronts. Militarily, it took Scotland out of the equation. For most of the Middle Ages, the Auld Alliance of Scotland and France had kept London honest. There were numerous campaigns against the kingdom of Scots – often revenge attacks for Scots incursions into northern England.

But the principal focus was always France. With the final French victories, that calculus changed. Now it was possible, if desired, to project English power more assertively on the island of Britain. This happened piecemeal: there was no grand plan. But there was a tradition of English involvement with the kingdom of Scots, an impressive polity – as authoritative north of the border as the English state was to the south, but obviously poorer and less populous. Many of the leading noble families of lowland Scotland – among them names as resonant as Bruce, Wallace and Menzies – had come there by invitation from Norman England. This was to help extend the writ of the Scottish crown beyond its lowland base, ever more northward into the Gaelic and Viking Highlands. In this, Edinburgh was successful over time, but it needed Norman muscle to do it. The Lowlands, being close to England, were more open to English influence and mores than the more remote and independent Highlands.

For all that, the two kingdoms had a prickly relationship, especially as Scottish national consciousness developed – aided by all those imported Normans, who by the time of Bannockburn (1314) were the very heart of Scots patriotism. Back and forth it went from time to time but England never had a grand plan to conquer Scotland: its moments of maximum aggression depended upon the occasional charismatic warrior-king like Edward I. Even he, the fabled Hammer of the Scots, could not destroy Scottish independence, as Robert the Bruce would prove in short order. Even later disasters like Flodden (1513), which saw the death of the cream of Scottish nobility – including King James IV – did not subvert the regal and national authority of the kingdom.

But the English were never far away. It only took another self-identified warrior-king, Henry VIII (r. 1509–47), to accelerate the process. It was his army that routed the Scots at Flodden. Thirty years later, he invaded Scotland to try to force a dynastic marriage between his son Edward and the infant daughter of the late King James V of Scotland. She was later famous as Mary Queen of Scots. The campaign, known ever after as the Rough Wooing, failed.

In the meantime, Henry had effected a revolution in church and state. He broke with Rome, appointing himself as Supreme Head of the Church of England, which quickly became ever more Protestant. He also affected the airs of a Renaissance king, centralizing power and curbing, as far as possible, the aspirations of over-ambitious provincial magnates. Rid of its French territorial incubus, the English state none the less copied the ways of the French court under the glamorous King François I, the contemporary *beau idéal* of Renaissance kingship.

And so to Ireland. It had been a lordship of the English crown since 1172, almost always ruled in practice by a mixture of Hiberno-Norman magnates and Gaelic chieftains, with the former more conspicuous. Of these magnate families, none was greater than the house of Kildare, the northern branch of the FitzGeralds. The southern branch comprised the house of Desmond, in Munster. Magnate rule made sense: Ireland was a long way off and, being the back door, of no great strategic significance. Every now and again, the Kildares would be ousted for a few years and a sort of *gauleiter* sent over from London to run things. But it never worked for long: the *gauleiter* lacked the vast network of connections and patronage that the Kildares held in their hands. So, after a decent interval, he was sent back where he had come from and the Kildares were reinstated. Thus it had been for as long as anyone could remember as the 1530s dawned.

That was the decade when Henry up-scuttled all existing arrangements: executing wives; breaking with the Pope; dissolving the monasteries; and putting in place the beginnings of the modern English state. This caused trouble in the English provinces, most obviously with the so-called Pilgrimage of Grace in the north. But it also caused an earthquake in Ireland.

Henry broke the magnate power of the Kildares. The head of the house, the 9th earl of Kildare, was the most consequential man in Ireland, who maintained control – nominally in the king's name – through a dizzying series of marriage and military alliances with other, lesser, magnates. He might best be thought of as a medieval mafia *capo*, and his alliance partners as local dons working their territories. This system had generally worked well under previous monarchs, but Henry VIII liked to keep his friends close. He was suspicious of the sheer degree of palatinate power exercised by Kildare, whom he summoned to London in 1534. It was not the first time this had happened but by now Henry's reforms in church and state were under way. On previous occasions when Kildare had been summoned to London and some form of direct rule attempted in Ireland in his absence, it had always proved a failure. Thus the serial ubiquity of the Kildares.

Not now. Kildare left his son and heir, Thomas, Lord Offaly, in charge. Kildare was full of suspicion and was particularly wary of Thomas Cromwell, Henry's new chief minister, whom he knew to be a centralizer and one who wished to have reliable English deputies established in Ireland. In the event, Cromwell could only find one volunteer, Sir William Skeffington, who did come to Dublin, only for the Kildares to give him the run-around. So now, Kildare was back in London, under the eyes of Henry and Cromwell, and Lord Offaly was continuing his father's policy of non-co-operation with Skeffington.

Lord Offaly is better known to history as Silken Thomas, a sobriquet given to him forty years later by members of the Kildare family anxious to ingratiate themselves with the new Elizabethan conquistadores.* His short career was a textbook example of muddle and miscommunication. Kildare wrote to his son in terms that expressed alarm at Cromwell's supposed plans for Ireland and Skeffington's agency in executing them, whatever they might be. Silken Thomas now engaged in a disastrous exercise in gesture politics. In June 1534, he pranced into the Irish privy council – attended by his retinue – and resigned the lord deputyship on behalf of his father.

It was a gesture designed to express the frustrations of the house of Kildare against creeping centralization, but it was a massive miscalculation. It was a revolutionary time; the certainties of the old stable order, which ensured the primacy of the house of Kildare, were weakening. The English Reformation was under way and Silken Thomas invoked the help of both the Pope and the Holy Roman Emperor Charles V, while trying to drum

---

* The name derived from his alleged love of sartorial display, the suggestion now being that he was little more than a trivial fop, with a none-too-subtle hint that he was homosexual.

up support closer to home among English and Welsh Catholics. There was no way Henry VIII could ignore this or regard it, as Silken Thomas naively imagined, as the basis for a negotiation to restore the *status quo ante*. Kildare was promptly clapped in the Tower of London; an earlier rumour of his murder had proved untrue, although it may have influenced Silken Thomas. At any rate, he died in the Tower, of what or by whose hand is not known. Silken Thomas was now the 10th earl of Kildare.

Fat lot of good it did him. His rebellion quickly ran out of control. His men murdered the archbishop of Dublin, an Englishman, and besieged Dublin Castle, the seat of royal power. As ever, the crown baulked at the cost of a military operation in Ireland – it cost the English exchequer money it did not want to spend in Ireland. But there was nothing for it, because the rule of the game had changed. The assertive, centralizing English state being put in place by Thomas Cromwell and Henry VIII was not content to play by the old medieval rules, respecting magnate distance. Instead, it imposed itself. Skeffington was furnished with an army and, crucially, with artillery support, and quickly reduced the Kildare stronghold of Maynooth Castle, just to the west of Dublin. That was that. Silken Thomas was promised his life, a promise soon broken. Packed off to London, he and five of his uncles lost their heads.

And that, more or less, was the end of the medieval house of Kildare. It meant that some form of direct rule would now have to replace magnate rule, thoroughly discredited by the rebellion and by the appeal to Pope and Emperor, neither of whom responded. The lordship of Ireland was declared at an end and in 1541 it was upgraded to the status of a kingdom, a sister of England with a union of crowns.

But if the 1530s represented the end of the house of Kildare, it also meant the end of medieval Ireland; the two things were not unconnected. If the English state was now to assume an active role in the governance of Ireland, it was going to have to pay for it. Hitherto, London had been able to devolve these responsibilities to magnates like the Kildares. Now it had to put its hand in its pocket. And, as with Hugh O'Neill's rebellion in the 1590s, the cost of suppressing the revolt nearly bankrupted England. It is still putting its hand in its pocket to this day: the annual Treasury transfer to prop up Northern Ireland now stands at a cool £12 billion net.

THREE

—❊—

HALF IN AND
HALF OUT

I T WOULD BE wrong to see Silken Thomas as a kind of dry run for Hugh O'Neill, but the pressures that bore on each were similar. For most of the sixteenth century, the English crown in Ireland hardly knew whether to stick or twist: a succession of chief governors or lords deputy alternated between coercion and accommodation. The FitzGeralds of Desmond rebelled against Elizabeth in the 1570s and were routed by crown forces who laid waste to the rich province of Munster. Among the most enthusiastic waste-layers was Edmund Spenser, the poet. English power gradually but fitfully pushed west and north while leaving Ulster largely alone. As we saw with Hugh O'Neill, English titles were granted to Gaelic chieftains in parallel with their old ones, but this contained the potential for confusion given the different succession and heritable systems.

What did the New English land-grabbers find in Ireland in the sixteenth century? First and foremost, an empty place: there are no reliable estimates of population but most scholars agree that the island contained fewer than a million people; the population recovered only slowly from the Black Death. (Compare this figure to a reliable one, just over *eight* million on the eve of the Great Famine.) Second, a land for the most part uncultivated and still densely wooded. As one historian has written: 'In 1500 the taming of the physical environment and the overcoming of its attendant perils were scarcely dreamed of.'

There were hardly any towns of significance and most of what there were were close to Dublin. To English eyes, the land was empty and uncultivated, an open frontier such as their countrymen were soon to find in America – and later in Australia. It was a land in which, as we saw, such legal system as existed seemed to them antique. Divorce was available, in defiance of canon law (never mind English Common Law), and concubinage was tolerated. Bishoprics were hereditary, because there was little in the way of clerical celibacy. The dean of Lough Erne and canon of Armagh and Clogher had at least thirteen children that we know of, which did not inhibit the *Annals of Ulster* from describing him as 'a gem of purity and a turtle dove of chastity'.

The New English parvenus of Elizabeth's time saw, therefore, what they regarded as a near-empty wilderness occupied by a barbarous people. Take Richard Boyle, a classic man on the make. A yeoman's son from Kent, he studied at Cambridge and the Middle Temple in London. He arrived in Ireland in 1588 and, using forged letters of introduction, managed to insinuate his way into government circles. He was rewarded by securing public office, well suited to his talents for corruption and peculation. He married twice, both times well. His first wife died; his second was seriously rich and set him up. Plus Queen Elizabeth, rather like Margaret Thatcher 400 years later, had a soft spot for energetic male chancers making their way.

He was knighted, made a privy counsellor and elected to parliament. By 1620, he was 1st earl of Cork and the richest man in Ireland, rich enough to lend King Charles I, no less, the colossal sum of £15,000 at short notice. And in his domain, he did something novel. He established towns: in Co. Cork, Charleville, Clonakilty, Midleton and Doneraile all owe their foundation to Boyle. In Youghal, he greatly expanded the existing little settlement. He chopped down woodland relentlessly to feed his ironworks, prompting one of the great laments in Irish poetry, from the pen of that distinguished poet, Anonymous:

Cad a dhéamfaimid feasta gan adhmad / Tá deireadh na gcoillte ar lár.

Or, in Frank O'Connor's translation, with Yeats's hand very visible:

What shall we do for timber? / The last of the woods is down.

The woods were down all right, just as they had been in England some centuries earlier. One of the great English mythic heroes, Robin Hood, had relied (if he had lived at all) on the dense protection of Sherwood Forest from the depredations of his new Norman masters, Guy of Gisborne and the Sheriff of Nottingham: foreigners, French bullies. It was the same in Ireland: the old order – Gaelic and Hiberno-Norman alike – sought the protection of the woods as a place of safe retreat from the assaults of the new conquistadores.

But now the woods were gone, chopped for iron-smelting charcoal and for the creation of pasture. If you were English, woods and forests were backward and forbidding places – the haunt of outlaws – and chopping them down in the service of commerce and industry was to bring the virtues of civilization to places previously denied them (through their own mulish obstinacy, of course). And so it went on from there, creating in the eighteenth century the enclosed Irish rural landscape, beautiful because it is artificial.

Thus we entered on the long eighteenth century, with the colonial ascendancy – Oliver Cromwell's legatees, now settled on the land – dominant in Ireland, both in parliament and in the Dublin Castle administration. A decorative viceroy or lord lieutenant was sent over from London to lend the city some tone but otherwise the local ascendancy was in charge. It was, for all the world, a return to magnate rule, albeit the ascendancy was very different in kind from the old medieval magnates. But in essence the logic was the same. Ireland was too far away and not enough of a threat to require a more assertive or direct English presence. In time of war or rebellion, such a presence was reluctantly agreed to; but once the dust settled, it was back to business as usual.

THAT WAS THE Irish condition, half in and half out of the English orbit. In some ways, Scotland had a similar semi-detached relationship with its southern neighbour. But the differences with Ireland were more material. Scotland, unlike Ireland, was an ancient, structured royal kingdom with its own administration and powers of internal coercion. It had maintained an orderly regnal succession – with only occasional bumps and grinds – for nearly as long as England. So although England conducted many wars against Scotland over the centuries, these were usually punitive affairs, not wars of conquest. England never seriously tried to conquer Scotland, although it did from time to time try to absorb it by dynastic marriage, as at the time of the Rough Wooing.

Eventually, the whirligig of royal genetics produced a union of crowns with the arrival of the Stuarts in London and, just over a century later, there was effected a political union between the two countries. But even then, Scottish particularism was too entrenched to be disturbed, and wisely the English did not try. Scotland retained its different legal system and its own church settlement – Presbyterian rather than Anglican, so that the monarch changes confession when crossing the border – together with its distinctive and different system of education. There was, in short, a Scottish establishment; under the Act of Union (1707) it was seduced, not violated. Scotland continued to be administered by its own elite, Ireland by a creole colonial junta.

Ireland had no tradition of unified statehood and no culturally unified establishment. Indeed, it had never known any kind of political unity until a version of it was imposed by Cromwell's sword: Oliver the first republican in Irish history? So the English Protestant interest, starting with the men sent to administer the newly minted kingdom of Ireland in the 1540s through to the beneficiaries of the Cromwellian land confiscations and subsequent settlements – which survived the Restoration because Charles II lacked the power to do anything about them – came to regard Ireland as a kind of *terra nullius*.

*

THE LOGISTICS OF mustering, arming, supplying and paying an army were not impossible. Nor was it impossible to transport it across water. After all, the English crown had been doing this on and off for centuries against internal rebellions, against the Welsh and Scots, and against the French crown during the Hundred Years War. Neither is it true to say that any of this was easy. Traditionally, kings had delegated the raising of armies to local magnates who in turn delegated to 'captains', in effect career officers who were their clients. Ordinary soldiers were dragooned from local riff-raff, the poor and prisoners: wars relieved pressure on prisons.

Commissariat and supply were managed by the captains but ultimately paid for by the crown, not always in a timely fashion. England had nothing that could be considered a standing army – an idea that long struck horror into the English breast – until the formation by parliament of the New Model Army in the 1640s. That experiment did not survive the Restoration in 1660. So both before and after the English Civil War, the business of raising a land army was a messy, devolved affair. Marching troops across country on pre-industrial roads and tracks together with kit and weaponry and hangers-on was a slow, laborious trudge.

Then, where Ireland was concerned, there was the additional chore of sailing them across a not always benign stretch of water: the Irish Sea. At both the port of departure and that of arrival, they were at the mercy of wind and tide. For example, when in 1741 Handel travelled from London to Dublin to conduct the first performance of *Messiah*, it took him about five days to get from London to the estuary of the Dee, whence he proposed to sail from Parkgate just below Chester. He did, eventually, after twelve days waiting for favourable wind and tide. Fourteen years earlier, Jonathan Swift – returning to Ireland for the last time – had had a similar experience. Sailing from Chester, his ship could make it no farther than Holyhead where it was detained for eight days by the elements. When he did arrive in Dublin, he put ashore not in the Liffey – whose estuary was notoriously prone to silting – but at a relief harbour outside the city.

Moreover, there was *mal de mer* to cope with: when Cromwell came with a huge force in August 1649, many of them were sick as dogs, not least the commander himself. It was Cromwell's first time out of England and first time at sea. The army chaplain said of him that he appeared 'as sea-sick as ever I saw any man in my life'. Like Swift, Cromwell could not drop anchor in the city but at Ringsend, a spit of land that stood proud above high water downriver to the east. Shipping in the pre-modern age was full of similar stories, of ships crossing the English Channel and having to tack up and down with the French coast in clear sight because of contrary tides and winds. The age of steam put an end to all this, but that was in the unimaginable future when Elizabeth I and her captains were struggling with what to do about Ireland.

The point is that an Irish military expedition was not impossible but it was extremely challenging: raising an army, sailing it across; and then engaging an enemy in his own back yard with inadequate maps. Moreover, it was hideously expensive: the cost of defeating O'Neill in the Nine Years War has been estimated as almost £2 million, an enormous sum of money.

In those sixty years, everything had changed. Henry VIII and his successors had abandoned magnate rule for direct rule through a series of English governors and this had had its effect. The English presence was now felt directly in parts of Ireland where it had been absent hitherto: in south Munster following the defeat of the Desmond rebellion in the 1570s; in north-east Connacht, touching on the borders of south-west Ulster, in the following decade. In the 1530s, there were only a few hundred English captains – freelance military officers – operating in Ireland; by the end of O'Neill's war, that figure was 21,000 officers and men. It had been growing steadily, *pari passu* with the gradual expansion of English influence as the century progressed.

All this generated an ideology, whose principal intellectual fountainhead was Edmund Spenser, better remembered as the author of *The Faerie Queene*. Spenser urged a policy of outright conquest by England but Elizabeth was never going to sanction that – for two reasons. First, the cost; second, because the logic of Spenser and his successors-in-thought was that Ireland was indeed a kind of *terra nullius*. Whatever it was, it was not that. There was an organized, if sparse, society there – archaic and backward, perhaps, in English eyes, but in no sense like the American west or the Australian outback later. Spenser's prescription would have required a kind of Final Solution for the Irish, either by death or forced exile, in order to repopulate the island with Anglo-Scots planters. No sensible person in authority, in London or Dublin, ever seriously contemplated this.

Yet England did finally get the job done. Cromwell consolidated the victory that Elizabeth's captains had finally achieved and William of Orange put the icing on the cake in the 1690s.

Then came the long eighteenth-century ascendancy and the return to a kind of magnate rule. What goes around…

In short, distance, indifference and cost were hugely inhibiting factors which denied England anything more than an incomplete victory in Ireland. Combined with what Philip Sidney, like Spenser another poet-courtier, called the Irish 'ignorant obstinacy in papistry', these factors ensured that Ireland stood at an angle to England more oblique than any other constituent element of the British Isles.

THE ENGLISH STATE conquest of Ireland had succeeded just as the religious conquest was failing. The New English – Protestants all – now established at the head of the Irish colony at Dublin Castle realized that if honeyed words of conversion were failing, then one alternative was to enfeeble, as far as they could, the sinews of the stubborn papists. From the 1570s on, there had been a systematic campaign of harassment against Catholic institutions, not least educational ones. For it was these that produced the literate, educated Catholic elite that provided indispensable social and spiritual leadership. That, plus the expropriation of monasteries which had served as centres of higher education, prompted the establishment of the continental colleges, where young Irish clergy could receive a Catholic education. Thus the officer corps of the Irish church was swaddled in a papal embrace, having vaulted over England. In the last quarter of the twentieth century, the Irish middle class – and especially its higher bureaucracy – made a similar leap in its embrace of the European Union. You bypassed London to get to a better place, to join a fully realized culture, one that was not England.

In the first half of the eighteenth century, the Irish colonial parliament passed a series of notorious penal laws against Catholics and, to a lesser degree, against Dissenters. That parliament had had a fitful history since the fourteenth century but was now an exclusively creole, Anglican assembly. The big winners of the Williamite wars of the 1690s had finally finished off what Elizabeth and Cromwell had started, and this was *their* parliament.

The penal laws had all to do with land and power and nothing to do with proselytism, but they were little more than the codification of a series of discriminatory practices against Catholicism that had been in train for over a century. It is no accident that they were enacted in Dublin and not at Westminster. Rather like the unreformed Stormont parliament of the twentieth century, these grandees – Cromwellian settlers now in the second, third and fourth generations – were nervous in their triumph. In their case, they feared a Stuart restoration, whose legitimate claim on the British crown was considerably stronger than that of the Hanoverians. But the Stuarts were now unrepentantly Catholic and the one thing that all British Protestants could agree on was the necessity for a Protestant monarch: thus the Act of Supremacy of 1701.

The various penal laws passed by the Irish parliament were ferocious on paper but less so in actuality. They echoed contemporary forms of discrimination on religious grounds elsewhere in Europe in that age of faith: Huguenots in France; Jews and Muslims in Spain; and so on. This is not to whitewash them, for they were the product of a panicked community determined that its providential deliverance by King Billy should not be compromised frivolously, as the peace settlement with Hugh O'Neill a century earlier had been perceived to be. And they vividly remembered the so-called patriot parliament of 1689 called by James II during his brief Irish ascendancy, which had carried pro-Catholic proposals, not least the restoration of landed estates to those families that had held them in 1641, that is, before Cromwell. Of course that hadn't happened, because King Billy beat King James, but it left the new Anglican ascendancy in no mood to accommodate people who would so recently have expropriated them and their property.

So they passed the Banishment Act of 1697 which expelled most Catholic clergy from Ireland. Of those remaining, most were required to register with the authorities under an act of 1704 and to give sureties of future good behaviour, under penalty of forfeiting the sureties in cases of infraction. Then an oath of abjuration of the Jacobite claim to the throne was foisted on all remaining Catholic clergy. This was too much. Very few priests swore the oath and the majority that refused suffered accordingly. But in reality the administration had over-reached. There were some years of genuine harassment and persecution but it gradually became clear that the reaction was too heavy-handed and the authorities quietly wearied of it.

Other acts forbade Catholics to own land, other than holding leases of no more than thirty-one years; they could not inherit from a Protestant; on death, a Catholic landowner was obliged to write a will in gavelkind, that is, partible inheritance among all sons – and if any one of these sons conformed to the state church, he acquired the entire inheritance. And so on. These laws did work, and in working they contributed to the neglect of the purely sectarian ones directed at the Catholic clergy, for once the land issue seemed settled the prime purpose of the laws was secured and pointless persecution of papist clergy drew fewer and fewer adherents. Still, this was a nervous society.

The grandees were nervous because they feared for the security of their land titles, so recently acquired, in the dread event of the Stuarts coming back. They were not completely hysterical in their fears: there was a Scottish rebellion in support of a Stuart restoration just a year after Queen Anne died, in 1715, with the Hanoverian George I barely settled on the throne. There was to be another one thirty years later. If in Scotland, why not in Ireland? It seemed more promising territory still. So the creoles applied the iron fist, rather like twentieth-century Afrikaners, and drank nervous toasts like this:

> *God bless the king;*
> *God bless the faith's defender.*
> *God bless – no harm in blessing – the pretender!*
> *But who pretender is and who is king:*
> *God bless us all, that's quite another thing.*

Even during the long ebb tide for Irish Catholicism in the eighteenth century, however, there had been an aspect of distance that had been entirely positive for Irish Catholics. That was the extraordinary network of Irish colleges established all over Catholic Europe under the protection of local rulers and ultimately drawing on the wealth and influence of the papacy. They were institutions of higher ecclesiastical learning for Irish Catholic exiles, and they played a critical role in maintaining a well-educated Irish Catholic officer corps. It is difficult to say exactly how many there were, for some were foundations of short duration, but the major ones amounted to about thirty. Foundation dates are quite early, as early in a few cases as the late sixteenth century. But the majority – including many that were of lasting influence – were founded in the seventeenth century. A few examples, with foundation dates, will indicate the geographical spread: Salamanca (1592), Lisbon (1593), Paris (1605), Leuven/Louvain (1607), Rome (1628).

These dates are significant because they echo what was happening in France as part of the modernization that followed the Counter-Reformation. In the words of one distinguished historian of France: 'A crucial element in this project – the establishment of diocesan seminaries for the training of the priesthood – had only been fully implemented in France between roughly 1650 and 1720. Paris, the most important diocese in the French church, had only got one in 1696.' So Irish church renewal was more than simply an act of charity offered to a poor, exile church: it also placed its Irish continental students at the heart of Counter-Reformation modernity.

There were other, less formal, connections between the Irish Catholic elite and the continent, and even in high Catholic milieux nearer home. Patrick Fitzsimons, later to be archbishop of Dublin, served in the private chapel of the Spanish ambassador to London in the 1720s. His successor-in-office, John Carpenter, had been secretary to Viscount Taaffe, also in London, as a young man. Fr John Brett, a Dominican, spent many years in Rome teaching and performing his pastoral duties in such spectacular examples of baroque ecclesiastical exuberance as Santa Maria sopra Minerva, San Clemente and San

Isodoro. No wonder the poor man felt cast out when appointed bishop of Killala in 1743, in the farthest western reaches of Co. Mayo, and later of Elphin, a little further east but not much. Writing to Rome, he wailed about being 'a poor exile in this Siberia of the west'.

—⇒⋟⋞⇐—

JACKIE GOES
TO BALLYBAY

H ISTORIANS DON'T AGREE about just when Irish exceptionalism took modern political form. However, the choice generally narrows to either the 1790s or the 1820s. Everything in the 1790s proceeded from the French Revolution. From it came the idea of popular sovereignty: legitimate government comes upward from the people – the nation, thus nationalism – rather than top-down from God via the monarch. In this manner, representative government displaced the royal, dynastic state – with the monarch as God's anointed – and gradually advanced as the eighteenth century yielded to the nineteenth. The aristocratic principle was in retreat, the bourgeois juggernaut on the march.

In Ireland, there were a number of key responses to the events in France. A Society of United Irishmen was formed in Belfast and Dublin in 1791 to assert the common citizenship of *all* Irish men (women came much later: there were limits to contemporary enlightenment) as distinct from the existing badges of identity: religious denominations.

The principal mover in all this was one of the most attractive people in the whole Irish saga. Theobald Wolfe Tone was born in Co. Kildare, the son of a coachman. His father had connections, however, not least with the influential Wolfe family, for whom he gave his eldest son his middle name. Tone went to Trinity College Dublin to study law, although hankering even more after a military career. He married young, eventually qualifying as a lawyer, but by now the ferment from Paris had turned his head, as it turned so many others, and filled it with the intoxicating brew *du jour*.

He was a gifted pamphleteer and wrote in support of the total end of legal disabilities on Roman Catholics. This did not always sit well with his fellow-Anglicans, whose whole political and social substructure was decidedly *ancien régime*. They were the so-called ascendancy, barely 10 per cent of the population of Ireland, but in a very *ancien régime* manner they constituted the entire political nation. Their ascendancy rested ultimately on the Protestant military victories of the seventeenth century and of the land grants that flowed from those victories. The ultimate guarantor of their position was the English crown but – like many ungrateful provincial creoles elsewhere – they chafed under the feeling that they were second-class citizens in English eyes (they were) and resented English restrictions on trade and governance.

Tone was never likely to appeal to this caste. One of its more colourful members, Jonah Barrington, has left an entertaining but unreliable memoir. In it, he analyses Tone, whom he knew:

Theobald Wolf [*sic*] Tone was one of the most remarkable of the persons who lost their lives in consequence of that wild democratic mania which... had seized upon the reason of so many otherwise sensible individuals... This gentleman's enthusiastic mind was eternally surrounded by the mist of visionary speculation: it was a fine sailor, but wanted ballast... I took him round in my carriage three times, and then thought well of him; but he was too light and visionary, and as for law, was quite incapable of imbibing that species of science... It was my belief that Tone could not have succeeded at any steady civil profession. He was not worldly enough, nor had he sufficient common sense for his guidance.

Tone was the guiding spirit of the United Irish movement, which started as a radical but peaceful group. But with the outbreak of the Revolutionary Wars in 1793 – which meant that England was more or less to be constantly at war with France for the next twenty-two years – it was driven underground. It sparked the rebellions of 1798 against English rule. By now, the movement had mutated into a very different animal. In addition to its French Revolutionary principles, espoused disproportionately by the educated and the literate, it effected a coalition with various secret agrarian societies, which furnished the numbers. They were decidedly unrevolutionary in any French sense. They nursed old grievances of a sectarian nature, as far removed from the inclusive idealism of the United Irish founders as it was possible to find.

The result of the rebellions of 1798 was the bloodiest month in modern Irish history. About thirty thousand people died in

June of that year, most of them in Co. Wexford, where events took a notably sectarian turn, resulting in many outrages against Protestants before the inevitable successful counter-attack – attended by equally disgusting official tortures, murders and reprisals – pacified the area.

I have used the plural – rebellions – quite deliberately. There was another uprising, in counties Antrim and Down in the north-east of the island. This was very different from the Wexford affair. It was almost entirely a Presbyterian enterprise. These were the two counties with the highest concentration of Presbyterians and, crucially, the fewest Roman Catholics. The principles of the French Revolution had had an immediate appeal to Presbyterians, who were a highly literate community with a quasi-democratic system of church government and a list of grievances against the Anglican elite.

In embracing the Revolutionary principles wafted in from France, the Presbyterians of east Ulster had a problem. Exercise of these principles meant making common cause with Anglicans and Roman Catholics – Wolfe Tone's basic formula – but as Calvinists they remained deeply suspicious of the Catholics. They knew that the Roman church was an inveterate enemy of the French Revolution and that many Catholics in western France – the *chouans* – were ostentatiously Catholic in their counter-revolutionary fervour.

As good, rational Calvinists, representing a radical statement of Reformation principles, they had every reason to distrust Catholics as incubators of superstition, priestcraft and distant authority. None the less, they were the critical material at hand and there was a sincere desire among Presbyterian United Irishmen in Belfast in the 1790s for the relief of Catholic disabilities. One of the leading Presbyterian intellectuals, William Drennan, summed it up thus, as if making the best of a bad job: 'It is a churlish soil, but it is the soil of Ireland and must be cultivated, or we must emigrate.' He was writing of Catholicism. Or again, defending the inclusivity of the United Irish movement, 'if the Protestants are much more enlightened in regard to civil and religious liberty they will by this mental intercourse most rapidly give light to the more opaque body... ignorance will become knowledge, bigotry liberality, and civil freedom must necessarily terminate in the pure principles of Protestantism.'

Then came the rebellion in June 1798. Those counties west of the River Bann did not rise. There, sectarian hatreds – finding expression in the recently formed Orange Order – made any co-operation across confessional lines impossible. So the rebellion in Ulster was confined to idealistic Presbyterians. They were routed in short order. The wider Presbyterian – and Protestant – community might have thought their sacrifice in vain when news filtered through of the sectarian jacquerie in Wexford.

That moment in 1798 put an end to idealistic fancies. All confessional groups huddled together for warmth. The Presbyterians abandoned revolutionary idealism: it had led only to the gallows, although the rebels are remembered warmly to this day in Presbyterian Ulster in a sentimental kind of fashion. The Anglicans allowed themselves to be bribed and bought by London to abolish the Dublin parliament and effect the Act of Union. The Catholics kept their heads down for the next decade or so.

And then, there emerged from all this the volcanic figure of Daniel O'Connell.

*

THE ACT OF Union created a unitary state and saw the end of the separate kingdom of Ireland, which had existed as a kingdom under the English crown since 1541 and as a lordship thereof since the twelfth century. Unlike the old kingdom of Scots, it had been in no sense an independent realm, rather a dependent one. The degree of dependence varied from time to time according to circumstance. Moreover, whether as lordship or kingdom, any claim that the English crown had had upon Ireland had been partial until Cromwell completed the total conquest of the island in the 1650s. Prior to that, the king's writ had run uncertainly if at all in large parts of the island, where local warlords cracked the whip.

Opposition to the Act of Union was strongest among those elements of the ascendancy for whom existing arrangements were very congenial indeed. The Irish parliament was open only to their kind, was cheerfully corrupt in the eighteenth-century manner and a matter of some considerable pride to that caste. Its members, therefore, needed substantial inducements to commit political hara-kiri and it was forthcoming in bribes from London on a scale that raised eyebrows in an age not excessively squeamish about such matters.

It is now generally accepted by scholars that the bribery required was impressive even by the standards of the age. Doubts had existed because one of the earliest accusations came from Jonah Barrington, as unreliable as he was entertaining. He was an MP in the old, unreformed Dublin parliament, a diarist of near genius and a vocal opponent of the Union. This did not inhibit him from applying without success for the job of solicitor-general in the middle of the controversy; he could not possibly have sustained his opposition to a government measure if he was a member of the ministry. But, rather like Churchill in the twentieth century, he ensured that history was kind to him by writing the history himself and painting his conduct in vividly principled colours. Barrington was, on the contrary, a chancer who may well have been a persuader for the Union on the quiet while denouncing it in public. There were rumours that he took bribes from both sides, unprovable but not implausible given his later conduct. Although subsequently appointed a judge, he had to flee Ireland to escape his creditors and charges of embezzlement – including the peculation of monies lodged in his own court – and spent the rest of his long life in Paris. Unlike Wolfe Tone, Jonah Barrington was very worldly indeed.

William Pitt the younger, the British prime minister, saw the Union as a sincere attempt to bind Ireland to the mother ship and to close the wounds opened by the ructions of the 1790s. A realist, he made Catholic Emancipation – the admission of Catholics to parliament and to high offices of state without the need to take the oath of supremacy, which no Catholic could in good conscience take – an integral part of the proposed measure. It was clear to Pitt that if the people of Ireland were to be bound to the new unitary state, the religion of the Irish majority must find a place in that state. Not everyone in England agreed. Religious conviction mattered in 1800 in a manner utterly remote from us today.

In the event, the only consequential conscience that was troubled by the emancipation proposal was that of the king. Dear old Farmer George, the third of that name, was violently opposed to what he saw as a betrayal of his coronation oath and would not have it at any price. Like a lot of stupid people, it took a great deal to get an idea into the king's head but once lodged there, there was no shifting it. Pitt got the Union through, but sans emancipation; and then resigned on a point of principle. So Ireland was now bound ever tighter to England and the Catholics were still out in the cold.

It is at this point that the name of Daniel O'Connell first began to be known. Pitt's proposal for emancipation came at a price: a government veto on Catholic episcopal appointments. Although the measure failed, the question of the veto persisted. O'Connell, the scion of a remote Catholic gentry family in south-west Co. Kerry that lived by its wits, had been born in 1775 and educated at St-Omer in France. There, the excesses of the Revolution put him off violence for life. He was called to the Bar – one of the earliest beneficiaries of the Relief Act of 1793 – and soon began to make a name for himself as an advocate.

For the next forty years, not much moved in Catholic Ireland that did not have O'Connell's hand across it. In mobilizing Irish Catholic opinion, he effectively invented mass populist politics in modern form, as remote from *ancien régime* usages as it was possible to be. But he first made his mark as a firm opponent of any proposed veto as a *quid pro quo* for emancipation. The question had lain dormant after 1800 but surfaced from 1808 onwards; proponents of emancipation were divided on whether or not the veto was an acceptable price to pay.

O'Connell was adamant that it was not, in that it would sacrifice the independence of the Catholic Church to its Protestant opponent. As London saw it, a veto was required precisely to exercise some degree of negative control over the leadership of this potentially dangerous body. So, in a sense, the anti-vetoists and London were agreed. To London – and to the pro-veto elements in Ireland – it seemed an unobjectionable proposal, for which there was a clear precedent in Lutheran Prussia, where the king exercised a veto on the appointment of bishops to the Polish Catholic Church.

The more radical, middle-class faction among Irish Catholics, with O'Connell ever more prominent, were unimpressed by Prussia or anywhere else. The older, more aristocratic leadership – both among the hierarchy and the laity – were open to the possibility of a veto but they were overborne. The controversy rumbled on through the 1810s: in part, the anti-vetoists represented a generational change, in part a class one. The Catholic middle class was still tiny and would not form a cohesive social project for the best part of another hundred years – a development that will be explored in more detail later in this book – but what there was of it knew what it wanted: an absolutely free-standing, autonomous church and community answerable to no external authority (other, perhaps, than the Pope who happily was far away).

The veto question was finally settled in O'Connell's favour, as were most things in his world in these years. Obscure in itself, it marks a critical moment in the story of the Irish exception. The leadership of Catholic Ireland was declaring ecclesiastical independence from the pan-Protestant state of which it was now formally a constituent element. It was part of a great change that was quietly transforming that community. The aristocratic old leadership had been prepared to accommodate itself to the state, however reluctantly, in a typically *ancien régime* way. The bourgeois radicals were not.

The Catholic Church had suffered the disabilities of the penal laws – most of them enacted by the old Irish parliament with its triumphant Anglican majority – for much of the eighteenth century. None the less, the church survived in good institutional order. All the dioceses had bishops in residence, there were numerous priests, the church was in full communion with Rome, and while many peasant practices persisted which the clergy deplored as superstitious, there was a movement towards doctrinal and liturgical orthodoxy which advanced steadily in the course of the nineteenth century.

The church was strongest where the community was strongest. One of the striking things about the early nineteenth-century church was its regional disparities. In the impoverished west of Ireland, it still remained for the greater part a pre-modern peasant body. In Ulster, as we shall see very shortly, it was swamped in a sea of Protestants. But in the south-east of the island, in the rich river valleys and towns – despite terrible poverty and beggary to which many contemporary travellers attested – there was a middle class of sorts. The Old English – descendants of the twelfth-century Normans who had remained Catholic – had sustained a modest middle class. They traded: the export trade from towns such as Waterford was vigorous and far-flung. They farmed and, through inter-marriage, they maintained extended family networks. As with O'Connell, they educated their sons abroad.

It was among these people that the church was strongest. The simplest way to illustrate this is to look at the foundation dates of Catholic institutions. The cathedral in Waterford – a fine neo-classical building, product of a self-confident wealthy community, dates from 1793. To be true, they were a small minority among their impoverished co-religionists, although it was the memory of the impoverishment that adhered in folk-memory while that of the wealth was occluded. The same year, 1793, saw the opening in Carlow of the first Catholic institution of higher education in the post-penal era. The cathedral adjacent in Carlow was begun in 1828, as was the parish church in Dungarvan, Co. Waterford. In nearby Youghal, Co. Cork, the parish church was built in 1796 in mock-Anglican style. Clongowes Wood College, the first Jesuit school founded in the British Isles since the Reformation, opened in Co. Kildare in 1814. These are all very early foundation dates: most of the institutional revival of Catholicism in the rest of the island – especially in church building – came in the second half of the nineteenth century.

The Catholic elite of the south-east, roughly east of a line drawn from Cork to Dublin, was a generation or two ahead of its co-religionists in terms of its social cohesion, wealth and influence. It is no coincidence that so many leading figures in the nineteenth-century hierarchy came disproportionately from this region. Paul Cullen, the first ever Irish cardinal, who dominated the Irish church in the generation after the Famine, was from Co. Kildare. His nephew, Patrick Francis Moran, was cardinal archbishop of Sydney and a key figure in the Irish Catholic diaspora of the late nineteenth century. Cullen's predecessor as archbishop of Dublin, Daniel Murray, was born near Arklow, Co. Wicklow. James Warren Doyle, the formidable and influential bishop of Kildare and Leighlin in the 1820s, was from Co. Wexford.

Similarly, it is remarkable how many of Daniel O'Connell's political lieutenants came from the south-east. Thomas Wyse from Co. Waterford, who married a Bonaparte, was one such. Another was Richard Lalor Sheil, from Co. Kilkenny. Denys Scully was from Kilfeakle, Co. Tipperary. All of them came from wealthy and professional backgrounds: Sheil and Scully, like O'Connell himself, were lawyers.

Irish nationalism, or at least the version of it that was to dominate the history of the island – and set its relationship with Britain thereafter – first developed among the privileged community of Catholics in the south-east quadrant. Their project was overtly confessional: the relief of remaining religious disabilities through the winning of Catholic Emancipation. Thereafter, they looked for repeal of the Union, confident in the superiority of Catholic numbers. Moreover, as we shall see in a little more detail in chapter 5, this elite looked beyond Britain to continental Europe, partly by dint of having been educated there, partly by confessional allegiance to Rome. Their mental world superseded the archipelago.

In 1823, Daniel O'Connell founded the Catholic Association. It was just the latest in a series of such political organizations that had been formed in the ten years or so since the veto controversy was at its height. None had prospered. Like the others, this new association was composed of the usual middle-class elite: the subscription was about a guinea a year, around six months' rent for a middling tenant farmer. A year later, in 1824, a new category of associate member was launched at a cost of a penny a month, the so-called Catholic Rent.

It transformed the association. More than that, it transformed the whole history of Ireland and had a volcanic effect on the politics of the United Kingdom. It announced the arrival of the politics of mass mobilization, the first such populist movement in Europe. It took the government a year or so to outlaw the association, which by then had raised about £17,000, a formidable sum; significantly, nearly all of this came from the provinces of Leinster and Munster. In addition, the association had created a national network of local committees and activists. The simplest way of doing this was to tap into the one existing organizational structure that was tailor-made for the purpose: the Catholic parish system.

(It is interesting to consider that Irish nationalist politics in the 1820s found an echo on the Indian subcontinent a century later. The Indian Congress Party had been founded in 1885 by educated westernized elites. In the 1920s, Gandhi, although a lawyer himself, transformed Congress into a vast mass movement of millions. Similarly, Jinnah – the Muslim leader and father of Pakistan, who was a tremendous snob – built the Muslim League up from an elite club to a mass movement that echoed and rivalled Congress. All very Dan O'Connell, but Dan had got there first.)

When the Catholic Association was suppressed by the government, O'Connell simply started a new organization called the New Catholic Association and renewed the rent. In 1826, there was a general election. Although Catholics were not permitted to sit in parliament, many liberal Protestants stood in support of O'Connell's association. The key contest was in Co. Waterford, right down in the far south-east corner, in the heartland of advanced nationalist consciousness.

The electorate was small. Its key element was the forty-shilling freeholders, that is tenants whose holding was valued at £2 (or forty shillings) per annum after rents and other charges had been defrayed. Traditionally, the forty-shilling freeholders had been creatures of their landlords: there was no secret ballot and each man had to declare his choice publicly. It was generally an unwise tenant who voted against his landlord's wishes; it was an invitation to eviction and ruin.

In 1826, the landlord in question was the marquis of Waterford, head of the powerful Beresford family. They had been a power in the land for generations and were accustomed to deference. The Tory candidate was the marquis's son, Lord George Thomas Beresford. Opposing Beresford was a young liberal landlord, Villiers Stuart, who won. The settled pattern of generations was broken: the forty-shilling freeholders abandoned the Beresfords and embraced the candidate supported by the Catholic Association. It was a transfer of loyalty on a seismic scale. Moreover, it was the first visible sign of the pattern that marked the advance of Irish nationalism: the deference previously extended to the grandees of the *ancien régime* was now to be replaced by Catholic communal solidarity. England's garrison in Ireland could no longer take the people for granted.

This pattern was repeated in the tumultuous by-election in Co. Clare in 1828, caused by the appointment of the sitting MP, William Vesey Fitzgerald, to a government post in London. Ironically, Vesey Fitzgerald was a liberal Protestant and a supporter of Catholic Emancipation. His re-election should have been a routine matter, a mere going through the motions. But the cat was thrown among the pigeons when O'Connell himself stood, although barred as a Catholic from entering parliament.

The Clare by-election was one of the foundation moments of modern Irish nationalism. The contest was drenched in the most uncompromising sectarian rhetoric: O'Connell knew his

St John's Castle, Limerick, commanding the lower reaches of the River Shannon; one of the great early Norman castles in Ireland.

Hugh O'Neill, simultaneously The O'Neill and 2nd earl of Tyrone, a military commander of exceptional talent who came close to defeating English royal power in Ireland in the 1590s.

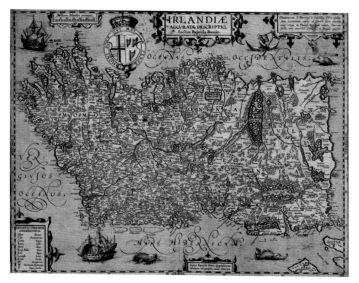

Baptista Boazzio's map is one of a number of maps of Ireland produced by cartographers working in Flanders in the late sixteenth century.

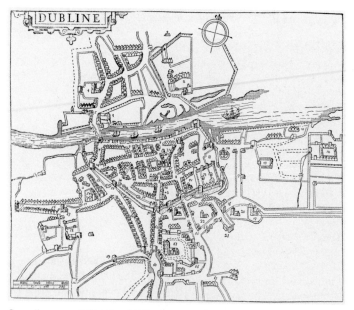

Speed's map of Dublin, 1610, showing the late medieval town before the great urban expansion that began in the 1670s.

The Battle of the Boyne, 11 July 1690, which was fought between James II and William III, as depicted by Jan van Huchtenburg. It was the only battle fought on Irish soil which was of consequence in a larger European war, as well as settling insular matters between King Billy and King James.

Oliver Cromwell brought to an end a process of English conquest of Ireland that had been in train for over a hundred years, and that almost faltered altogether in the 1590s. By the 1650s, the English state had, for the first time, complete control of Ireland.

Bantry Bay viewed from Seskin Hill in West Cork. It is spectacular, but the French had no luck here in 1796, the last attempt by a continental power to assist an Irish rebellion against Britain.

Façade of Roman Catholic cathedral in Waterford. The interior is more exuberant than the cool classicism of this façade. The architect, John Roberts, also designed the nearby Anglican cathedral. There, he maintained the classicism within, appropriate to the calm of that confession. Here, his interior was more exuberant, reflecting the theatrical exuberance of Catholic liturgy.

View of Upper Mount Street to Pepper Cannister Church. This street runs off the south-east corner of Merrion Square and forecloses the vista along the southern side of the square, one of the finest urban views in Georgian Dublin.

Portrait of Daniel O'Connell, the Irish political leader who developed modern mass nationalism, dominated Irish life in the first half of the nineteenth century and influenced all who followed him.

James Stephens was the first Fenian leader of real importance. A civil engineer by profession and an energetic, indeed relentless, organizer, he helped to introduce a movement into Irish nationalist life whose hour finally struck at Easter 1916.

Illustration depicting starving peasants at a workhouse gate during the Irish Famine (1845–1849).

Joseph Gillis Biggar,
Vanity Fair, 1877.

Ham Cuffe, 5th earl of Desart,
Vanity Fair, 1902.

St John's Church of Ireland, Seafield Road, Clontarf, in north Dublin, dates from 1866 and replaced a pre-Reformation church (now ruinous) which stands in a cemetery adjacent. It was the last major parish church built in Dublin prior to disestablishment.

Inistioge, Co. Kilkenny. The playing field of The Rower-Inistioge GAA club can be seen just beyond the bridge.

The quarter-final match of the GAA Hurling All-Ireland Senior Championship between Kilkenny and Cork at Croke Park, Dublin, July 2019. Cork (in red) and Kilkenny are two of the oldest rivals in the game, the third traditional power being neighbouring Tipperary. The Kilkenny team of the early 2000s were arguably the finest ever proponents of the game. They won the championship eleven times between 2000 and 2015.

market. Although his rival was a supporter of the Catholic cause and a popular landlord who had opposed the Act of Union, O'Connell played the two cards that were to sustain popular Irish nationalism for more than a century to come: faith and fatherland. He represented himself to the electors of Clare as one whose 'forefathers were for centuries the chieftains of the land and the friends of her people'. Describing Fitzgerald as 'the sworn libeller of the Catholic faith' – this because he had taken the oath of allegiance, anti-Catholic bits and all, as all MPs were obliged to do – he drew the contrast with himself: 'one who has devoted his early life to your cause, who has consumed his manhood in a struggle for your liberties'. In effect, as one of O'Connell's biographers notes, his 'energies [were] directed to prising the peasant vote from the proprietors by the lever of religion'.

It was an uncompromising display of Catholic power. Every parish priest in Co. Clare bar one worked on O'Connell's campaign. In the course of the poll itself, conducted in Ennis, the county town, by open roll-call vote over a number of days, one priest helpfully explained to the crowds that an elector who had voted against O'Connell had just dropped dead! Another exhorted the voters to support O'Connell in terms that left nothing unsaid: 'You have heard the tones of the tempter and charmer [Fitzgerald] whose confederates have through all ages joined the descendants of the Dane, the Norman, and the Saxon, in burning your churches and levelling your altars, in slaughtering your clergy, in stamping out your religion. Let every renegade to his God and his country follow Vesey Fitzgerald, and every true Catholic Irishman follow me.'

This self-dramatizing farrago of victimhood hit a powerful nerve in Co. Clare in 1828. A version of it continued to serve Catholic Ireland as a rough epitome of its history well into the twentieth century; there are many in modern Ireland who might argue with the tone but not with the substance. The Irish nation was forming itself in uncompromisingly Catholic terms. It was going to be hard for Protestants not to recoil from this new nation. If Vesey Fitzgerald's face did not fit, what Protestant face would? Ireland had moved a long way in a generation from the blithe idealism of the United Irishmen.

O'Connell won. He polled 2,057 votes to Fitzgerald's 982. The Tory government jointly led by the Duke of Wellington and Sir Robert Peel was now in a bind. O'Connell was the duly elected member for Clare with over two-thirds of the vote. But he was unable to take his seat, if only because of the anti-Catholic clauses in the oath of allegiance. Peel himself was horrified by O'Connell's 'tens of thousands of disciplined fanatics' but prudently concluded that it was worth facing down King George IV and the Tory ultras in order to mollify O'Connell's 'hereditary bondsmen'. Faced with outright electoral revolt in Ireland, and the implicit threat of something worse, the government capitulated. Catholic Emancipation was granted: Catholics could now sit in parliament, being required only to take a revised and inoffensive oath; hold office; and become judges. The price extracted to save some of the government's face was the raising of the franchise threshold in Ireland from forty shillings (£2) to £10. Thus the forty-shilling freeholders, who won Catholic Emancipation, were disenfranchised for their pains – at least for the moment.

It was O'Connell's greatest hour. He was fifty-four years old and beyond question the dominant figure in Irish life. To his contemporaries, he was a mixture of hero and enigma. He had titanic energy and organizing ability; a sulphurous temper; torrential eloquence; deep reservoirs of charm. He was a genuine liberal in many respects, as his parliamentary career was to prove: he was a free trader and anti-slaver at a time when these were litmus tests of liberalism – but he led a movement that was nakedly confessional. His political organization was based on the Catholic parishes and with the parishes came the priests. O'Connell stands accused of introducing the priests into Irish politics, from which they have only recently been extruded. He might have replied that he simply used the most practical means to hand and that, after all, the confessional rivalry between Protestant and Catholic was the decisive line of division in Irish life.

It was. The problem for O'Connell was that Ireland was not all Catholic. The three provinces of Leinster, Munster and Connacht were overwhelmingly so. But the northern province, Ulster, was not.

O'CONNELL'S ASSOCIATION HAD established no presence in Ulster. As we saw, it raised its finances in Leinster and Munster. Connacht was too poor. But Ulster was too Protestant. Indeed, O'Connell had never visited Ulster and knew nothing about it. The only time he ever went there was as late as 1841; he got short shrift from the locals and was glad to head back south expeditiously.

So, in 1828, as the final campaign for Catholic Emancipation was in full surge following O'Connell's election win in Clare, and just a few months after that historic victory, one of his most enthusiastic lieutenants, a certain John Lawless, decided to take the campaign to Ulster.

Lawless had been born in Dublin around 1780, the son of a brewer. On his father's side, he was related to Nicholas Lawless, the 1st baron Cloncurry. So he was typical of O'Connell's associates, being from the small but influential Catholic well-to-do class. We know less than we would like about his career. He attended Trinity but appeared not to take a degree; nor do we know what he studied. In later life, he appeared to have established himself as a lawyer but in his youth he started out with his father in the brewery.

He also espoused radical politics and may have been 'out' in 1798. He was an associate of Robert Emmet but appears not to have taken part in Emmet's farcical rebellion in Dublin in 1803, a sad aftershock of the '98 uprising; it is speculated that that is because he was in preventative detention, held by the authorities on suspicion. If that was the case, he was lucky because any close involvement with Emmet might have ended on a scaffold.

When Percy Bysshe Shelley and his wife Harriet first came to Ireland early in 1812, Lawless befriended them and the poet referred to him as a republican. On Shelley's return visit a year later, there was a cooling of relations between them for reasons unknown. But it was clear that Lawless kept, and liked to keep, radical company.

He turned to journalism and inevitably, given his radicalism, got himself in trouble with the authorities from time to time. He established himself in Belfast, opened and closed a succession of papers and journals, and acquired a reputation as a trenchant opinion-monger. This reflected his personality: he was outspoken and indiscreet. For this, he acquired the sobriquet Honest Jack Lawless, although how much of his honesty was of the clumsy holy fool variety we can only guess. Certainly, O'Connell was less than enthusiastic about Lawless, who had become a person of substance in the Catholic Association by the mid-1820s. 'I cannot say', O'Connell wrote to a correspondent in 1830, 'that Lawless ever satisfied me of the soundness of his views or the perfect integrity of his purposes. He was almost always a <u>nuisance to be managed</u> and it was difficult to manage him.'

Although Lawless had been a vocal and tireless supporter of O'Connell, especially in Clare, he later criticized him loudly for the concessions made to secure emancipation, especially the disenfranchisement of the forty-shilling freeholders. This was typical of Lawless, who trumpeted the purity of his principles and appointed himself a man of the people; he was exactly the kind of irritant that a political heavyweight like O'Connell came to despise. Indeed, O'Connell made sure that Lawless was refused a nomination to stand in the 1830 general election.

But back in 1828, swollen with the great victory in Clare, Lawless decided to do something about Ulster. The existing social leadership of the Ulster Catholics, especially the higher clergy, were extremely nervous about Lawless's proposed démarche, being acutely aware of local sensitivities and of the potency of popular Protestant organization. Of all these things, Lawless was blithely unaware; moreover, he appears to have turned a deaf ear to any minatory advice from persons who had some knowledge of the realities.

Nothing daunted, Lawless persisted in believing that any opposition in Ulster to Catholic ambition was thinly rooted in the local aristocracy and had no purchase among ordinary Protestants, the very opposite of the truth, as Lawless was to discover the hard way. He organized a group of supporters and set off north from Dublin in September 1828, picking up more people on the way. Some estimates tell of his supporters numbering almost one hundred thousand people but this is obviously absurd and inflated. Even Lawless himself never called for more than twenty thousand people, still a formidable number and one that he may or may not have realized. The first sign of trouble came at the little village of Collon, Co. Louth – still in Leinster – where there was a brief affray. But from there Lawless kept going north and debouched into the southern reaches of Ulster at the town of Carrickmacross, Co. Monaghan. From Carrickmacross, Lawless proposed to push slightly north-west towards the village of Ballybay. With typical lack of tact, he referred to this whole enterprise as 'the invasion of Ulster'.

He and his followers never quite made it to Ballybay. Troops were deployed: the authorities were that concerned about Lawless and his 'invasion'. And it was a good thing that they were, for when the 'invaders' approached Ballybay, they got a nasty dose of Ulster reality. Ballybay was a Presbyterian village and it was the most southerly point in Ulster where Protestant numbers could be confidently deployed in force. They were so deployed, courtesy of the Orange Order. In general, the Orange had not had a great presence among Presbyterians, being for the most part composed of lower-class Anglicans. So Ballybay was something new: communal Protestant solidarity across intra-confessional lines.

They mustered – and with menaces. They were armed and meant to use their arms. The army kept the sides apart and eventually persuaded Lawless to retreat. He made his way across country to Armagh, where there was more trouble. After this, the invasion of Ulster pretty well collapsed in on itself and slunk off back to Dublin. It had been an utter humiliation and a reminder that no significant projection of Catholic ambition was possible even on the southern reaches of the northern province.

So, in one sense nothing much happened when Jackie went to Ballybay. After all, it amounted to little more than a threatened affray. But something very profound indeed happened there, just as was happening – but in a different way – all over Ireland in 1828–9. Outside Ulster, the Irish exception was announcing itself in blatantly confessional terms. Catholic ambition focused on re-setting its community's relationship with the pan-Protestant state of which it was now a constituent part. O'Connell would, in the coming years, look to re-set that relationship even further by trying unsuccessfully to repeal the Union. That demand set the basic aspiration of Irish Catholics for the rest of the century, until the Irish exception – after many twists and turns – eventually detached itself altogether from the United Kingdom in 1922.

But within the Irish exception, there was the Ulster exception; and Ballybay was its first coherent, public manifestation. That, too, was to persist and it persists to this day. When nationalist ambition, pressing north, meets unionist resistance on the Ulster marches, it falters. It may not falter forever but Ballybay in 1828 is the moment when what became Ulster unionism – the solidarity of all Ulster Protestants against nationalist advance – is first manifest *in utero*. This was the force that almost brought the UK to the brink of civil war in 1914 over home rule. It was the force that eventually led to the betrayal of the southern Protestants – a scattered regional minority – and the acceptance of partition.

It has been said a thousand times and bears repeating here that the divide in Ireland is not religious in any theological sense: it is not a religious war. But religious or confessional allegiance is the most visible marker of all differences in the Anglo-Irish imbroglio. In the end, the pan-Protestant United Kingdom could not hold onto the part of Ireland that was overwhelmingly Catholic. It, in its turn, could not absorb pan-Protestant Ulster. It, in *its* turn, found itself with a large, alienated and disaffected minority of Catholics within its own territory. These were impermeable tribal boundaries, layered rather like Russian dolls, in which the principal markers were religious affiliation.

Had the Reformation taken in most of Ireland, would we be where we are? Impossible to say. It wasn't the Reformation that delivered the Scottish Act of Union in 1707, but it helped that that arrangement was one between two varieties of Reform. Catholicism – the religion of those continental powers most threatening to Britain – proved too indigestible in the end. And it, in its turn, could not digest the Protestant redoubt in Ulster. So here we are.

—❊—

GALLANT ALLIES IN EUROPE?

I F IRELAND WAS a long way from England – or at least from that part of England from which power was projected – it was *a fortiori* even farther from potential continental allies. Despite a repeated pattern of Irish dreams about deliverance from the English yoke by the appearance – *deus ex machina* – of continental muscle, it generally failed to materialize. These disappointed dreams of deliverance informed a lot of eighteenth-century Irish-language poetry, specifically the genre known as the *aisling*.

The *aisling* had a long run in Irish poetry, with surviving examples from Old and Middle Irish. They are dream poems, in which the protagonist imagines some attained state of bliss, as with the conquest of a beautiful woman. But in the eighteenth century, it assumed a more allegorical mode, especially in the hands of an exceptional school of poets in Munster.

These poets were Jacobites, dreaming of Ireland's deliverance from the Georges and the restoration of the Stuarts. But the Stuarts could not come on their own. By the time these poems were written, the Stuarts were either a busted flush or on the point of becoming so. When the Pope finally recognized the legitimacy of the Hanoverian dynasty in 1766, on the death of the Old Pretender, James VIII and III – who never reigned – the son of James II and father of the sot Bonnie Prince Charlie.

None the less, the poetry continued, probably because the Stuarts had never been much more than a means to an end. The end was to effect a fundamental re-set in relations between the two islands. This would entail the replacement of the Hanoverians with a Catholic king, wherever one might be found. Furthermore, it would entail the reversal of the Cromwellian land settlement. Later, these ambitions developed into modern nationalism. All that, however, was for the future: in the age of the *aisling*, the dream was of deliverance from current woes. At most, the Stuarts might act as agents and persuaders, but the muscle would be provided – were it to be forthcoming at all – from England's continental Catholic enemies, first Spain and later France.

In the eighteenth-century *aislingí*, Ireland is imagined as a violated woman, raped by a stranger who has displaced her rightful lover or husband. The symbolism is transparent. Yet the persistence of these poems – some of them of quite superb quality – seeded a tradition of resentful sensibility that never quite disappeared. In the eyes of the dispossessed – all those whose lands had been rendered forfeit and settled by English – this was simple theft and appropriation. The entire transaction was illegitimate. It did not matter what the English and their lawyers thought: what mattered in the long run was that this is what Irish people thought – and remembered.

And it was not just the dispossessed landowners but persons farther down the social scale as well. The poets were not entirely disinterested: they had depended on the patronage of Gaelic and Old English lords. They described the new English as boors, barbarians, vulgarians. All words on the wind, but the wind carried a virus that would eventually be fatal to the English. Towards the bottom of the Gaelic heap, with all its poverty, there was added to the cocktail the toxin of religion. In Irish Catholic eyes, Protestantism and land theft marched together. These new men now in possession of ancestral lands were not just thieves: they were heretic thieves.

Much of this lay quiescent. But, rather like a long-dormant volcano, it suddenly materialized in the ferocious sectarian rhetoric of Daniel O'Connell's by-election campaign in 1828 (p. 79, chapter 4). The verbal ferocity of Dan himself and of his acolytes – with the priests enthusiastically in the van – was not directed at poor Vesey Fitzgerald because he was a landlord (or not just) but because he was a Protestant. The principal point of O'Connell's attack was that Fitzgerald had taken the oath of allegiance, which no Catholic could even contemplate in good conscience. These verbal assaults had not been conjured out of thin air; they had drawn on an underground sensibility, previously nurtured by the *aisling* poets. It hadn't gone away.

Nor was there anything peculiar to Ireland about all this. The historian James Hawes, writing about Germany east of the Elbe, notes that the German presence there was colonial and incomplete, surrounded by Slavs with their own languages, traditions and communal memories. Religious antagonism was also part of that mix: Lutheran versus Catholic. The Slavs 'were a constant reminder... that this was colonial land, taken by force from someone else who was still around and might one day fight back.'

He then illustrates this point in a footnote, in which he recalls meeting a small farmer in the south of Ireland in the 1980s who resentfully pointed out a large Protestant house standing on land which, the farmer claimed, was once his family's. The house was more than two hundred years old at the time. I can corroborate Hawes's anecdote from my own recollection, specifically the pride on the face of a substantial Catholic professional now living in the big house abandoned by its previous ascendancy owner. It stood on land that had been in this man's family before the confiscations: his pride was that he had recovered it, and righted the wrongs of centuries.

The *aisling* dream of deliverance could, however, only be realized with help from the continent. That dream was there from the moment that the Reformation wrought its transformation. The sixteenth-century rebels against the crown had looked abroad. Silken Thomas in the 1530s and the Munster Catholic rebels in the 1570s – from the other, southern branch of the FitzGeralds – had each invoked papal help. None materialized.

But when it came to the serious stuff, O'Neill's rebellion in the 1590s, the picture changed. Spanish help did come. But it came with a divided command and landed at the wrong end of the island and it all ended badly. O'Neill had cultivated King Philip II – who proved easily bored by Ireland, and unreliable withal – and would have enthroned him as King of Ireland had the war been won. As it was, it had been a very close shave for England.

*

WHAT FOLLOWED WAS a case of the dog that did not bark. It was clear that Ireland was an awkward sort of place. Even in quiet times – which means most of the eighteenth century, when the Scottish Jacobites rebelled twice but Ireland was silent – its differences were marked. Unlike Scotland, which had a highly developed form of administrative home rule even after the union of 1707, Ireland was ruled more like a recalcitrant colony after the union of 1801.

The continental great powers were the dog that did not bark. After the Spaniards at Kinsale in 1601, there was only ever one serious attempt to render assistance to an Irish rebellion. That was the French Revolutionary expedition of 1796. It too failed – if only just: like the Armada, it had all the bad luck going. But luck is part of the calculation in these things as well. Napoleon was not simply being amusing when he enquired of putative generals if they were lucky. Luck, in that sense, seems to be what a modern business executive would refer to as measuring the downside risk.

The downside risk for the French – by the late eighteenth century, Spain had shot its bolt and was out of the game – was tied up with distance, and with front and back doors. France was a continental power whose army would always outrank its navy, whereas with Britain it was the exact opposite. For France the front door was Germany and the Low Countries. That was where the military threat to the Revolution had come from until the cannonade at Valmy in 1792 broke the First Coalition and set France on its dizzying waltz all the way to Moscow and Waterloo.

The back door was no threat at all militarily. The Royal Navy may have had control of the seas but there was never the slightest chance of Britain launching an invasion of France. Britain could make trouble for France by financing counter-revolutionary agitations, something vexatious enough in itself, but its military commitment to the various coalitions assembled against Revolutionary and Napoleonic France was modest until relatively late in the day.

So why, in the winter of 1796, did France launch a naval expedition from Brest to sail to Ireland with 15,000 of the best troops in Europe – troops that had beaten everything put before them for the previous four years and would continue to do so for the next fifteen – when Ireland itself was disturbed but not (yet) in open rebellion against the crown?

Revenge was a principal incentive for the French Directory. A counter-revolutionary royalist rebellion in the Vendée – southern Brittany – had been suppressed with exemplary brutality by troops under the command of General Lazare Hoche. The rebels had been aided and abetted by Britain, but now Hoche's army was idle and close to Brest. In the meantime, Wolfe Tone – who had been in America – had arrived in Paris. In America, he had come to know James Monroe, later to be President of the United States and the author of his eponymous doctrine, who was by now ambassador to France. Through Monroe, Tone had got to know Lazare Carnot, the key figure in the Directory.

Tone urged Carnot to send an expedition to Ireland, representing the country as ripe for rebellion. It suited the Directory to accede to this opportunity, for there was Hoche and his men within striking distance of Brest, the obvious port of departure for any such expedition. Prussia was out of the war and peace had been made with Austria, so Britain was France's only remaining antagonist. The chance to make trouble in the

British rear proved too good to miss. That was the ambition: Irish freedom was of no account to the French, but irritating Britain was.

So they sailed – and every misfortune that could attend them happened. They got to Bantry Bay in December 1796 but contrary winds forestalled them: not a single French foot stepped onto Irish soil. Eventually, what was left of the expedition cut their cables and headed back to Brest. There is little doubt that, had they got ashore, they would have captured Cork and the south with ease. Some contemporary British army reports stated that Dublin itself could have fallen. All this is speculation, of course, but it was by any measure a narrow escape for Britain. Tone ruefully commented that England had not had such an escape since the Armada.

But that was as much continental assistance as Ireland got: the Spaniards at Kinsale in 1601 and the French in Bantry Bay in 1796. Apart from that, nothing. In 400 years, only two serious attempts to assist Irish rebellions against the crown. If Ireland was distant from England, it was even more so from those continental powers that might have assisted Irish rebels, in whom those powers generally took little interest. Ireland was a sideshow, a game not worth the candle. It was hard to reach, and the two serious attempts to do so had been cursed with ill-luck, enough to suggest that even the luckiest general might be well advised to steer clear of Irish adventures.

Even then, had a landing been successful, there was the problem of resupply. The Royal Navy held the whip hand at sea, so that even a successful expedition was in danger of finding itself stuck up a distant cul-de-sac. It just wasn't worth the trouble and the risk. And so, there were no more serious attempts to assist Irish rebellions. When, in 1916, the Proclamation of the Republic spoke of 'gallant allies in Europe', it was a reference to the feeble assistance offered by Germany to the Easter Rising. It was of necessity feeble: there was a proper war on in Europe, from which the Germans were hardly going to divert serious resources in aid of a distant frolic.

Irish hopes of deliverance by Britain's continental enemies were deluded. Ireland was a potential strategic nuisance for Britain but not enticing enough to hold the sustained attention of a major continental power. There is a world of difference between being a nuisance and possessing an acute strategic value. For potential gallant allies in Europe, there were invariably bigger and more urgent concerns and crises nearer home.

BY AN IRONIC coincidence, the same year that the French were on their futile expedition to Bantry Bay, 1796, a Breton royalist did make it to Ireland. Jacques-Louis de Bougrenet de la Tocnaye, a Chevalier of the Order of St Louis, had good reason to flee France. He might not have survived the decade had he stayed, especially as the centre of counter-revolutionary activity was in his native Brittany.

He was one of a number of travellers to visit Ireland in the fifty years prior to the Great Famine of the mid-nineteenth century. In varying degrees, these travellers were also measuring distance. What fascinated them was the mental distance between the more developed societies from which they had come and the marginal place they were discovering. There is more to distance than mere mechanical measurement.

What is especially valuable in these various accounts is that the visitors, with a few exceptions such as Thackeray, were not

English. La Tocnaye was French, as were de Tocqueville and Beaumont who were in Ireland in the 1830s; Pückler Muskau, a German, ten years earlier. So the charge of English bias could hardly be laid against them. We shall return to them from time to time. But the image of Ireland as remote, other, perplexing and poor did not start with La Tocnaye and the others: it had been part of a sensibility consistently present in overseas travellers who fetched up in Ireland, whether by accident or design, but most clearly marked in the English because they had the primary interaction with Ireland – and they came as conquerors.

The English colonized Ireland. Even before the English were properly English – when they were French-speaking Norman conquistadores back in the twelfth century – they did what all conquerors do. They left an account of the natives they had displaced that was less than flattering. That tradition begins with Giraldus Cambrensis, otherwise Gerald de Barry or Gerald of Wales (c.1146–c.1223). He was Cambro-Norman, a cleric and a scholar, being an alumnus of the University of Paris. He visited Ireland in the 1180s and left two books, *Topographia Hiberniae* and *Expugnatio Hibernica*. The second, in particular, is an apologia for the first twenty years of the Norman settlement of the island. It is fair to say that in neither book does he offer a favourable view of the Gaelic Irish.

Gerald was related in blood to several of the leading early Norman lords. For all his acuteness of observation, he writes from an unapologetically superior perspective. He detested the Gaelic Irish, whom he regarded as little better than barbarians. In this, he stands at the head of a long tradition which was later carried on by New English travellers at the time of the Reformation and after, in which the same theme occurs over and over again. The English presence in Ireland is a *mission civilisatrice*, bringing enlightenment to benighted indigenes.

Some of this was simple incomprehension. In one respect, Gaelic Ireland was decidedly not backward. There was a legal system, uniform through Gaelic society and of ancient provenance. But it was a system based on retributive justice: theft was answered by material restitution and compensation. Murders were sometimes settled by the payment of blood money. Crimes were seen principally as offences of one individual against another, rather than the more modern (and English) concept of an abstract rule of law in which offences were a breach of social order and therefore required punishment by the state. Gaelic law was not just strange to the sixteenth-century English – who regarded the compensatory system as a thieves' and murderers' charter – but ever more remote from European norms. These norms depended on the development of robust state structures, so that where these were strong and strengthening, as in England and France, the concept of the rule of law might find a greater purchase. Where they were weak, as in Ireland, that was less likely. So perhaps the English had a point after all.

There is a ready answer to all such charges of native savagery, namely that it is the merest flimsy cover for predatory bullying and land-grabbing. Nor is such characterization confined to the English in Ireland. The original idea of a civilizing mission was French, as they purported to offer the peerless fruits of their civilization to their colonial subjects: it was all for their own good, don't you know. Recently, Facebook has been embarrassed by the discovery that the American Declaration of Independence contains racist language and hate speech. There are references to 'merciless Indian savages' which Facebook now deems unacceptable and has removed from its platform. Thus is one of the foundation documents of the United States bowdlerized in the service of modish obsessions: talk about Victorians and piano legs! As to the white Australian attitude to Aboriginals, it has hardly been a model of liberal accommodation for most of the time since 1788.

WITH THE DEATH of the Stuarts, the papal recognition of Hanoverian legitimacy, the failure of the French Revolutionary expedition in 1796 and the incorporation of Ireland fully into the British metropolitan state, there was a basic change of rules. Ireland forgot about gallant allies in Europe for more than a century. They had, after all, been rather a let-down.

So, in the course of the nineteenth century, Ireland focused on trying to redress its grievances in a British parliamentary context, presenting as a different kind of nuisance. First O'Connell with Catholic Emancipation in 1829 and later Parnell and his successors from the 1870s and '80s upended treasured conventions in British public life. Home rule, in particular, paralysed British politics for forty years. The Irish parliamentary tradition worked: it got the job done. It settled the land question in favour of the tenants and it was on the point of delivering home rule – devolved autonomy within the Union – when World War I transformed everything.

So, whether in parliament or on the barricades, the Irish had learned to shift for themselves if they wanted to have their heart's desire, because there was no help coming from Europe. In the second half of the nineteenth century, however, while Europe was largely forgotten, it was replaced by the influence of the Irish-American diaspora. Initially, this affected the internal organization of Irish nationalist politics, with the joint transatlantic launching of the Fenians/Irish Republican Brotherhood in 1858 destined to have the greatest influence as time went on. This was of particular significance during World War I, when Britain was trying to induce an ever-more reluctant America, with its deeply isolationist instincts, to join the conflict on the allied side. No American president, especially a Democrat like Woodrow Wilson, could ignore the Irish-American lobby which was furiously, and understandably, anglophobic. That is one reason why Ireland was the only part of the United Kingdom that did not suffer wartime conscription. It may also be the reason that Éamon de Valera was the only garrison commander in the Easter Rising *not* to have been executed: Dev had been born in New York City. It is generally not a good idea to shoot people with American passports when you are trying to solicit American assistance at a moment of existential crisis for your country.

None the less, the nature of American influence was materially different to the old Jacobite dream of military deliverance from Europe. No Fenian army was going to sail the Atlantic to help liberate Ireland. So from O'Connell in the 1820s through to Dev and Michael Collins in the 1920s, Irish nationalism had to look ever more to its own resources, to what it could achieve in a specifically British Isles context. The brief flirtation with imperial Germany before the 1916 rising was the last rumble of the gallant allies tradition. It proved as empty as its predecessors. The game was now played out either through parliament, as with O'Connell, Parnell and John Redmond, or through revolutionary republicanism. Always, however, the primary focus was on what we could do for ourselves. Any outside help, as from Irish-America, was welcomed but the primary impulse was to stop dreaming of deliverance and to shift for themselves. And shift they did, eventually securing what was in effect independence for the most heavily Catholic parts of the island, leaving Ulster behind in the United Kingdom with its own potentially destabilizing nationalist minority trapped in the unionist statelet.

All these successes looked fine for as long as the nationalist gaze was averted from Protestant Ulster, which it usually was. Irish nationalist leaders from O'Connell onward had a blind spot about Ulster, seeing in the resistance to nationalist ambition in that small, maddening, costive community little more than bluff. But it was no such thing, and no amount of denial could conjure the Ulster problem out of nationalist existence. Nationalist Ireland had found the limits of its success roughly at the same point that Honest Jack Lawless had reached nearly a hundred years earlier.

THE STUARTS DID not come back. And the penal laws – other than the ones bearing most heavily on land ownership – either did not work, or were relaxed and ignored. At any rate, things eased for Catholics from about 1730; the definitive moments came in 1745 – when Ireland did not echo Jacobite Scotland – and 1766 when Bonnie Prince Charlie died in Rome and the Pope recognized the Hanoverians in the person of King George III as the legitimate king.

What is remarkable is that, through all this, the Catholic Church in Ireland retained its institutional structures in better working order than a bald reading of the penal laws might have suggested. By 1750 or so, most dioceses had a resident bishop, even though bishops had supposedly been banished under the 1697 act. There were absentee bishops as late as the 1730s – and a particularly flagrant case in Armagh, of all sees, as late as the 1760s – but the overall pattern of resident bishops was established by the mid-century. And under the bishops, the parish system was being rebuilt. Clergy educated in that network of continental Irish colleges provided the spiritual infantry, notwithstanding another penal law that had forbidden the education of Catholics abroad. That had proved utterly unenforceable; education in one of the continental colleges was a requirement for ordination. The Irish colleges all over Catholic Europe represented an educational Counter-Reformation and made available to the old country a steady supply of returning priests and other clergy. The quick recovery of the church in the eighteenth century was an astonishing achievement. It was a process rather than an event: the quality of the lower clergy was often unsatisfactory – there are numerous complaints on this score from exasperated reforming clerics, deploring everything from doctrinal ignorance to the toleration of archaic superstitious practices to concubinage and the soliciting of female penitents in the confessional* to drunkenness – and it was well into the nineteenth century before conformity to Roman orthodoxy had finally achieved total victory. One other thing that had saved it in the penal era was pure numbers: other forms of religious discrimination in Europe were directed at minorities; uniquely, the Irish penal laws were directed at the majority.

---

* Confession boxes, first introduced in Milan by Carlo Borromeo, one of the most notable Counter-Reformation reformers, in the sixteenth century were, like so many other things, slow to reach faraway Ireland.

The recovery gave a social definition to Irish Catholics, by furnishing them with a spiritual officer corps. Together with the robust mercantile Catholic middle class, traders and shippers disproportionately found in the south-east quadrant of the island, the clergy provided the social leadership that facilitated an emerging community self-consciousness. In a sense, something like this had been going on since Cromwell declined to discriminate between different kinds of Catholics. If someone says 'you are all the same, and you're not us' and if his descendants pass laws that specifically attempt to exclude you from the public square simply because of your confessional allegiance, it is understandable that such a process of self-conscious identity might emerge over time. Combine that emerging self-identity with the memory of dispossession and you have the chemical mix that would prove so explosive at the end of the century.

This emerging self-conscious community had found an alternative locus of moral power to London: Rome. It was in the second half of the eighteenth century that the Irish Catholic Church acquired that ultramontanism that was ever after its distinguishing characteristic. There was very little market in Ireland for a Gallican church *à la française*, although there had been a minority of eighteenth-century bishops whose French educational formation had inclined them in that direction.* But the Romans outgunned them. By the early nineteenth century, only occasional bishops such as MacHale of Tuam demonstrated Gallican inclinations but were by then very much the exception rather than the rule. The recovery of the institutional

---

* Gallicanism, especially strong in France – thus the name – espouses greater national church control without totally rejecting Rome.

church in Ireland after the penal era was led by bishops and priests whose religious sensibilities had been formed in the papal forcing houses of the continental colleges. Names forgotten to all other than specialist scholars, but important in their day, were all moulded in these establishments: Nicholas Sweetman (1695–1786), bishop of Ferns, educated at Santiago; Luke Fagan (*c*.1655–1733), archbishop of Dublin, educated at Seville; James Warren Doyle (1786–1834), the formidable bishop of Kildare and Leighlin, educated at Coimbra; John Thomas Troy (1739–1823), archbishop of Dublin, educated at Rome. And so on.

Troy was important in this connection. In Rome, prior to his return to Ireland, he had been master of San Clemente al Laterano, a minor basilica, and had enjoyed the confidence of the Holy See. That confidence was well placed, for on his appointment to Dublin he put a great emphasis on ensuring that orthodox Roman disciplines were enforced on congregations still given to archaic and superstitious practices. His influence ran beyond Dublin, and his voice carried weight with his fellow-bishops. This tightening of discipline along Roman lines laid the basis for the institutional musculature of the Irish church during the nineteenth century, a process that was continuous and was brought to full fruition after the Famine by one of Troy's successors in Dublin, Paul Cullen, the first Irish cardinal and another man formed as a young priest in the ecclesiastical hothouse of Roman politics.

Thus the Irish church was cast in a Roman mould. Irish Catholicism acquired the habit of silently looking to Rome as the ultimate source of moral authority, while acknowledging London however reluctantly as the source of political authority. The ultramontane bishops were conservative and cautious men in political matters, in no sense revolutionaries or ardent nationalists – quite the contrary, for the most part – but they were conscious of being the spiritual leaders of a community that was psychologically remote from London, and that offered no spontaneous political loyalty to London commensurate with the moral loyalty that it so conspicuously offered to Rome. This was demonstrated as early as the veto controversy (p. 72, chapter 4). There was an acceptance of the political status quo *faute de mieux* and a serious hostility to revolutionary conspiracies such as the Fenians. Still, there was a tension between political and moral allegiances that lay unresolved for most of the nineteenth century.

The continental colleges either did not survive the French Revolution or were greatly weakened by it. Their critical role in ecclesiastical education and formation was made redundant by the establishment of an Irish national seminary at Maynooth, just west of Dublin, in 1795. St Patrick's College was established by an act of the Irish parliament in 1795, with enthusiastic support from London, where the fear of continental revolutionary infection was a factor. The college was sustained by an annual grant from the British Treasury. Not only that: fears of intellectual contagion from Revolutionary France were shared by senior figures in the Irish Catholic hierarchy, especially those with a Roman educational background rather than a French one – where a long-standing aversion to Gallicanism had already pre-disposed the 'Romans' to a suspicion of France. Foremost among these Romans was John Thomas Troy, who wrote of Revolutionary France as its armies rampaged across Europe: 'Look... to the different countries and states they have conquered or republicanized under the mask of friendship. In every one of them you may observe that anarchy has succeeded to regular government... and competency, infidelity and licentiousness to religion and morality.'

The hope was that Maynooth would be seen as a generous concession to Catholic ambition and an institution that would reconcile the spiritual leadership of Irish Catholicism to the British state. This hope was only half realized. Troy may have been as conservative as any member of Pitt's cabinet, to the point that if history had taken another turn, there might well have been a gradual rapprochement between the Irish Catholic establishment and the British state. That is, obviously, one of the many things we shall never know. But history actually took a turn that was as inimical to Troy's world as to Pitt's. The establishment of Maynooth coincided with the rise of nationalism, which gradually gave to Catholic communal self-consciousness a political definition. The tension between a growing spiritual allegiance to Rome and a weakening political allegiance to London snapped. Irish Catholicism had by the 1820s acquired a public face and a political project, which was to weaken, as far as possible, the political connection to Britain. There was, it is true, a significant Protestant element to nineteenth-century nationalism – Parnell, after all, was a Protestant – but it was always unrepresentative of Irish Protestantism in general. The salient feature of nationalism was its Catholicism.

—>‹—

SIX

THE EMPTY CENTRE

I N 1842, WILLIAM Makepeace Thackeray was in Cork. He noted that there were handsome retail shops but that 'most look as if too big for the business carried on within'. He illustrates this point by observing that there was 'a want of ready money'. In three of the principal shops he 'purchased articles, and tendered a pound in exchange – not one of them had silver enough; and as for a five-pound note, which I presented at one of the topping [*sic*] booksellers his boy went round to various places in vain, and finally set forth to the bank where change was got'. He had a similar experience in another shop where he tendered half-a-crown for a sixpenny item and was therefore due change of two shillings. It had to be found in another premises.

While in Cork, Thackeray also tells of receiving six postal orders for £5 each. He visited the post office on four different days before the full £30 was forthcoming. On the third day, the post office was able to produce £20 once Thackeray had made a fuss, saying that such a thing would be impossible in England.

He witnessed poor people who, he speculates, may have come in from the country refused payment of postal orders for £2. 'Such things could not take place in the hundred and second city in England; and as I do not pretend to doctrinize at all, I leave the reader to draw his own deductions with regard to the commercial condition and prosperity of the second city in Ireland.'

He found a lack of vitality even in the 'respectable quarter' of Cork but noted that the poorer quarters were swarming with life, 'but of such a frightful kind as no pen need care to describe; alleys where the odours and rags and darkness are so hideous that one runs frightened away from them. In some of them, they say, not the policeman, only the priest can penetrate. I asked a Roman Catholic clergyman of the city to take me into some of these haunts, but he refused very justly.'

Thackeray's comments on the ubiquity of Irish poverty, and its comparative wretchedness, is endorsed by all contemporary travellers to the country, regardless of their own origins. Arthur Young (1780); Chevalier de la Tocnaye (1796); Hermann von Pückler Muskau (1825); de Tocqueville and de Beaumont in the 1830s; Mr and Mrs S.C. Hall at the start of the 1840s, just before Thackeray: they and others all represented Irish poverty as the most abject in Europe, by which I think they meant the nearer and richer parts of the continent.* We know of no comparisons with the condition of Balkan peasants or Russian serfs. Still, the point stands. They can't all have been deluded.

---

* To this list could be added others: Wakefield, 1812; Bicheno, 1831; Kohl, 1844; and more. All agreed on the main point. An English Quaker, James Cropper, stated this in the 1820s as if it was the settled consensus, although one imagines that, as with other travellers, his idea of Europe did not venture east of the Elbe or south of the Danube.

There was another side to Cork, which Thackeray also saw. 'That the city contains much wealth is evidenced by the number of handsome villas round about it, where the rich merchants dwell; but the warehouses of the wealthy provision merchants make no show to the stranger walking the streets...' And of these merchants, there was no shortage. Cork is blessed with a superb natural deep-water harbour plumb in the centre of the southern Irish coast. By about 1700 or so, it had taken advantage of its geographical position to eclipse all the smaller southern ports. It was a major export point for wool, but as the eighteenth century wore on, it was the provision trade that came to dominate the city's commerce.

The boom years started in the 1750s with the beginning of the Seven Years War and continued until Napoleon's final defeat in 1815. In those fifty-nine years, Cork defied the conventional wisdom that war is bad for commerce. To the contrary, the series of wars against the French and the American Revolutionaries were the making of the place. The south of Ireland – with a climate made for the rearing of cattle, sheep and pigs – became one of the bread baskets of the British army. The beef trade, in particular, flourished. Even before the wars, Cork controlled more than 40 per cent of the Irish food export market. By the end of the eighteenth century, its dominance had grown so overwhelming as to be almost total. And the infrastructure went with the growth of trade: harbour development advanced and slaughterhouses were built.

The long series of wars brought high prices for the staples that sustained Cork's prosperity: beef and butter and, more and more as time went on, pork. The rise of pork was a direct consequence of the wars. Pork and bacon had risen from a low base to equal beef in quantities exported by the 1790s: the demand for pork from the military increased spectacularly. The relative ease with which pork can be salted and preserved was a key consideration here.

The net effect is that, for the more successful provision merchants, great fortunes were made. And the makers of those fortunes, their pockets suitably stuffed, fled the city for the nearby rising ground. Cork is *Corcaigh* in Irish, a swamp, and indeed its central area, divided by the two channels of the River Lee (just like Paris, except not really), is almost at sea level. But all around, especially to the north and east, are pleasant hills which were given suggestive names: Montenotte, Tivoli and so on. It was on these pleasing uplands that the great merchants – their money made in the noisome slaughterhouses and dockyards down below – built their villas. And there they stayed. The majority of them were Catholics: the ascendancy would not deign to soil its hands with filthy commerce. But money talks, and what follows is evidence of it – if any further evidence were needed.

Seven years before Thackeray was in Ireland, Alexis de Tocqueville was here. He too visited Cork – or Kork, as he rendered it. He had come across country from Kilkenny, acknowledging the now familiar rural misery of mud cabins, ragged people and beggarly children. Then he arrived in Co. Cork, at the town of Mitchelstown, about 50 kilometres north of the city. There, the local grandee was Lord Kingston, whose residence stood at the heart of his 75,000 acres. He notes that the estate bears all the signs of civilized improvement; so does the town, not having, 'as much of the rest of the country, so wretched an appearance'. The theme of unimproved market towns is one of the more dismal motifs in Irish history. The relatively few places that did benefit from the benison of improving landlords demonstrate a sense of order and architectural proportion that mark them apart: estate towns, they are called. Mitchelstown was one such, although it brought no material benefit to Kingston.

De Tocqueville enquires after Kingston, to be told that two years previously, his lordship had gone mad. This was as a consequence of being 'charged with 400,000 pounds sterling of debts, without hope of ever being able to pay them. The money had been lent him by the Catholic merchants of Cork who hold mortgages on the vast estate... and who receive nearly all the income.' His comments on this are brisk: 'It is the same in nearly all Ireland. See the finger of God! The Irish aristocracy wished to remain separated from the people and to remain English. It has striven to imitate the English aristocracy without having its spirit and resources, and dies where it has sinned. The Irish have been dispossessed by force of arms. They return to the estates by industry.'

The point hardly needs labouring. Here is the landlord who has improved his own lands as well as the town adjacent, now hopelessly in hock to the papists from Montenotte who in their turn are neglecting the urban working class upon whose labour they have depended for their villas and all that pleasant fresh air, all the while chuckling at the thought that they have the heretic up the road by the balls. But £400,000 in 1835, in Ireland! The modern equivalent is about £30 *million*.

Ireland was a third-world province of a first-world country, indeed *the* first-world country. Great Britain had not only helped to restore the balance of power in Europe with its money – much more potent than its army, although not than its navy – but it led the way in the industrial revolution. It was often a cruel and ugly business, as anyone who has read Engels's accounts of contemporary Manchester can confirm, but it reached most parts of Britain: London and the south-east remained rich, its wealth grounded in the City of London; manufacturing and textiles were centred on the Midlands and north-west; coal mining, producing the essential resource for the steam age, in south Wales, Yorkshire and Scotland; ship-building on the Tyne, the Mersey and the Clyde and soon on the Lagan in a small corner of the neighbouring island.

As to the rest of the island, nothing. Ireland remained almost entirely pre-industrial outside east Ulster. Industrialization and all other facets of a modernizing capitalist economy depended overwhelmingly on an enterprising merchant middle class, backed by a free flow of credit and capital. In one form or another, almost every important region of Britain – and east Ulster – developed the sinews of this new society as the nineteenth century went on. The major exception to this rule was the Scottish Highlands, which was left a beautiful wilderness after the Duchess of Sutherland's clearances. So while the Highlands were no good for people, they were grand for sheep.

Ireland, however, was full of people. The population started to grow around 1780 and continued to do so until the cataclysm of the Famine befell the island in 1845. All estimates of population before 1841 are just that: estimates. That year produced the first national census which was generally accepted to be enumerated to a high degree of accuracy. That said, most estimates antecedent are now relied upon by scholars as being there and thereabouts – not as rigorous as 1841 and after, but based on reasonable scholarly inferences rather than pure guesswork. For 1780, the estimate of Ireland's population is about four million; by 1821, it was almost seven million; in the 1841 census, it was counted at 8.2 million. That is a doubling of the population in a single lifetime, on an island that was for the most part economically sclerotic. And yet this vastly increasing population – the growth seems to have slowed, without stopping, from the mid-1820s – was wonderfully healthy and well nourished. Successions of travellers, going all the way back to that dyspeptic but shrewd Englishman Arthur Young in the 1770s and '80s (he always judged places by comparison to England, and always unfavourably), noted not just the poverty and squalor but the robust good health of even the poorest people.

The cause was simple: diet. The Irish poor lived in a subsistence agricultural economy and subsisted on a monotonous diet of potatoes, milk and buttermilk. But even Young applauded the diet and said, quite correctly, that it accounted for the ruddy cheeks of the poor. It wasn't just Young: Adam Smith declared in *The Wealth of Nations* that in London the Irish-born porters could bear the strongest loads. He also complimented Irish-born prostitutes for their beauty; like Young, he ascribed these pleasing qualities to diet. A statistical estimate of male heights in the early nineteenth century bears this out: Irishmen were consistently about an inch taller than their English and Welsh counterparts. And so we have a paradox: a population that was regarded in comparative terms as among the poorest in Europe is also among the healthiest.

That good fortune, as everyone now knows, and knew then, was utterly dependent on the reliability of each year's potato harvest. There were occasional failures, as in 1816, which led to a famine in the following year. The young Robert Peel was chief secretary for Ireland and applied direct government assistance to alleviate starvation. The full flowering of laissez-faire was some time away, with disastrous consequences for Ireland and also for Peel's Tory Party. But for the moment, humanity trumped ideology, and the day was saved. Normal service was resumed at the next harvest; in general, the potato was wonderfully reliable. And so the population grew, immiserated but in blooming health.

That growing population was a net growth, for there was emigration as well. The idea that Irish emigration does not take off until after the cataclysm of the Great Famine at the mid-century is simply wrong. Apart from the mass exodus of Ulster Presbyterians to the United States from the mid-eighteenth century on, there was a huge outflow in the thirty years from 1815 to 1845: it is estimated that 1.5 million left Ireland, about one-third of whom went to England, drawn by the employment offered – however degrading the conditions – by the industrial revolution. They were hated, as are all swarms of the poor coming in at the bottom of society, and thus depressing wages. And there are numerous testaments to their squalid conditions of life, not least from that acute and keen-eyed observer, Friedrich Engels, who as the director of his father's textile mill in Manchester was in closer contact with the immigrant Irish than many.

Engels was what Ireland lacked: a genuinely modernizing capitalist. The co-founder of communism and Karl Marx's private banker was also *un vrai bourgeois*. He may have hated commerce – he claimed to stick with it only to be able to fund the genius of his improvident friend – but he none the less assumed most of the outward laminate appropriate to his status as a commercial gentleman of means and position. He joined the right clubs, rode to hounds and was seldom short of champagne. But he also had what by the standards of his class and time was an extraordinarily irregular sex life. He lived with his lover Mary Burns, a redheaded Irish factory worker. It was a genuine love affair; Engels was bereft when she died. So he may be absolved of any kneejerk anti-Irish prejudice when he described the condition of the immigrant Irish in that part of 1840s Manchester known as 'Little Ireland':

masses of refuse, offal and sickening filth lie among standing pools in all directions; the atmosphere is poisoned by the effluvia from these, and laden and darkened by the smoke of a dozen tall factory chimneys. A horde of ragged women and children swarm about here, as filthy as the swine that thrive upon the garbage heaps and in the puddles. In short, the whole rookery furnishes such a hateful and repulsive spectacle as can hardly be equalled in the worst court on the Irk.* The race that lives in these ruinous cottages, behind broken windows, mended with oilskin, sprung doors, and rotten door-posts, or in dark, wet cellars, in measureless filth and stench, in this atmosphere penned in with a purpose, this race must really have reached the lowest stage of humanity. This is the impression and the line of thought which the exterior of this district forces upon the beholder.

---

* A Lancashire river on whose banks a large number of the early industrial mills were established, with all the filth and pollution that early industrial process facilitated.

But what must one think when he hears that in each of these pens, containing at most two rooms, a garret and perhaps a cellar, on the average twenty human beings live...

Engels's concern was not with the Irish poor *per se* but with examining – as the title of his book puts it with splendid concision – the condition of the working class in England. None the less, at the bottom of a very nasty heap – no one denies that the early phases of the industrial revolution were anything other than frightful for the new industrial poor – was a clearly identifiable group, the new immigrant Irish, huddled in their very own slum which was the worst slum in the city. And the story could be repeated for every industrializing city in Britain, not least London itself where the St Giles district, near the modern Centre Point, was teeming with Irish and was reckoned to be the worst rookery in the capital. Marx began to form his philosophy not just on the back of Engels's largesse but also on the back of his forensic sociology. And Engels, in his turn, would hardly have ventured into Little Ireland – few, if any, of his contemporaries dared – without his Irish lover as shield.

Yet the co-founder of communism was, by day and however reluctantly, a capitalist captain of the new industry, sitting with whatever degree of reluctance on the board of his father's cotton business, Ermen & Engels, and enjoying all the pleasures and rewards that his enterprise yielded up. This form of new manufacturing capitalism was innovative, revolutionary and for better or worse the way of the future. Its momentum was carrying it forward to a transforming new kind of society. Part of Marx's genius was that he was one of the first, if not the very first, to spot this. Marx celebrated the new industrial capitalism as a necessary evolutionary advance until the next phase of human development. That would assume the shape of a proletarian revolution of economy and society. In its turn, it would overwhelm the bourgeois consensus then forming and inject a different kind of transformation.

Ermen & Engels had very little in common with the provision merchants of Cork. Both traded and exchanged commercial goods for profit, but there the comparison ends. Ermen & Engels and all such businesses were engaged on a series of economic processes that were new and that contained within themselves the potential – realized in due time – for a social transformation. The gradual extension of the parliamentary franchise in a series of acts from 1867 on was a direct consequence of the social changes and the adjusted class alliances wrought by industrialization. But the merchant princes of Cork were behaving more like the nabobs of the East India Company in Bengal. They enriched themselves through their enterprise and commercial acumen, rather than through outright theft and plunder, as in India, but they had no concern to alleviate the state of the teeming poor on their own doorstep. Neither did many of the new industrial capitalists in Britain, but the changing nature of capitalism conduced in that direction, whether they desired it or not. In Cork, as in any part of the antique world, a man of enterprise, pluck and resource could make his fortune and retire. Robert Clive retired to London, groaning with the wealth of Bengal. The Cork merchant princes retired up the road. Still, you feel that Clive would have felt quite at home above in Montenotte.

And wherever in Britain there was heavy industry, which as we saw by the mid-century was very large parts of it – and especially those parts north of the Trent previously considered

underdeveloped but now charted as the central powerhouses
of the new economy – that industry prompted the series of
social shifts and recalibrations that led not only to the franchise
reform acts but, over a couple of generations, to the introduction of a state pension system and the early shoots of what
would become the welfare state. The pioneer in this welfare
process was another new industrial powerhouse, Germany.

Marx was quite right to celebrate capitalism as a necessary
bridge to the future. The fact that his version of the future
ended badly most places it was seriously tried is neither here nor
there in this context: being a brilliant historical analyst does not
equip you for prophecy. The very economic process itself was
making the future, in whatever direction it might be steered.
But without significant industry, you were stuck in the archaic
past. That was Ireland's problem, outside of north-east Ulster.
It had no industry, few natural resources – and certainly no iron
and coal worth talking about, the essential building blocks of
an industrial economy. That in turn meant that while it had
a kind of commercial middle class, it was small and practised
bad habits, such as making its pile and going up the hill. It was
rather like the extractive economics of much of the contemporary developing world. The game was zero sum: for me to
win, you must lose. So it's better that I win, even if it leaves you
exactly where you were, in the mire.

Modern capitalism, for all its enormities and its impulse to
concentrate wealth, has none the less lifted more people out of
abject poverty than any other system yet tried. Such capitalism
as there was in early nineteenth-century Ireland was not of that
kind and contained none of that potential, any more than the
East India Company brought prosperity to Bengal. The same

might be said of the small Irish commercial and financial class, for in an economy that is so sluggish and underdeveloped it is hard to see how the sinews of a commercial middle class can develop. It is one explanation for the cautious, unentrepreneurial attitude to such commerce as there was in the nineteenth century, as observed by many scholars. Likewise, the shortage of capital and the late and hesitant development of a banking system – not really up and toddling until the 1820s – contributed to the traditional lament about the paucity of capital available. It was an unvirtuous circle: a sclerotic economy is hardly going to attract large sums of working capital from an infant banking system. And without sufficient capital, modest entrepreneurial ambition probably makes sense. Whatever the reasons, the evidence is blatant. A survey of industrial capacity in the British Isles in 1871 is deeply unflattering to Ireland. Rather than elaborate, it is easiest to make the point by comparing the results for Ireland and Scotland. Scotland had 98 cotton plants; Ireland had 14; for wool, the respective figures were 218 and 61; for shoe factories, 3,266 to 251. Only for flax was there near-equality, although even there Scotland was slightly ahead. (The long-established Ulster flax industry accounted for the near closing of the gap.)

The absence of economic dynamism was displaced into politics, to which Paddy took with astonishing facility. The Irish nationalist community had given a political expression to their previously cultural and confessional integrity. They had conjured their myths and memories into a political narrative and programme. But their social leadership base was very narrow indeed. There was no robust, native administrative bourgeoisie, as there was in Scotland, although that situation did improve somewhat in the last decades of British rule. There was little or no modern industry, other than brewing and distilling. The basis for a self-confident and large middle class did not exist. It is one of the critical factors in the Irish nationalist inability to fold quietly into some sort of larger British Isles political settlement that it did not possess the indispensable class, for whom some such accommodation might have made sense *as a class*, in sufficient numbers. The longer the century went on – and certainly after the disaster of the Famine – the less likely that sort of accommodation looked every day. Instead of seeking any kind of role in the greater United Kingdom, Ireland's small bourgeoisie grew ever more resolutely nationalist in ambition. Every radical and revolutionary group from O'Connell to 1916 contained a disproportionate number of leaders from that small middle class. Who else would have provided the requisite leadership? But they were too few and lacked the industrial, administrative and financial skills required to punch their weight. That process – the development of a middle class properly equipped with those skills – had to await independence and even then only acquired them slowly and haltingly. But acquired they were over time, so that nationalist Ireland gradually evolved – after many errors and *bêtises* of policy – into a modern, rich and reasonably virtuous bourgeois republic.

BY THE TIME of independence, in 1922, Ireland had pretty much universal literacy. But that conceals a bigger picture. Its middle class was small and that was reflected in retention levels in the education system, which remained shamefully low until as late as the 1960s. Secondary schooling, whether in fee-paying institutions – run by orders such as the Jesuits and the Holy Ghost Fathers for Catholics or endowed schools run by various Protestant denominations – or in free schools run by the Christian Brothers and others, expanded impressively from the Famine to independence. But it was growth from a very low base and in general it offered a Gradgrind kind of education. This was especially the case in the free Catholic schools: the Christian Brothers had a well-earned reputation, not just for enthusiastic corporal punishments, but also for cramming. And the object of cramming was to help boys to 'get on'. More than anything else, this meant preparing them for the lower reaches of the civil service. That was the best that most of these lower middle-class boys could aspire to. It worked. The number of Catholics employed at junior civil service level between 1870 and 1919 grew significantly. In all that time, the higher positions in the civil service were held by Protestants, but they were regarded with suspicion in London, for the Dublin Castle administrative machine was regarded as a comfortable featherbed for mediocrities who just happened to dig with the right foot. In one of the great ironies of late British rule, a crack Treasury team came over to Dublin – just around the time that the War of Independence was getting going – and accomplished a thoroughgoing clean out of the stable, giving Ireland an administrative system reformed along best contemporary Treasury lines. Three years later, they bequeathed it to the new Irish Free State.*

---

* There is a story, which I have never been able to verify, that early in the life of the new state, after the civil war was settled, a delegation from the French government was sent to Dublin, with instructions to make the good offices of the French administrative system available to the new Ireland. Little Willie Cosgrave, the new head of the government, was able to thank them very much but to tell them that, well, the Brits had done the job for them before they had left. If it's not true, it should be.

Overall though, while there were visible improvements in Irish educational performance in the second half of the nineteenth century, these were still relatively poor by comparative standards, and the most obvious comparison is once again with Scotland. In 1911, the last national census conducted under the old United Kingdom, the four Scottish universities produced around 1,450 graduates, while the equivalent figure for the four universities in what would shortly be independent Ireland – Trinity and the three constituent colleges of the National University of Ireland at Dublin, Cork and Galway – was only about 750.[*] In short, Scotland had a bigger and more established middle class and was better at reproducing it generationally.

Once independence came in 1922, the higher reaches of the Irish civil service were filled by more and more Catholics, most of whom had cut their teeth and acquired their skills in late British days. This was an important development, not just for crude sectarian reasons or because it ensured a degree of administrative continuity. It certainly furnished the latter: the Department of Finance was a ferociously conservative and orthodox upholder of Treasury values in the early years of the state, with some formidably intelligent and forceful reactionaries at the tiller. But the real significance of this development overall is that it created a growing administrative class. And so, after centuries of being governed by a top-down colonial elite, remote from ordinary Irish life if not downright foreign to it, a new class was emerging. And it was *their* state that they were

---

[*] These numbers are estimates, the records being incomplete. I am grateful to Dr Ewen Cameron of the University of Edinburgh for the Scottish figures and to the Registrars of Trinity College Dublin and the National University of Ireland for the Irish ones.

running, not someone else's who had given them a junior job. In little time, this cadre of civil servants developed an *esprit de corps* that bound them emotionally to the institutions of the new state in a manner impossible under the old regime. This was a seminal development, for one of the strands that would be woven into what became the Irish middle class was on the loom here. It was still an embryonic middle class. The administrators came first in the 1920s and '30s; the businesspeople and the financiers would have to wait another generation to get started, for levels of financial and commercial accomplishment in the early years of the new state were nugatory. But it was a start.

There was, however, a shadow cast alongside. The Catholic Church wielded almost irresistible moral influence in the new Ireland. Indeed, every political leader of Irish nationalism, going right back to Parnell in the 1880s, had had to accommodate himself to the church. The basic deal was church support for the politicians in return for, first, the protection of the church's educational interests under British rule, and then a controlling free-for-all after independence. The great pedagogic ideologue of the new state was a Jesuit called Timothy Corcoran. He was Professor of Education in University College Dublin – one of three constituent colleges of the National University of Ireland mentioned earlier – from 1909 to 1942. He had been born into a well-to-do Tipperary farming family, precisely the kind of strong farmers who had survived the Famine in good order and would become owner-proprietors under the Wyndham Land Act of 1903. He was educated at Clongowes, the oldest and best Jesuit school in Ireland, and subsequently was a figure of substance in the Irish academic and intellectual firmament.

Corcoran was an ideologue. He insisted on Irish particularism, even when it made little sense. He supported the old Sinn Féin economic policy of protection and autarchy, which was ignored by the Cosgrave governments of the 1920s – under the influence of the Finance mandarins, every bit as formidable as Corcoran and free traders to a man – but which was adopted by de Valera's governments after 1932. It wasn't a completely senseless economic policy: many developing economies mature behind tariff walls and systems of import substitution. But whatever merit the system had, Irish governments persisted with it for far too long. After World War II, free trade became the order of the day in most western capitalist economies and resulted in the astonishing economic recovery that hardly faltered until the first oil crisis of 1973. Ireland simply failed to hitch a ride on this boom until the start of the 1960s, and when it did the effects were transformative. For the first time since the Famine, the country was invested with a sense of optimism, a key moment being the 1966 census which showed the first growth in population since the Famine. Ireland persisted with Sinn Féin 'economics' long past the point where any utility it may have had was gone. This stubbornness had nearly wrecked the country in the dismal 1950s, when Ireland became the only country in the capitalist world whose economy actually contracted. Between 1955 and 1957, right in the middle of *les trente glorieuses*, Ireland was the only country in the developed world where the total volume of goods and services consumed declined. But for Corcoran and those who thought like him, free trade was British and Protestant, and that was enough for him.

It had taken Ireland fifty years to weary of being Not England. After that, it really wanted to be like any other country. So

we joined the EU, as it later became, and remain enthusiastic members – unlike some I could mention. The lads in the
Wexford pub, in the heartland of hurling, felt no qualms about
watching and cheering Liverpool and Newcastle. Nationalist
Ireland has many similarities to England, especially once that
desire just to be a normal country elbowed aside the old autarkic impulses. But it is also different. It is quite like England, but
it is still not England.

THAT FIRST GENERATION of civil servants after independence
furnished what Ireland had so conspicuously lacked, a proper,
self-referential administrative middle class. They were not merely
effective drivers of the state machine. They were scholarly. And
when the generational change came from the 1960s on, it was
their sons and daughters – and the children of people like them
– who did not, for the most part, follow their fathers into public
administration, but rather acquired those other middle-class com-
petencies: in academic life, in the law,* in finance and banking,**
in journalism, in engineering, in computing, in marketing, and
so on. In short, the Irish acquired the range of skills required to
run a modern, complex, open economy and society. And their

---

* The number of solicitors admitted to practice trebled between 1986 and
2019, even after correcting for the very large number of those who had originally qualified in England and Wales and who inflated the 2019 numbers
as a 'Brexit backstop'. [Figures courtesy of the Law Society of Ireland.]
** The number of qualified accountants grew by 83 per cent between
1996 and 2011, from 14,822 to 27,116, while the number of Catholic clergy in the latter year was a mere 6,729; thus one clerisy replaced
another. [Tony Farmar, *The Versatile Profession: A History of the Account-
ancy Profession in Ireland since 1850*, Dublin: Chartered Accountants
Ireland, 2013, p. 224.]

mores have changed: how those old bishops from long ago must be turning in their graves at the thought of Holy Ireland replaced by a secular republic that has had a taoiseach who is both gay and ethnically diverse; that has legalized abortion and gay marriage; and that is basically deaf to any opinions their episcopal successors might venture from time to time.

It is easy to see the older Ireland as an anti-modern project, with all that attempted introversion and withdrawal from the wider world. It did have such features, but more importantly Irish independence – seeing the British off in 1922 – was an essential prerequisite for modernity. To have remained in the United Kingdom in some shape or form, which was the optimum expectation of most Irish nationalists prior to 1916, would hardly have created that administrative bourgeoisie as quickly or as thoroughly. Instead, that group became the coping stone of a new, urban, gradually secularizing middle class that eventually completed the journey to modernity.

It was the absence of such a class in British days that was another key marker, along with religion and distance, of just how nationalist Ireland sat so ill-fittingly in the archipelagic little world of the British Isles.

IT WAS THE grandsons of the Catholic tenants who had done well out of the Famine who inherited the state in 1922 and who provided the middle class, both rural and urban, whose virtuous dominance is the glue that holds Irish society together.

It is not usual to attach an adjective such as 'virtuous' to describe a class that was often costive and mean-spirited. But they did not create their social world; they inherited it, and then gave it definition and purpose without in any way challenging the internal social settlement put in place after the Famine. The priests and bishops threw their weight around – although, to be fair to de Valera, he clipped their wings from time to time, while never subverting the source of their authority.

That social settlement, with the church at its centre, persisted for as long as it did because it possessed that most precious of all political assets: legitimacy. The population consented, connived and submitted to its strictures. It knew about the horrors that were the price paid for it: the brutal physical violence in Catholic schools; the shameful treatment of 'fallen' women by other women, nuns, in institutions of incarceration; the tragic emigration of poorly educated men from the bottom of the heap, which ensured for them a life of near-peonage on the building sites of Britain, and so on. They knew, but they looked the other way. Why? Because they deemed it a price worth paying for a society that was stable, peaceful and at ease with itself. The smug petit bourgeois paradise rested on these and similar evils. Yet it rested comfortably.

The subversion of this social settlement began in the 1960s and one way and another has gone on ever since, latterly adopting the modish glad rags of identity politics. But the 1960s saw the breakthrough: a new post-revolutionary generation, many of them cowboys and chancers on the make; television; the beginnings of a consumer society and of an industrial policy; and, best of all, the introduction of universal state-funded secondary education.

To top it all, emigration ended. The 1966 census in the Republic showed the first increase of population in any inter-censal period since the Famine. It was small and focused most heavily in the east of the country; but even in the west, the rate of decline was slowing significantly. The Dublin suburbs spread ever outwards. The land was emptying, the towns and cities filling. In short, Ireland began a process of *enrichissement*, secularization and a social rebalancing to the European norm that is basically the narrative of the last fifty years.

This reign of bourgeois virtue – with the church now cast aside like a serpent's old skin – needed a context, an opposite with which it could contend. And that context was the smug, philistine republic that had preceded it. So why did I describe it in terms of virtue?

It represented a necessary evolutionary step, for all its lack of retrospective attraction. Ireland had been a society of land-lords and peasants – all very Yeatsian – but with an exiguous middle class. Independence expanded that middle class, if only by providing jobs in the civil service, and furnished it with the sinews of a social project. To be sure, that project nestled in the bosom of the overall post-Famine settlement. But it also introduced a new bourgeois dimension, previously absent, which waxed over time. It was the children of that generation of the new bourgeoisie, come of age around 1960, who began to distance themselves from the puritanism and rigour of their fathers. More than any other identifiable group, it was they who made the new Ireland. And they made it by Dumping Daddy.

But Daddy had broken the ground for them. Whatever you can say about de Valera's little neutral republic, it now had what the British had lacked in their day: a self-conscious bourgeoisie that saw itself as a mandarin officer class of the state. Later came the industrial, financial and commercial elements of that class, as the private sector gradually took off from the 1960s on. But the presence of that class through the de Valera years was the source of virtue – for without it no next step was possible. A foundation stone had been laid.

The great comic novelist Flann O'Brien, writing under (yet another) pseudonym as Myles na Gopaleen in *The Irish Times* in the 1940s, made gentle fun of this key process of social improvement: 'No Irish farmer appreciates his young strapping son for the attractive, healthy agricultural type he is (and must intrinsically remain). The Irish farmer sees his son as a potential Higher Executive Officer [in the civil service], Grade II, Temporary, Unestablished, full of grievances about bonus.'

That's a joke grounded in reality. The newly forming Irish middle class, unlovely in many respects, were disproportionately the children of farmers, now translated to an urban milieu to serve not just their immediately local and family interests but those of the entire state and community. There was much self-serving fantasy in that self-image and much that was betrayed by behavioural reality but it did reflect an aspiration, an ethos, an *esprit de corps* that in the first generation of the new state represented a radical departure from British days. It was also effected, crucially, by physical removal from countryside to city.

It meant an end to Yeats's mad dream of a coalition of aristocrat and peasant, joined in hostility to philistine merchants, hucksters and other such riff-raff. But it was the riff-raff and their kind that did the business; and moreover, no one else could have managed it. Thackeray wouldn't recognize the place.

INTERLUDE

SEVEN

—⋙⋘—

LOOKING DOWN ON INISTIOGE*

I F YOU DRIVE south from the small city of Kilkenny, along the valley of the River Nore, you arrive in due time at the pretty little village of Inistioge. It used to be an estate village, that is, one kept neat and orderly by a benign landlord – sufficiently rare in Ireland to merit a denominator. The local big house was up the hill above the village. It was called Woodbrook. That brave and singular man, Hubert Butler – for my money, the very finest Irish essayist of the twentieth century – lived nearby in a family house called Maidenhall. His was a cadet branch of the Butlers, successively earls and dukes of Ormonde, and his shadow will fall across much of what follows in this chapter. They had been lords of this part of Ireland for most of the time since the arrival of the Normans in 1169. Their castle in Kilkenny city is one of the most impressive in the country. One of the family, James Butler, 12th earl and 1st duke of Ormonde,

---

* Tough name to pronounce if you're not Irish: it's Inish-theeg.

was effectively the ruler of all Ireland after the restoration of King Charles II.

Hubert Butler was born in 1900 and, like so many of the Anglo-Irish elite, he was educated in England, in his case at Charterhouse and Oxford. In the 1930s, he travelled widely in Europe – especially in the Balkans – before returning to Ireland on his father's death in 1941 to take possession of Maidenhall. His essays are masterly in their range: his writings about recent and contemporary European politics were grounded in personal experience, far ranging in their erudition and limpid in their prose.

They won him few friends in Ireland, especially when they pointed out the uncomfortable fact of the wartime collaboration – at least tacit and often overt – between the Roman Catholic Church in Croatia and the neo-Nazi Ustashe regime, not to mention the attempted forced conversion of over two million Serb Orthodox Christians to Catholicism. When Tito and the communists came to power in Yugoslavia after the war, they took it out on the church and in particular on Archbishop Aloysius Stepinac, whom they incarcerated. In Catholic Ireland – at that time experiencing its Tibet of the West phase – this was regarded as typical communist hatred for Catholicism, and the legal proceedings that sent Stepinac to jail no more than a vulgar show trial.

There was, no doubt, every truth in the charge of a show trial. Communists everywhere behind the Iron Curtain had previous form, and were loathsome. But in Ireland, the idea that there had been a cosy relationship between the church and the Ustashe was regarded with outrage. Even more so was any suggestion of forced conversion, for the Catholic Irish had a horror of proselytism that went back to some attempts during the nineteenth-century Famine to induce conversion to Protestantism in return for soup. The church could only have the cleanest of hands, whether in Ireland or anywhere. So, when Butler the big-house Protestant pointed out material facts to the contrary, with supporting evidence which included testimony based on personal experience and observation, and all rendered in a detached Olympian style, he was kicking a hornets' nest.

Friends shunned him. He was forced to resign from a local scholarly society that he himself had founded. The papal nuncio turned up to one of Butler's lectures only to indulge in the pleasure of walking out of it. As Flann O'Brien, writing in another connection in his *Irish Times* column as Myles na Gopaleen, said: the nuncio left the premises 'in that lofty vehicle, high dudgeon'.

Hubert Butler did not completely retire to private life. He maintained a minor public presence in the marginalized world of little literary journals but his voice was lost to a wider public until 1985 when, in his old age, there was published in Dublin by a small, independent publishing house called, with commendable tact, Lilliput Press, a selection of his essays under the title *Escape from the Anthill*. I was not alone in staying up half the night to read it. Many others did as well. Here was a voice unlike any we had heard before: it was like finding buried treasure, which, in literary and intellectual terms, is precisely what it was.

In the remaining six years of his life, there were more selections including one published in New York by Farrar, Straus and Giroux, one of the most celebrated literary publishing houses in the anglophone world. Butler's eye may have ranged far but he was what Yeats said of Synge: he was a rooted man. He had an intense love of his native Co. Kilkenny: 'I have lived for most of my life on the Nore and own three fields upon its banks, some miles before it turns to the south-east and forces its way under Brandon Hill to join the Barrow above New Ross.'

It is that 'upon' that delivers the emotional register. Many found Butler chilly. Well, like many an outwardly chilly man, he was passionate. And he recalls, in that same essay, travelling to Woodbrook, above Inistioge, for supper dances as a young man. It was part of the social round for the Anglo-Irish.

Woodbrook did not survive the civil war of 1922–3. Like so many other big houses, it was burned by the IRA. The ruin is still there and you can drive up to it. But as you do, there is something of greater interest below. Halfway up the hill, you look back down towards the village. The main street runs towards you before bending right as you look at it to cross the bridge over the Nore. In the meadow between the street and the river, there is a rectangle of green that catches your eye.

This is the home ground of The Rower-Inistioge GAA club.* I should say hurling club because hurling is the only game taken seriously in Co. Kilkenny. If this was England, you'd say that here was a well-loved and minded village cricket ground. And, indeed, it looks as if you could get a mower and a roller on it and play a three-day match on the wicket you had made. They mind it that much.

So why are they *not* playing cricket in Inistioge, in the meadow by the river? After all, cricket was a major sport and a popular one in this county and also in Co. Tipperary adjacent,

---

* The GAA is the Gaelic Athletic Association, of which a lot more later.

as we are reminded by Gerard Siggins in his authoritative history of the game in Ireland. It was organized on an estate basis, so that Woodbrook would have a team, patronized by the landlord and manned by the tenants. It would play other, similar estate teams, a country summertime sport accompanied by drinking and gambling.

Most of the places where cricket was strongest in Ireland in the eighteenth century had certain features in common. It flourished on flat – or flattish – limestone country, avoiding mountains and rising ground, and which happened – not coincidentally – to be the areas of densest Norman settlement in the twelfth century. All the places where we know cricket to have been strong are now strong for hurling.[*] An arc running north by west from Wexford to south Galway takes in all the big hurling counties. No county outside that arc has ever won the All-Ireland Senior Hurling Championship[**] although it has been contested annually since 1887.

So, one stick and ball game replaced another stick and ball game. So what? Well, much what actually. Sports, once established, can be very tenaciously rooted. It can take a lot to grow a sport in unwelcoming soil: just think of the struggle to make soccer – by far the world's most popular game and the one with

---

[*] This caused *The Economist*, of all improbable organs, to speculate some years ago that hurling might have been a game of Norman origin, not Gaelic at all; enough to make a fíor-Ghaeil choke on his cornflakes.
[**] With the exception of Dublin, which won it six times when they were allowed to select non-Dublin players domiciled in the city, most of whom came from counties within the arc. That regulation was changed, obliging Dublin only to select Dubliners, which accounts for the fact that Dublin's last championship victory was in 1938 and their last appearance in a final was in 1961.

the biggest international reach – take root in the United States. So what happened in Ireland to elbow cricket aside and put hurling in its place?

The timing is suggestive. We are in the 1880s. Sports were being codified all over the place. Rough-and-tumble local pastimes were now being made subject to uniform national and – by extension – international rules. England led the way in this process, possibly because of the Victorian belief in the virtue of manly, muscular sports (a prophylactic against masturbation?) but also because the technology that made uniform national rules necessary – the railway – was farther advanced and most densely developed in England. Before the railway, it hardly mattered if the rules – sorry, laws – of the game were a bit different in Yorkshire and in Kent. With the development of the iron road, however, it meant that teams from Kent could now play in Yorkshire and vice versa. So there had to be an agreed standard.

Even before English cricket's county championship began officially in 1890, inter-county rivalry was well established. In the 1880s, bank holiday games between Surrey and Nottinghamshire – the two leading counties of the day and significantly rather distant from each other – drew huge crowds. *Wisden Cricketers' Almanack*, the game's annual authoritative statistical and opinion review, was first published in 1864 and is still with us. Test cricket dates from 1877. The Football League was formed in 1888. The first rugby union international was played in 1871. Tennis dates from the same decade. Likewise, baseball developed its modern form in the second half of the nineteenth century. The first professional team, the Cincinnati Reds, was formed in 1869 and the National League in 1876. The World Series – ludicrously inflated title – dates from 1903. The British Open Golf Championship goes back all the way to 1860.

You get the point, but what the hell has this to do with Inistioge, Co. Kilkenny? Quite a lot. Because what *should* have happened, all things being equal, was that these codifying processes afoot in England would simply have crossed the water and established themselves in Ireland. They didn't, at least not all of them. In terms of major sports, Ireland went its own way. Or, to be rather more precise: Catholic, nationalist Ireland went its own way, because all things were not equal.

The principal reason was the Great Famine of 1845–52. It was catastrophic, the last big subsistence crisis in Western Europe. And it didn't just happen any old where: it happened in a (notional) part of the United Kingdom, then by far the richest country in the world. It fell heaviest on the poorest of the poor, who died or emigrated. But it ruined many landlords, too (see next chapter), because their rent rolls dried up; many of them were already heavily mortgaged, anyway.

The landlord system weakened progressively after the Famine and came under fatal strain in the 1880s, with the successive campaigns for tenant rights and home rule. Such bonds of affection as had subsisted between landlord and tenant were weakened. Two issues – the restoration of Catholic lands improperly stolen 200 years earlier and political autonomy for a Catholic people – were mixed. They did not quite put it like that, but that was about the size of it.

THE ATTITUDE OF the British government to Irish poverty was not unique. We are fortunate to have the testimony of many travellers to Ireland in the decades immediately preceding the

Famine. As we have seen, their judgments were not always flattering and not as far removed from those of the British government as you might suppose.

Here is Thackeray travelling through Co. Kilkenny in 1842:

> troops of slatternly, ruffian-looking fellows assembled round the carriage, dirty heads peeped out of all the dirty windows, beggars came forward with a joke and a prayer… they come crawling round you with lying prayers and loathsome compliments, that make the stomach turn… How do all these people live?… The Irish Poor Law Report says that there are twelve hundred thousand people in Ireland, a sixth of the population, who have no means of livelihood but charity…

Or again, in Thomastown, a few kilometres north of Inistioge:

> most picturesquely situated among trees and meadow on the river Nore. The place within, however, is dirty and ruinous – the same wretched suburbs, the same squalid congregation of beggarly loungers that are to be seen elsewhere.

Thackeray was English and might be supposed to be sharing an English sensibility that went all the way to the top of government. No such excuse can be advanced for two other contemporary travellers in Ireland, the great Alexis de Tocqueville and his friend Gustave de Beaumont who first visited the country together in 1835 with de Beaumont returning alone in 1839. They too found poverty and squalor on a scale that shocked them. This is de Beaumont:

Imagine four walls of dried mud, which the rain, as it falls, easily restores to its primitive condition; having for its roof a little straw or some sods, for its chimney a hole cut in the roof, or very frequently the door, through which alone the smoke finds an issue. One single compartment contains the father, mother, children and sometimes a grandfather or grandmother; there is no furniture in this wretched hovel; a single bed of hay or straw serves for the entire family. Five or six half-naked children may be seen crouched near a miserable fire, the ashes of which cover a few potatoes, the sole nourishment of the family. In the midst of all lies a dirty pig, the only thriving inhabitant of the place, for he lives in filth. The presence of a pig in an Irish hovel may at first seem an indication of misery; on the contrary, it is a sign of comparative comfort. Indigence is still more extreme in the hovel where no pig is to be found.

De Tocqueville makes precisely the same point about the pig within. In later generations, the 'pig in the parlour' was regarded by Irish people as an insult so vile as to be almost if not actually racist. As for Thomastown, it is today a thriving market town, neat and orderly. Something profound has happened in Ireland – and specifically in this corner of it – to make Thomastown prosperous and to banish the pig from the parlour.

With the collapse of the landlord–tenant bond, what was to replace it? Something already there and well noted by de Tocqueville and the others fifty years earlier: the structure of the Catholic Church. The focus of local loyalty now shifted from the old estates to the Catholic parishes. When the Gaelic Athletic Association was founded in 1884, that is how it organized itself: a club in every Catholic parish, with the estates completely sidelined. And with the estates went the cricket: the GAA's declared purpose was to revive the ancient game of hurling – and it has succeeded, but mostly in the places where cricket had been strong before, as if some muscle memory of stick and ball was needed to embrace the change.

And that's why the pitch at The Rower-Inistioge looks as it does and why there is hardly any cricket played in Kilkenny today.[*] And as to Thomastown's prosperity, it happened because the big tenants who eventually became owner-proprietors had matured into what Ireland had lacked historically: a rural, yeoman class – an aspirational middle class.

ON THE OTHER side of Co. Kilkenny to Hubert Butler's house at Maidenhall sat a far grander house. This was Desart Court, about 24 kilometres south-west of Kilkenny city near the county border with Co. Tipperary. It was a splendid Italianate palazzo built in the 1730s for John Cuffe, the 1st baron Desart. The Ur-Cuffe had been one Joseph, a Cromwellian officer who had been rewarded with these lands in the 1650s for services rendered. Down the generations it went, and in 1898, the house passed into the possession of Hamilton Cuffe, who thus became the 5th earl of Desart.

---

[*] While the latter point is correct – there is only one club in the county as I write – the decline was not as sudden as my account may suggest. It was a fluctuating pattern, from a robust thirty cricket clubs in the county in 1860 to a high point of fifty clubs in 1896, during the fledgling GAA's time of troubles; following which the fall became inexorable: twenty teams in 1906, sixteen in 1926 and a dead-cat bounce to thirty teams as late as the mid-1930s, before World War II marked the final collapse of the game in Kilkenny.

He had been a younger brother and therefore had not expected to acquire the title. His early career was as a barrister in London. He made a success of it and rose to be Director of Public Prosecutions. Even after his succession to the title, he continued his career in London – sitting in the House of Lords – but coming to Desart as frequently as business would allow. This account is based on his granddaughter's memoir: Iris Origo made her life in Italy but had been born into a rich family with one branch in the United States and the other at Desart.

To young Iris, Hamilton Cuffe, 5th earl of Desart, was Gabba, her pet-name for him. To his tenants, he must have seemed absurdly remote and grand and we can be certain that not one of them would have dared to address him thus, even had they known – which assuredly they had not – that anyone in the world called him Gabba. He was, according to his granddaughter's account, kindly and not one to press his tenants in arrears.

We have a photograph of him in 1904. He is standing by the steps of Desart with his wife, dressed in a three-piece plus-fours Irish tweed suit, knee stockings and Oxford brogues and a Homburg hat, looking every inch the milord. But his was a dying, Chekhovian world: the Wyndham Land Act had been passed the previous year, finally breaking up the great estates and establishing the strong tenants as strong farmers – yeomen proprietors now in their own right.

He wasn't stupid, Ham Cuffe, 5th earl of Desart; nor was his wife. But could they possibly have anticipated the ruin that was to come, carrying their world away as surely as if it had been the Byzantine Empire? Everything familiar and solid stood all around. Yet within twenty years it would all be ashes.

But nobody knew what was coming. James Joyce set *Ulysses* in that year, on the fateful day of Thursday 16 June. In the Cyclops episode of that peerless masterpiece – chapter 12 of 18 – he takes the reader to Barney Kiernan's pub in Little Britain Street off Capel Street in central Dublin. The chapter is a mixture of demotic conversational realism and inflated satirical lampoon, the squalidness of Irish reality counterpointed with high-falutin' romances about the Irish mythical past and future fantasy. The British royal family is cheerfully and scatologically traduced in a manner unimaginable in any other city of similar size in the United Kingdom. The drinkers were all nationalists. The context makes it clear that they expected home rule, devolution of regional autonomy, soon. But the idea of separation – which is what happened in reality – was unconsidered, except by the least sympathetic character in the group: a demented fanatic, a cadger, a blowhard and a soak. Nobody, whether in Barney Kiernan's or at Desart Court, knew what was coming.

Otway Cuffe was Ham's younger brother, an exotic, and one memorialized in retrospect by Hubert Butler. He in turn relied on the only source for Otway of which he had knowledge, a memoir written by his niece, Lady Sybil Lubbock, sister of Iris Origo's mother. Otway was an ascendancy nationalist, a species not unknown but increasingly rare by the last decade of the nineteenth century. In general, their nationalism ran to cultural matters rather than to the outright political. So tweeds, the Irish language, local artisanal enterprises of one sort or another (their sensibility was cross-pollinated by the English Arts and Crafts movement), literature and the theatre, co-operative agriculture and other worthy causes attracted their often passionate support.

In the 1890s, after the defenestration of Parnell, the tide flowed for cultural nationalism. Politics was in bad odour and Ireland looked elsewhere to express its non-Englishness. One of the key developments was the foundation of the Gaelic League in 1893 whose first president, Dr Douglas Hyde, had delivered an inaugural address to the National Literary Society in the previous year. Its title was unambiguous: 'The Necessity for De-Anglicising the Irish People'.

This cultural revival took many forms and included a steady campaign against the demoralizing effect of cheap English literature: this was a time when British book publishing expanded dramatically and the popular press was born. This was represented as a culturally deplorable development which would enfeeble the collective resolve of the Irish nation. It would echo down the decades, starting in the 1890s with high-minded idealists such as Hyde and finishing in the 1920s with the introduction of ferocious literary censorship, designed to create a cultural *cordon sanitaire* to protect Ireland from Saxon impurities.

Otway Cuffe was immersed in this world of Hyde and Yeats, with its ambition for a new Irish cultural consciousness. They all had a suspicion of modernity, which tended to come in an English wrapper and a vulgar one at that. He was indulged by his family, perplexed by his eccentricities as they saw them. Hubert Butler, in one of his essays, put the words in their mouths: 'Why, with his gifts and advantages, did he choose to sacrifice himself for people who would only exploit him and ridicule him behind his back?' Well, perhaps they did all those things; yet, when he died years later in far-off Australia, there was a genuine expression of public grief in Kilkenny. Shops closed and the flag on the Tholsel – city hall – flew at half-mast. Far too easy, as with the Desarts, for an uncomprehending caste to ascribe ridicule and bad faith to people of whom you have imperfect knowledge.

One story that Butler[*] told of Cuffe is this: that he was driving with his sister-in-law Lady Desart one day when the conversation turned to a neighbour who had put up a prize for folk dancing at a local school. Lady Desart had been very high born indeed; she was a Lascelles, daughter of the earl of Harewood and related to the queen. She did not approve of the neighbour's prize, thinking it frivolous given the prevailing poverty. Otway dissented, saying that the villagers needed 'poetry, poetry and music'. To this Lady Desart replied: 'A course in cleanliness and practical housewifery would be more to the point. In my opinion what the villagers need most are buttons and teeth.'

Indeed, Lady Desart; but who was to furnish the buttons and teeth? Not the Desarts, it would seem. As with so many ascendancy families, they had calcified into a caste as their social energy and influence declined, a Junkers garrison in the western world. And in an age of nationalism, what did the adjective 'Irish' mean to them? Lady Desart was English through and through. Her husband, although Irish born, had made his whole career in the upper reaches of the English state. To the Desarts, to be Irish was roughly cognate with being from Yorkshire or the West Country, a regional marker within the overall embrace of Englishness. This is not at all to say that they did not love Ireland: they did, and there is abundant evidence of it. But to

---

[*] Relying on Lady Sybil Lubbock's account, although it was corroborated in Iris Origo's memoir, which Butler appears not to have read.

the people who needed buttons and teeth – and she was quite right, they did – to be Irish meant to be not English at all, to be separate. It was a distinction as wide as the Danube.

The people eventually got their buttons and teeth, although in many cases not until well into the twentieth century. And they got them from an independent Irish administration from which the Desarts and their kind – for all their good sense and benign wishes – were effectively excluded. It took some generations of independent Irish politics and bureaucracy to deliver these sensible improvements. They had been improvements correctly diagnosed by the old ascendancy, but which were beyond its prescriptive reach.

Otway's enthusiasms held no more attraction for Lord Desart than they had for his wife. Ham was severely critical of the likes of Yeats whose embrace of folklore he deplored: 'All country folk tell the same tales and a backward people like the Irish keep theirs longest… The harm begins when men like Yeats come and make solemn pilgrimages to see the fairies and… then encourage all the world to think that ignorance and superstition are better than reason and common sense. Of course, there is charm in these fancies but there is cruelty too and there is a danger in any denial of reason.'

The Desarts were not wrong about everything but were incapable of setting Irish wrongs to rights. They could analyse – some of Desart's observations were to prove acute – but were incapable of amelioration. As I write, in the first quarter of the twenty-first century, how many Irish secular liberals will dissent from Desart and embrace the fairies? Not many, I think.

When Desart said his piece, the Famine and the land war were recent. The 1916 rising and all that followed from it were still occluded below the horizon. During the civil war of 1922–3, fought over the terms on which Ireland gained independence, Desart Court was, like Woodbrook, burned in what may have started as a revolt against a constitutional settlement but ended as little more than a mindless peasant jacquerie. Ham had made the mistake of accepting office in the Senate of the newly independent state, whose institutions were regarded as illegitimate by those opposing the peace treaty terms. The Desarts returned to England and when Ham Cuffe died in 1934 his title died with him: he had no male heirs.

In 1904, the year in which Lord and Lady Desart are photographed on the steps of their big house, something else happened. Kilkenny won the All-Ireland Senior Hurling Championship for the first time. To date, they have won it more often than any other county. This was the game of the people who needed buttons and teeth. Did Lord Desart even register the victory? We don't know.

Still, the Desarts were not totally lost to hurling. Otway Cuffe died at Fremantle in Western Australia in 1912 and was buried there, as far away from home as one could imagine. His pallbearers were all Kilkenny men, members of the Perth hurling club.

PART TWO

—⁌⁍—

A JOURNEY
TO THE EXIT

EIGHT

—⟩✦⟨—

ENCUMBERED
ESTATES

TELEOLOGY IS THE deterministic view of the past, proposing that all that happened was an inevitable process getting us from there to here. How we got from there to here is certainly worth exploring. Otherwise why bother with history at all? But to suppose that what happened was the only thing that could have happened, that the sequence of events was some kind of providential procession leading inevitably to the glorious (or disastrous) now, is wrong. Along the way, there were all sorts of random events or choices that might have been made differently.

Leopold Lojka couldn't be expected to know the route to the new city museum. He wasn't a local. But the car in front of him, acting as a kind of pilot fish, should have. It contained Fehim Effendi Curcic, the local mayor, who was acting as navigator. None the less, he inexplicably told his driver to take a wrong turning and naturally enough, Lojka followed. But the provincial governor, Oskar Potiorek, who was in the second car, immediately realized the error and told Lojka to reverse. As he was trying to do so, Gavrilo Princip, a nineteen-year-old Bosnian Serb fanatic, leapt forward with a loaded gun and killed two of Lojka's passengers, Archduke Franz Ferdinand, heir to the throne of Austria-Hungary, and his wife Sophie. We know what followed. But despite the fact that there had indeed been a plot to assassinate the archduke which had failed earlier in the day, the final act itself was more accident than design and the Austrian response was in no sense inevitable. Still, a world ended that day.

It is just one particularly well-known example to illustrate a general point. People enjoy the game of counterfactual speculation when contemplating what might otherwise have happened if some utterly unexpected event hadn't happened at all, or had happened differently.* The chapters that follow comprise a series of linked narratives concerning post-Famine Ireland. The events they describe were in no sense inevitable or providential but they do contain a pattern. That pattern is one of twin impulses: in nationalist Ireland, growing alienation from the British state; in Britain, a weakening of resolve to support the key social and political foundations of the Union.

THE GREAT FAMINE of 1845–52 is the moment of fracture in the Irish story. Out of a population of eight million in 1841, a million died and a million emigrated. As always, the catastrophe

---

* Gore Vidal once illustrated this point, when asked what might have happened if, on 22 November 1963, Nikita Khrushchev had been assassinated in Moscow rather than JFK in Dallas. He said that it was hard to tell but that he was pretty sure that Aristotle Onassis would not have married Mrs Khrushchev.

bore heaviest on the poorest. The landless or near-landless peasant cottiers were the principal victims. But many landlords were ruined as well because their impoverished tenants could not meet their rent obligations, thus robbing the landlords – many of them heavily mortgaged and otherwise indebted – of the oxygen of income.

The London administration had little affection for the landlords, whom they considered feckless; or for the peasantry, whom they represented as idle, torpid, fatalistic papists to whose collective arse a brisk, no-nonsense English-speaking Protestant god was now applying his size 12s.

Understandably, this did not commend itself to the starving Irish. Even less did it do so to those of them that survived the Famine. Rather like post-Holocaust Israelis, there was a silent determination that we would never allow this to happen to us again. This bred a conviction, especially strong among those who had made it to America: that England had betrayed Ireland in its hour of need and indeed had seen the advantage of the whole affair by clearing out the useless poor at the bottom of the heap and fatally weakening the improvident landlords at the top.

Subsistence crises had almost disappeared from Western Europe by the nineteenth century. While the blight that attacked the Irish potato crop, *Phytophthera infestans*, affected other parts of North-west Europe as well – Belgium, for instance – nowhere else did it produce a catastrophe of such biblical proportions. The response of the London government was driven by a mixture of economic ideology, godly providentialism and a cultural condescension that had a long history antecedent.

The ideology, in the form of laissez-faire, arrived with the Whig government of Little Johnny Russell which assumed office in July 1846. Up to that point, Peel's Tories had been in power but were fatally weakened by the split caused by the repeal of the Corn Laws. Peel now acted as he had as Irish chief secretary back in 1817 when there had been a crop failure. He established a relief commission in Dublin and local relief committees throughout Ireland before the end of 1845. He also caused £100,000 worth of Indian corn to be secretly imported from America for direct famine relief. It arrived but was inedible because it was unground. Grinding it proved to be vastly more complicated than anyone might have imagined. But in the meantime, the government in London changed. There had certainly been members of Peel's cabinet who were sceptical – to put it no stronger than that – about direct government intervention. But for all the doubts, it was at least done.

The Whigs were not entirely unanimous on laissez-faire but in general they were much more enthusiastic about non-interference in the market, which should instead be allowed, without government interference, to apply the balm of its logical hand to all problems. While Russell himself was not an out-and-out true believer, his chancellor of the exchequer, Charles Wood, certainly was. And Wood found a congenial confrere in Charles Trevelyan, the permanent secretary at the Treasury, who was evangelical (and in more ways than one) in his embrace of laissez-faire. At all costs – and those costs were to turn out to be disastrously high – he was determined that the financial burden of relief was not to fall upon the public purse. The Irish landlords and other property interests in Ireland would have to shoulder the load.

This neither Irish property nor the Irish Poor Law were remotely capable of doing. They simply did not have the wherewithal. Even government officials in Ireland grew increasingly to doubt that such local relief schemes were in any way practical. Before long, the sickness and mortality rates were simply overwhelming. As tenants began to default on their rent payments, the landlords' rent rolls began to shrink. Given that Irish landlords were properly notorious for raising mortgages on their properties, their liquidity was frequently an issue. We saw earlier the distressing case of Lord Kingston in Co. Cork: he was not alone. It meant that the landlords – with the best will in the world, which admittedly was not always there – did not have the ready financial resources to fund local relief schemes. The government insisted mulishly that in law it was properly the responsibility of local landlords to finance relief. The Treasury fretted that direct government assistance might allow the landlords to evade this obligation. This was hopelessly to miss the point: the law was a dead letter by dint of the landlords' financial distress.

As to the Irish Poor Law, it had arisen from a commission of enquiry established in 1833, its members being Irish for the most part and well acquainted with Irish conditions. It contained both the Roman Catholic and the Anglican archbishops of Dublin. It had recommended a series of measures but counselled against the simple extension of English law to Ireland, proposing instead measures better adapted to the very different social conditions prevailing in the smaller island. Their report was ignored by the government, which instead despatched George Nicholls, an English Poor Law commissioner who had no intimate knowledge of Irish conditions, to review the situation. Nicholls – yet another Englishman who knew what was best for poor Paddy – simply extended the English law to Ireland, the very thing that the earlier commission of enquiry had warned against. This was done by an act of parliament in 1838.

The system thus established was overwhelmed by the sheer scale of the Famine. No system could have been designed to cope with a catastrophe on this scale. Yet the government and the Treasury stuck to their ideological guns and held to their laissez-faire principles with a conviction worthy of a religious fanatic.* Between them, Wood and Trevelyan reduced grain importation and attempted to run down public works schemes. Such schemes breached a key provision of the Poor Law, whose reliefs were intended to be financed at local level and upon whose shoulders London wanted above all else to throw the principal burden of famine relief. Public works schemes, which offered outdoor relief in the form of basic menial labour, were by definition publicly funded. To orthodox Treasury eyes, this was a legal and a moral scandal.

THE BIG WINNERS in the aftermath of the Famine were the Catholic Church and the larger tenant farmers, the ones who survived the hurricane. The church embarked on its long century of moral monopoly from which the more recent, secular liberal

---

* The in-house journal of all laissez-fairies from its foundation in 1843 to the present, *The Economist*, declares in its mission statement, occasionally still run on its contents page as a reminder of baptismal vows, that it exists 'to take part in a severe contest between intelligence, which presses forward, and an unworthy, timid ignorance obstructing our progress'. No Jesuit was ever more certain of transubstantiation.

bourgeoisie is recoiling in embarrassment. But it was potent while it lasted, that power. De Tocqueville, de Beaumont and Thackeray all emphasize the extraordinary bond of affection and loyalty between priests and people in pre-Famine Ireland, counterpointed by a poisonous sectarianism and an unapologetic hatred – it is not too strong a word on the evidence – for Protestantism. Thackeray notes at one point in Co. Kildare, just to the north of Kilkenny, the following: 'There are Catholic inns and Protestant inns in the towns; Catholic coaches and Protestant coaches on the roads; nay, in the north, I have heard of a high-church coach and a low-church coach, adopted by travelling Christians of either party.'

The reference to the north is presumably to Ulster, which, as the world knows, has its peculiarities in these matters. But no one reading these three pre-Famine travellers, and other contemporaries, could doubt the depth of sectarian animosity or the historical memory of dispossession going back to the seventeenth century. That's why Cromwell keeps popping up sooner or later in most accounts of the Irish past. It was following his victory in the 1650s that Catholic landowners – the vast majority – were expropriated and their lands settled on English Protestant parvenus. It was their descendants who constituted the feckless ascendancy landlords ruined by the Famine.

Their surviving big tenants shared the historical memory of dispossession and, compounded with sectarian animosity, it made for an unstable brew. All was relatively quiet for about twenty years after the Famine but then a collapse in agricultural prices renewed the pressure on the system. The price crash was largely due to imports from the United States and Argentina, the products of enormous industrial farming that nowhere in Europe could match for economies of scale. The upshot in Ireland in the 1880s was a vigorous – indeed intimidatory and violent – campaign for land reform which eventually resulted in the Land Act of 1903 which transferred ownership of the land from the landlords to the tenants. Thus was Cromwell undone.

THE MORAL ELEMENT in the British response to the Famine mattered. There had been a long and dismal English tradition of regarding the Irish as an inferior people, in some cases outright barbarous, going all the way back to Giraldus Cambrensis. Is this what happens when an invading culture collides with an indigenous one and displaces it, especially when the invader brings a more advanced technology? Conquest begets superiority, a contempt for the defeated and a blatant indifference to their culture. Take this little gem, for example:

> I am not, nor ever have been, in favour of bringing about in any way the social and political equality of the white and black races... I am not nor ever have been in favour of making voters or jurors of negroes, nor of qualifying them to hold office, nor to inter-marry with white people... There is a physical difference between the white and black races which I believe will forever forbid the two races living together on terms of social and political equality.

Thus Abraham Lincoln, in the course of the fourth of his seven debates with Stephen Douglas in 1858. Douglas had argued that American independence was an entirely white affair; its constitution and laws were for whites only. Blacks were excluded. As for Native Americans, his views are not known but can be readily imagined.

So the long English tradition of cultural condescension towards Ireland, going right back to Giraldus Cambrensis, is part of a larger, repeating pattern. That throws its judgements in doubt, as prejudiced, but does it invalidate them? It is all too easy for Irish people to say that it does. Every people wants to think well of itself and will readily attribute bad faith to the negative opinions of others, especially if those others have arrived with fire and sword. But attribution of bad faith is not invalidation of evidence, any more than it is an endorsement of it.

SO THE TREASURY's negative view of Ireland had centuries of tradition and disobliging opinion behind it. By the time the Famine hit, it was an article of faith in London that Ireland was a backward social and economic mess. Its landlords were viewed as feckless and reactionary, ignoring the modernizing improvements that had transformed English agriculture, such as consolidation and enclosure to create larger holdings, sophisticated crop rotation techniques and modern fertilizing methods. The tenants were characterized as a slothful human mass kept in a permanent state of backward subsistence by their overwhelming reliance on the potato and the ignorance of their heretic priests. The free traders wanted a wholesale shakeout of Irish society and in particular of its agriculture. They wanted enclosure, modern farming methods that echoed English practice, assisted passage to the colonies for tenants surplus to requirements – the Duchess of Sutherland's prescription renewed. They saw the Famine as a providential opportunity to achieve these desiderata. It was a moral pleasure as well as a legal obligation.

In the end, they pretty well got their way. The Irish Poor Law collapsed financially in 1848, with thousands of tenants evicted for non-payment of rent now thrown upon its mercies. An act of 1847, known ever after as the Quarter-Acre Clause, decreed that 'occupiers of more than a quarter acre of land are not to be deemed destitute, not to be relieved out of the poor rates'. Thus starving tenants – the very poorest of the poor in a poor land – were made to surrender their miserable little hold-ings, all they had in the world, in order to embrace the horrors of the workhouse, where at least they might eat. The inten-tion of the clause was to make eviction easier and thus help to rationalize Irish land holdings, but it felt like an exercise in theoretical economics with the human consequences – which were anticipated and criticized by opponents of the legislation at the time – reckoned to be of no account. The sponsor of the notorious clause was one Sir William Gregory, a Co. Clare landlord who later married a younger neighbour, Augusta Persse, who survived him and who, as Lady Gregory, was one of the prime movers of the Irish literary and cultural revival at the turn of the twentieth century.

There was a wider context to this laissez-faire fetish in the Anglo-Saxon world, and one that gradually insinuated itself even into such bastions of statist *dirigisme* as France. It wasn't just wickedness or carelessness; it was worse than that: it was fashionable. In the 1830s, a few years before the Famine, there was a stock market crash in New York – yes, yet another one, now obliterated from the collective memory – which prompted Henry Clay, the leader of America's Whig Party (precursors of the Republicans), to call for federal aid for the afflicted. The people, said he, were 'entitled to the protecting care of a parental government'. The president, Martin Van Buren, a laissez-faire man to the marrow, wouldn't hear of it and let things take their course. Nor was there to be 'the protecting care of a parental government' in the case of Ireland. There was badness in the British response to the Famine, but much modish orthodoxy as well.

The Treasury got its desires not just because of the mortality and the emigration. It may have regretted the former but it applauded the latter. There remained the problem of the landlords, many of whom were ruined by the Famine. With impoverished, starving and dying tenants, the landlords' basic income stopped flowing. Many of them, already indebted, simply went under. Insolvent or encumbered estates were taken into temporary public ownership under two acts passed in 1848 and 1849. Under the acts, an Encumbered Estates Court was established and charged with selling off these properties. Creditors were paid a fraction of the outstanding debts, depending on the funds raised from the sales, and the new owners were granted a clear legal title. Nearly three thousand estates aggregating to 5 million acres of lands changed hands in this manner between 1849 and 1857. That represented about a quarter of all the land in Ireland. Ninety-six per cent of the new owners were Irish: as we saw with the merchants of Cork, not everyone in Ireland was short of money.

The bankruptcy of so many landlords was the *reductio ad absurdum* of laissez-faire. The state simply had to step in, if only to act as a temporary clearing house for the disposal of so many distressed properties. It was not unlike the effective nationalization of banks following the financial crash of 2008, something taken on with the greatest reluctance and under-pinned by a desire to return the troubled entities to the private sector as quickly as possible. The government, in the person of Charles Wood, declared that there was no chance of Irish agri-cultural reform unless distressed properties were transferred to solvent proprietors who would have both the will and the means to modernize. These turned out to be a mixture of speculators with ready cash and provident landlords. It had the desired effect: the very smallest pre-Famine holdings began a long and continuing decline; larger holdings increased as a percentage of the total; and their tenants, who had survived the storm, were the biggest winners of all. They were to prove the backbone of Irish nationalism until (and after) independence, reaping the material rewards of the disaster while blaming the entire thing on the British government.

The whole business of the encumbered estates marked a crit-ical psychological shift in British government thinking about Ireland. The landlords whose lands were transferred had been the descendants of the Cromwellian settlers. They were what could, with justice, be regarded as the English colony in Ireland. Yet the English and Scots held them in contempt, as we saw. When it came to it, the state simply had to insert itself into the process of clearing up the mess, however temporarily. If parlia-ment could legislate for the disposal of encumbered estates, there was no reason why it might not, at a later date, legislate again for Irish land reform, which is indeed what happened from 1870 on. The coping stone of the whole process was the Wyndham Act of 1903 which undid the whole landlord system and turned the tenants into owner-proprietors.

The Encumbered Estates Acts were the first small pebble in this pond. The government in London had given up on its recalcitrant colonists in Ireland. Ironically, the first post-Famine land act was the Landlord and Tenant (Amendment) Act 1860, known as Deasy's Act after its principal sponsor, the attorney-general Richard Deasy. It was a heroic attempt to turn the clock back by asserting the absolute rights of landlords based on contract law and placing no legal value on occupation, improvements or tenancy. It was a reiteration of fundamental English property law. But once again, parliament was tinkering with the Irish land question in a manner unthinkable before the Famine. Deasy's Act stood for a mere ten years until the first of Gladstone's Land Acts (1870) gradually began the process of acknowledging tenants' rights, the first step away from Deasy and towards Wyndham.*

No legislation to secure the rights of tenants, along the lines of Gladstone's Land Acts and their successors, was ever contemplated for England and Scotland. It was not just that conditions similar to Ireland did not obtain but that the acts themselves represented a compromising of English property law, the security and absolute position of which was regarded as a key feature of English liberties. It runs deep in the English psyche: in modern times, Margaret Thatcher, a worthy intellectual successor to Wood and Trevelyan, was vocal in promoting 'a property-owning democracy'. Nor is

---

* It is worth acknowledging that during the nineteenth century, state intervention was more common in Ireland than in England in areas such as education, policing and economic activity; this more active state was a tacit admission of the Irish difference and of the existential deficiencies of the entire Union project.

there any doubt that secure property titles are a hallmark of free societies.

Yet it proved impossible to hold the line on this core legal principle in Ireland. The various land acts of the late nineteenth century did compromise the absolute property rights of landlords by acknowledging and endorsing the rights of tenants. Once again, the Irish hand proved that it couldn't fit into the English glove. The English found Ireland exasperating, maddening and time-consuming. As the nineteenth century turns into the twentieth, you can almost feel a sense of fed-upness in some English attitudes to Ireland, swinging between stupid Tory ultras – they haven't gone away, you know – who wanted to hold onto Ireland at all hazards despite the steadily rising tide of nationalism and others who were willing to compromise but gave the impression of wishing that the whole damned thing would just go away.

Of course, it didn't go away. It got worse. The Easter Rising of 1916 may not have invented Irish nationalism, which had been on the road for at least a hundred years at that stage, but it transformed it. The nationalist demand suddenly became more radical and more urgent, as expectations that had seemed impossible before the rising suddenly appeared very possible indeed.

NINE

DISESTABLISHMENT

THE SHIFTING ATTITUDE to land was not the only manner in which London began to rethink Ireland in the wake of the Famine. Nor was it the only signal that its will to rule – at least in conformity to English pieties and orthodoxies – was weakening. The disestablishment of the Church of Ireland was another case in point. An established church, as defined in the *Oxford English Dictionary*, is one which obtains 'legal form and recognition… as the official church of a country'. So to remove that status by legislation is no small step. As we shall see shortly, the established position of the Church of Ireland was integral to the Act of Union of 1801. Thus it was a key part of the Basic Law that governed relations between the two islands in the nineteenth century, almost like a kind of written constitution.

THE CHURCH OF Ireland is part of the international Anglican Communion. It was established contemporaneously with its sister church in England at the time of Henry VIII's break with the Roman papacy in 1536. It regards itself as Catholic in the sense that the Henrician reforms were a restoration of propriety, returning Christianity to a state of good accord by ridding it of the corrupt excesses of the medieval papacy. So the 1530s are regarded as a moment of reform and cleansing, not of foundation. This enables the Church of Ireland to claim a continuous existence right back to St Patrick and early Irish Christianity, just as the Church of England traces its origin to the arrival of St Augustine to Canterbury in 597.

England embraced Anglicanism more or less; Scotland accepted the more severe Calvinist version of the Reformation; while various dissenting sects flourished in Wales. But, as we saw, the Reformation struggled in Ireland and never established itself securely outside parts of Ulster, mainly in the east of the province, and even there the influence was principally Scots' Calvinist. For most of its existence, the Church of Ireland has commanded the spiritual loyalty of about 10 per cent of the island's population. Yet, following in lockstep with its sister church, it was declared to be the established church of the country. Even as Reform failed to gain a purchase over time, that status did not change. Uniquely for an established church, the Church of Ireland did not command the allegiance of the majority of people in the country where it was so established.

None the less, the Anglican minority pretty well ran Ireland in the eighteenth century. They alone constituted the political nation; their political power was anchored in their ownership of land. Then, at the end of that century, there came the turbulence following on from the French Revolution, the Revolutionary and Napoleonic wars, and the bloody rising of 1798 in Ireland. The result was the Act of Union of 1801 which bound Ireland into the unitary British state. The old Irish parliament voted itself out of existence and instead began to send MPs direct to Westminster. Thus was formed the United Kingdom of Great Britain and Ireland.

The Act of Union had consequences for the Church of Ireland. Just as the island was now joined in a single parliamentary union with Britain, so it was in ecclesiastical matters. The Church of Ireland was no longer merely to be a sister of the English church; it was to be united to it in a single body. Article 5 of the act stated that:

> the Churches of England and Ireland, as now by law established, be united into one Protestant Episcopal Church, to be called, *The United Church of England and Ireland*; and that the doctrine, worship, discipline of government of the said united Church shall be, and shall remain in full force for ever, as the same are now by law established for the Church of England, and that the continuance and preservation of the said united Church, as the Established Church of England and Ireland, shall be deemed and taken to be an essential and fundamental part of the Union...

None of this did anything to endear the Irish majority to the Church of Ireland, towards which that majority continued to demonstrate an undisguised hostility. De Tocqueville, visiting Ireland in the mid-1830s, summed it up with his unfailingly acute eye, writing of an Anglican rector:

> a holy man, whom God has not overwhelmed with work; he has twenty or so thousand francs [£800] income, forty

parishioners, and a small gothic church, which is built at the top of the park. The Catholic priest has a small house, a much smaller dinner, five or six thousand parishioners who are dying of hunger,* and share their last penny with him; and he fancies that this state of things is not the best possible one. He thinks that if the Protestant minister had a little less and the poor Catholic population a little more, society would gain by it, and he is amazed that five thousand Catholics are obliged to pay twenty thousand francs in taxes to support the religion of forty Protestants.

De Tocqueville was in Ireland in the middle of what became known as the Tithe War, and it is to the system of tithes that he referred at the end of that passage. Tithes were a tax – notionally one-tenth of earnings levied either in cash or kind for the upkeep of the Church of Ireland clergy. Tithes had always been resented and had been the proximate cause of sporadic campaigns of agrarian violence ever since the 1760s. These campaigns had escalated in the early 1830s, resulting in serious violence in the countryside. In general, attempts to enforce payment – or, worse, to distrain goods for non-payment – met with fierce resistance. The ferocity was a product of the time: what had previously been a grievance now became a source of bitter resentment, buoyed by the increased set of Catholic expectations in the wake of emancipation in 1829. As we saw, O'Connell's rhetoric could be brutally sectarian when it suited

---

* By which I think that de Tocqueville means impoverished, which was true. But they were not dying of hunger – yet – because of all those potatoes and all that buttermilk. But his choice of words would prove prophetic before long.

him, and he found a responsive audience. Fresh in the Catholic memory, as well, was the evangelical proselytising campaign of the 1820s known as the Second Reformation.

In this heightened sectarian atmosphere, it was unsurprising that the tithe system was so inflammatory. By 1830, almost two-thirds of the total income of Church of Ireland clergy came from that source. And the main burden of payment fell upon a majority population not in communion with the Church of Ireland. Moreover, from 1735 to 1823 pasturage was excluded from the scheme, which meant that people holding the best land were exempt. Given the reality of land-holding patterns, this meant that wealthy members of the Church of Ireland paid less than their due share for the upkeep of their own clergy, throwing the principal burden onto poorer Catholics and – in Ulster – Presbyterians.

The Tithe War started in Graiguenamanagh, Co. Kilkenny, in October 1830 when the cattle of the parish priest, Fr Martin Doyle,* were distrained for non-payment. A campaign spread out from the south-east to embrace twenty-two of the thirty-two Irish counties. Although formally a campaign of passive resistance, it inevitably turned violent. The use of police and troops to distrain goods and livestock resulted in serious clashes. In Newtownbarry, Co. Wexford, an affray on 18 June 1832, the seventeenth anniversary of the Battle of Waterloo, led to the deaths of seventeen people and injuries to twenty more: a company of yeomanry had fired into a protesting crowd. A few weeks later, in Castlepollard, Co. Westmeath, another seventeen

---

*A relation of the formidable James Warren Doyle, bishop of Kildare and Leighlin.

were killed by troops in similar circumstances. In October, the government was sufficiently alarmed to pass the Tumultuous Risings Act, which substituted transportation for execution for certain capital crimes; it was thought, perhaps correctly, to be the greater deterrent. None the less, on 14 December, a mob of some two thousand people attacked troops at Carrickshock, Co. Kilkenny: sixteen died.

In all, over 43,000 decrees were issued against defaulters while Lord Gort claimed in 1832 that the anti-tithe campaign had so far claimed 242 homicides; 1,179 robberies; 401 burglaries; 568 burnings; 280 cattle maimings; 161 assaults; 203 riots; and 723 attacks on houses. By 1833, the withdrawal of police and yeomanry from tithe enforcement duties took much of the heat out of the situation. By then, arrears were more than £1 million, which the London government quietly gifted to the church, acknowledging in effect that the tithe system was no longer sustainable. The problem was finally conjured out of existence by legislation in 1838 when O'Connell, who had kept his distance from the agitation while benefiting politically from it – he was not the last Irish nationalist to master this trick – contributed to a proposal which meant the state taking over responsibility for clerical payments. The Tithe Rent Charge (Ireland) Act turned the tithe into a rent charge at 75 per cent of the old value; it was payable twice annually by the head landlord, who could then recover its value in whole or in part through his tenants' rents.

SO THE TITHE question was settled and faded in the collective memory. In a few years, Ireland had more to remember than tithes. The Famine of 1845–52 was such a social and demographic catastrophe as to mark the greatest disjunction in its history. It coincided with the coming of the railway and the institutional expansion of the Catholic Church. In aggregate, these three forces or events make the pre-Famine world impossible to recall imaginatively. It was another world to ours.

After the Famine, Irish public life atrophied. The church, with its moral monopoly now established beyond question, entered into its century or more as the unchallenged arbiter of public morals and personal behaviour. Paul Cullen – a severe ultramontane rigorist whose youthful formation had been in Rome itself – became archbishop of Dublin in 1852 and the first Irish cardinal in 1866. He was no friend of Britain, although he maintained such proprieties with the public authorities as he could not avoid. But his coolness towards the heretic without was as nothing compared to his ice-cold ferocity towards political conspirators within. These were the Fenians, founded, as we saw, jointly in Ireland and America in 1858. Their structure was based on the revolutionary secret societies of the continent – especially France and Italy – and it was this that drew Cullen's adamantine hostility. The British may have been poor heretics, deluded in their absurd beliefs, but they were more to be pitied and prayed for than hated. You never know, they might yet be saved for the true church of Christ. But the Fenians were an existential enemy, partly because the church had always been neurotic about political secret societies, and partly because they represented a potential focus for mobilizing public loyalty that could only succeed by diminishing the loyalty offered to the church. There was a further reason: towards the end of his time in Rome, Cullen had seen what conspiratorial secret societies were capable of. He had had to flee Rome in 1848 along with

Pope Pius IX, having seen the papal minister of the interior murdered – all this the doing of republican secret societies that flourished briefly in that heady year. And now, back home in Ireland, Cullen found himself with similar conspiratorial cuckoos in his nest.

As the 1860s went on, the Fenians flourished organization-ally. Their leader, James Stephens, displayed unflagging energy in establishing Fenian cells in nearly all of Ireland, although he foolishly exaggerated the total number of members, something that greatly angered the American wing of the movement when the truth emerged. Once again, Protestant Ulster fell outside his remit, nor was he so foolish as to try to persuade them: no Jackie Lawless he. But Fenian roots went deep, offering a radical, militarized solution to British rule in Ireland – it had no time, at least in the beginning, for parliamentary blather. Moreover, it mobilized young men in the urban lower middle class, young people of modest educational accomplishments but sufficient to furnish them with ambition and the prospect of social mobility. That was new.

The year 1865 was set for an insurrection against British rule. It never happened. There was a split* between Stephens, who knew that they were not ready in 1865, and the American wing, which was urging him on in the belief that his numbers were sound; many of these Americans were Civil War veterans, newly demobilized and full of fight. The 'rising', when it even-tually came in early 1867, was a shambles. But in September and December that year, the Fenians pulled off two outrages that

---

* Brendan Behan famously said years later that the first item on every Irish agenda is the split.

were consequential. In September, a prison van in Manchester carrying two senior Fenians was attacked in an attempt to free them. In the ensuing affray, a policeman was shot dead. Three men, known in Ireland ever after as the Manchester Martyrs, were hanged on dubious evidence. On one later account, the person who fired the fatal shot was never brought before a court. Then in December, an Irish Fenian, Ricard [sic] O'Sullivan Burke, who was a veteran of the Union army in the American Civil War, came to Britain under an alias and began to buy up arms. He also imported rifles from America and stored them in a premises in Liverpool. On the night of 20 November, he was in London but unaware that he was under surveillance. The Metropolitan Police had found a Fenian informer, one John Devany, who fingered O'Sullivan Burke. After a hearing at Bow Street magistrates' court, O'Sullivan Burke found himself lodged in the Middlesex House of Detention at Clerkenwell. It was a bad blow for the Fenians, for O'Sullivan Burke was a senior man and had even been 'out' in the earlier effort in Dublin in March 1867.

So it was resolved to spring him. Despite prison security, Fenians on the outside made contact with O'Sullivan Burke and resolved upon an explosion which would breach the external wall at Clerkenwell and allow the prisoner to run off through the gap during the confusion. O'Sullivan Burke was a former engineering officer in the Union army and had been present at the explosion of an 8,000-pound mine at Petersburg, Virginia, in 1864. On his instructions, gunpowder was purchased and the escape attempt was set for 12 December. A barrel of gunpowder was to be rolled up against the weak point in the wall during the prisoners' exercise time and a rubber ball thrown over the wall to signal that things were about to happen. Burke saw the ball sail over and dropped out. But the fuse, when lit, didn't take. A warder pocketed the ball for his children and nobody thought any more of the whole thing.

Until later: for a message was received the same day from the Dublin Metropolitan Police who had got very precise details of the plan – presumably from one of their own informers as it was accurate in every detail, including the bit about the ball – which eventually reached the desk of Sir Richard Mayne, the commissioner of the Met. He alerted the governor at Clerkenwell, who promptly increased security. Exercise time was moved from the afternoon to the morning; O'Sullivan Burke was shifted to a new, double-locked cell. Next day, 13 December, the Fenians tried again at the usual exercise time, around 3:45 p.m., throwing their ball into the now-empty exercise yard. This time the plan worked – all too well. A sixty-foot section of the wall was destroyed but so was a row of houses across the street. Twelve people died directly and five more indirectly; more than fifty were injured. One woman went mad; about forty women gave birth prematurely; there were claims that a further twenty babies died as a consequence of the trauma suffered by their mothers, although that latter claim may be taken *cum grano salis* given the high rate of infant mortality at the time. The dead and injured were all working-class people.

Naturally, there was outrage. Queen Victoria called for summary justice for Irish suspects and Benjamin Disraeli, now prime minister for the first time, would have been happy to suspend *habeas corpus*. There were arrests and trials but it was impossible to convict on the basis of the testimony of many traumatized and confused prosecution witnesses. But one

Fenian, Michael Barrett, was convicted and executed, attaining in death the minor accomplishment of being the last man to be hanged in public in England. But Manchester and Clerkenwell had another effect. They got William Ewart Gladstone thinking about Ireland.

IT WASN'T JUST Gladstone. Disraeli also thought that something should be done about Ireland and was considering a proposal to extend ecclesiastical endowment – then reserved solely for the established Church of Ireland – to the Roman Catholic and Presbyterian churches as well, thus putting the major confessions on a more equal financial footing. Whether Disraeli could ever have got this proposal past British public opinion, solidly Protestant and further convinced of the irremediable treachery of Irish Catholics by Manchester and Clerkenwell, will never be known. He might have had a tough time trying to get British taxpayers to fund such an arrangement. At any rate, it never happened, because Gladstone, still smarting from having received the parliamentary run-around from Disraeli the year before in the matter of the Second Reform Act, upped the bid.

In the House of Commons, Gladstone declared that he was now in favour of the full disestablishment and disendowment of the Church of Ireland. Moreover, he proposed to make it part of his manifesto in the forthcoming general election, which was only months away. If Disraeli was the brilliant, serpentine tactician, Gladstone was the strategist. He had concluded that something had to be done for Ireland, not home rule or anything like that – that was for the future and well below the horizon in 1868 – but to reconcile Ireland to British rule by doing away with its most egregious anomalies. And the established position of the Church of Ireland was certainly one such, given that it claimed the allegiance of such a paltry proportion of the Irish population, albeit the most influential and wealthy element. The move was not without risk for Gladstone, because the Liberal Party had a solid backbone of non-conformist, low-church supporters who had no love for Anglicans but at the same time had no obvious desire to deliver what would inevitably be seen as a victory for the Roman Catholics.

All this represented a *volte-face* for Gladstone, for in his youth he had been a high-church Tory opposed to concessions to Irish Catholicism. But he drifted away from the Tories following the split over the Corn Laws in the 1840s and gradually moved towards that junction of Peelite Tories and Whigs that became the Liberal Party in 1859. He made disestablishment of the Church of Ireland a central plank in the Liberal election manifesto for the general election of 1868, and it became one of the principal discussion points of the campaign. Gladstone won the election, delivering a majority of 112 to the Liberals in the House of Commons. He was at Hawarden, his estate in north Wales, when the telegram arrived announcing his victory. He was chopping down a tree at the time and his first response was, 'Very significant,' before turning once more to the tree. After a few more strokes, he stopped and said, 'My mission is to pacify Ireland.'

Perhaps it was, but Gladstone, for all the thought he may have given to Ireland, knew remarkably little about the place, never having been there, and this lack of knowledge on Irish matters merely reflected British opinion in general, including all of Gladstone's incoming ministers. *Plus ça change*. The Tories were no better informed, although they opposed the measure as if they knew something about the subject. They did, however, have two points that resonated in English (and Irish Protestant) ears. First, there was the awkward matter of article 5 of the Act of Union. The act was effectively a Basic Law, setting out the constitutional relationship between the two islands; and if language meant anything, the words of article 5 should have been fatal to Gladstone's cause. The union of churches was declared to be 'an essential and fundamental part of the Union'. It was therefore asserted by opponents of the measure that if the union of churches was so fundamental to the whole constitutional arrangement, then surely disestablishment was a betrayal of the Union *tout court*. If you permit one thread in a cloak to be unravelled, might not the entire garment fall apart?

There were also concerns about the endowment proposals, which relieved the Church of Ireland of much of its considerable land holdings; these were henceforth vested in a body known as the Commission for the Irish Church Temporalities. Compensation of £16 million was paid to the church, an amount reckoned to be little more than half the market value of the properties thus transferred. This troubled some Tories because it compromised the purity and absolutism of English property law: the terms of compensation, by discounting the market value of the lands transferred, could be represented as a form of expropriation.

Despite these doubts, and despite a robust campaign of opposition from the bench of bishops of the Church of Ireland, the bill became law in July 1869, with remarkably little fuss, and was operative from 1871. It was a sensible measure to undo one of the most anomalous aspects of relations between the two islands. But it was also a moment of hesitation for both great British parties. Henceforth, all the Liberals' Irish reforms under four Gladstone governments were one way and another recognitions of Irish difference. This was especially true in matters of land and agrarian reform which could only be achieved by further compromising the purest principles of property law, something that made the English skin itch. Likewise, the Tories gradually came to acknowledge the need for some social reforms, in recognition of the different conditions prevailing in Ireland, but they set their faces against any further weakening of the constitutional position. And so, their opposition to disestablishment, emphasizing the potentially negative effect of setting aside article 5, gradually snowballed into a hysterical opposition to Irish home rule that carried the party of throne and altar to the point of open treason in 1912.*

Ireland and its discontents were to consume much of British public life for the next fifty years. In that time, no fewer than eleven land acts, some more important than others and none more important than the 1903 act, were passed in parliament. Home rule for Ireland would become in short order the most pressing question of the age. But with the disestablishment of the Church of Ireland, something had snapped. The whole basis on which the union of the two islands had been predicated

---

* In a suggestive modern parallel, the Tories' contemporary hysterics over the European Union have followed a similar trajectory. When the UK joined the Common Market (as it then was) in 1973 only a tiny minority of Conservatives, of which the charismatic and sinister Enoch Powell was the most prominent, opposed entry. Within twenty years, that minority had grown, had made a thorough nuisance of itself under John Major's government in the 1990s, and eventually became possessed of a messianism that finally delivered Brexit by plebiscite in 2016.

was subverted. It was a small act of subversion but a telling one. Henceforth, a large part of the British establishment acknowledged that the Irish difference had to be appeased in recognition of reality. A minority, the Tory ultras, saw only their own reality of imperial pride, which they absolutely refused to compromise, at the very centre of their possessions and at the apogee of their power. Disestablishment was, in the end, not all that important in itself and worked out fine. But the fact of disestablishment was the loosening of the first brick in the wall. Those Tories who opposed the measure as a subversion of the Act of Union had a point, as cultural pessimists often do. There was no straight line from disestablishment to the republic, but something had changed – and it had changed in people's heads.

What was changing was the automatic cultural cringe felt in the smaller island towards the larger. All colonial arrangements depend upon the deference of the colonized: accepting their masters' manners and mores as superior and imitable. When that weakens, the colonial enterprise itself begins to wobble. This does not entail political or constitutional change – the usual headline stuff – but it is an indispensable precursor to it. Which brings us to the curious figure of Joseph Gillis Biggar.

TEN

—>< —

OF MAN'S FIRST DISOBEDIENCE

B Y ANY REASONABLE standard, Joseph Gillis Biggar was a pain in the arse. He was from a prosperous mercantile background in Belfast – his father was chairman of the Ulster Bank, which placed the family in the first rank of provincial society – and he managed the family provision business from 1861 to 1880. He also turned to politics, embracing radicalism as part of the dying embers of that particular Ulster Presbyterian tradition. He joined the newly formed Home Government Association and was elected to the House of Commons in 1874. He was, therefore, important as a prominent early home rule MP, part of a process that – like just about everything that follows in the rest of this book – was detaching nationalist Ireland from the British embrace, or at least weakening that embrace.

The Home Government Association had been founded in 1870, with Isaac Butt, a barrister, as its most prominent figure.

Butt was a Dublin Protestant and the association drew an impressive number of Protestants to its membership. Allegiances were still somewhat fluid but this was a surprising development, if only because the great majority of Anglicans gave visceral loyalty to the Union. This also applied with increasing effect to the local Ulster Presbyterian majority. But there were still some dissenters, holding to that old radical Ulster tradition, as was the case with Biggar.

The southern Protestant membership of the Home Government Association has been attributed by some historians to anxieties arising from the disestablishment of their church. This was regarded as an act of *force majeure* by London, done over the heads and against the furious protests of the Irish church hierarchy. Might it not be better to regain some measure of local autonomy, not to facilitate nationalist ambition – heaven forfend! – but to get some aspects of Irish governance out of the hands of ignorant and irresponsible Englishmen and into the hands of the local Irish elite, who knew the country and understood its imperatives and usages? It represented a kind of political inoculation: by injecting a small measure of harmless autonomy into the body politic, it might be possible to immunize the entire body against more virulent strains of the virus.

Alas, if that was their motivation, they were not for long deceived. Any proposal, however modest, for Irish autonomy was bound to find some favour with nationalists. Moreover, the Fenians were changing. After the fiasco of 1867, James Stephens was pushed aside and a new management structure established for the organization. It was, for a while, numerically the largest organized political grouping in Ireland, and its earlier outright rejection of parliamentary politics had softened. The Home

Government Association was founded in the Bilton Hotel, Dublin, on 19 May 1870; two of those at the inaugural meeting were members of the supreme council of the Irish Republican Brotherhood (the Brotherhood and the Fenians were effectively one and the same thing). They gave their blessing to this new initiative. It was as a member of the Home Rule League, a successor body to the Home Government Association, that Joseph Gillis Biggar was returned to Westminster in the 1874 general election that saw Gladstone ousted from Downing Street to be replaced by Disraeli, who had delivered the first Conservative majority in the Commons since the 1840s. The Tories had no interest in Ireland other than to keep it quiet.

There were fifty-nine MPs returned in that election under the banner of the Home Rule League. Butt, their leader, had won nationalist kudos at the bar by defending Fenian prisoners, although his own political sympathies were remote from theirs. He had even been briefly a Tory MP in the 1850s. But like Gladstone, he shifted. In Butt's case, the drift was away from stout defence of Protestant ascendancy towards a reconstituted form of civil society in which nationalist grievances would be addressed seriously under a compact of Protestant and Catholic interests, although with the social leadership of the former to be retained as an insurance against social dissolution. It was a position ripe with prevarication and ambiguity. But the drift in Butt's politics was unmistakeable, from unbending Tory before the Famine to a very soft nationalism – perhaps even a kind of Tory nationalism – by the end of the 1860s. He was also the president of the Amnesty Association, a body established to demand an amnesty for convicted Fenians, many of whom Butt had defended and whose good faith and sincerity he never doubted.

Home rule was from the beginning what one historian has described as a coat of many colours. There were nervous Protestants hoping to patch things up in the wake of disestablishment; Tories like Butt who shared many of these aspirations and anxieties but had a closer understanding of and respect for advanced nationalism; Catholics who were more urgent in their demands for autonomy; some careerists; and oddballs like Biggar. As yet, there were no Fenians in the parliamentary ranks, although that development was not far off.

Biggar was a hunchback with the sort of Belfast accent that might sound musical on Royal Avenue but which grates in most other places. It grated in the House of Commons where, to compound the matter, he proved a poor orator. However, he made his mark, to the fury of members, hon members, hon and gallant members, hon and learned members and Uncle Tom Cobleigh and all. Unlike Butt, he was no Tory gent but a troublemaker in the best Belfast Presbyterian tradition. In April 1875, the Peace Preservation Act came to the floor of the House. In opposing it, Biggar droned on for four hours, thus introducing the Commons to the delights of the filibuster. With little original to say himself, he used up the time by reading from official documents and government reports. He concluded by saying that he 'was unwilling to detain the House any longer'.

He reprised this performance repeatedly over the next few years, making himself thoroughly obnoxious in the eyes of other members and something of a hero back in nationalist Ireland. Basically, he was buggering up the system because the rules of the House did not allow for any motion of closure, or guillotine, although inevitably that arrived in due time, largely in response to the antics of Biggar and his pals.

For he did attract support from his own side, although not from Butt who was repelled by such egregious offences to the dignity of the House. Not only were they distasteful, in Butt's eyes they were counterproductive, because their only practical effect was to get members' backs up. After all, these were the very people whose support would be required in pursuit of any of Butt's desiderata. Not everyone among his own MPs agreed with Butt and many came to enjoy Biggar's antics.* Of all the adherents to his methods, none was more important than a man returned for the constituency of Co. Meath at a by-election in 1875: Charles Stewart Parnell.

Parnell was one of the most brilliant – and certainly the most enigmatic – figures in all of British and Irish history. He was of a landlord family in Co. Wicklow whose remote origins had been in Cheshire: an ancestor had been mayor of Congleton. The first Irish Parnell was one Thomas, who was a beneficiary of the Cromwellian plantation back in the 1660s. Whether Thomas Parnell had supported the parliamentary cause in the English Civil War with money or with arms is unclear but he secured an estate in Queen's County for whatever services had been rendered and settled to life as a country gentleman. A number of descendants distinguished themselves, but the first to make

---

* It need hardly be said that by the time of his death in 1890, Biggar was widely mourned and had, in the finest British tradition, been embraced with affection in the bosom of parliament and was regarded as what we would now call a national treasure. In addition to his other accomplishments, Biggar was an enthusiastic and serial philanderer, which should have damaged him in the eyes of his Ulster constituents but didn't. When a parliamentary bill was introduced in 1883 to ease the financial impositions on men in breach-of-promise cases, it was known popularly as the Biggar Relief Bill.

an impact on Irish public life was Sir John Parnell, the second baronet, who rose to be chancellor of the Irish exchequer and an opponent of the Act of Union.* This did no harm to his great-grandson's political prospects, because by the time Charles came on the political scene in the 1870s, opposition to the Union was a mark of good pedigree in nationalist eyes. One of Sir John's sons, William Parnell, inherited the house and estate in Avondale, Co. Wicklow, from a cousin, Samuel Hayes, whose family was inter-married with the Parnells. In turn, his son, John Henry Parnell, inherited it and lived there with his American wife, Delia Stewart. She was the daughter of Admiral Charles Stewart of the US Navy – known to all as Old Ironsides – who had distinguished himself during the war with the British in 1812.

Charles Stewart Parnell, named for his maternal grandfather, was born in Avondale in 1846. He was reared in the manner of an Irish country gentleman, sent first to a girls' school in Somerset and later to a private academy in Oxfordshire, both of which he hated. In 1865, he went up to Cambridge and came down as quickly as he had gone up, for he was expelled without taking his degree. He played cricket for, among others, the Gentlemen of Co. Wicklow, at which game he cheated – just like W.G. Grace. All in all, it was an improbable curriculum vitae for an Irish nationalist MP.

He was barely a year in parliament before he made his mark. The Tory colonial secretary, Sir Michael Hicks Beach, soon to be chief secretary for Ireland, made a reference to the murders

---

* In fact, Sir John's opposition was similar to that of other anti-Union ultras: he was no friend of Catholic and nationalist ambitions and wished to retain the old Irish parliament, cheerfully corrupt as it was, in support of the narrow ascendancy interest, rather like Stormont prior to 1970.

committed in Manchester, whereupon Parnell shouted, 'No, no!' Hicks Beach then said that he regretted that a member of the House should condone murder. Parnell then stated flatly: 'The right honourable gentleman looked at me so directly when he said that he regretted that any member of this house should apologize for murder, that I wish to say as publicly and directly as I can that I do not believe, and never shall believe, that any murder was committed at Manchester.'

Butt had founded the Home Rule Confederation of Great Britain in 1873 as an umbrella group which aimed to draw the support of the Irish in Britain for his evolving cause. The Fenians did not take long to see the potential of such a group for accessing the huge numbers of Irish people working in industrial Britain. Butt's focus, however, remained firmly on a kind of Tory federalism which might make Ireland an equal partner in the burgeoning imperial enterprise. The real Tories, with a predictable stupidity which is almost endearing in its consistency, represented Butt as variously a dreamer or an impractical radical. Poor Butt, he was the best friend they had, if only they had eyes to see it.

Parnell and the real radicals on his own benches saw it and found Butt ever less to their taste. Parnell ousted Butt as leader of the Home Rule Confederation of Great Britain in 1877. It effectively ended the public career of a man whose virtues were ill-suited to the times. Public life is not for the pure of heart; besides, Butt's Tory imperialism was as much a feature of his politics by now as his modest home rule aspirations. He was a good man, but the wrong man in the wrong place. Two years later, he was dead of a stroke four months shy of his sixty-fifth birthday.

Biggar's bad manners were much more like it. He and the other obstructionists had not just caught (or caused) a change of mood. They had made a key psychological break. All stable political systems depend upon unwritten conventions and codes of manners in order to function. The unspoken conventions of British parliamentary usage were no exception. But they were *British* rules. And Britain was showing Ireland the back of its hand, never more so than in the time of Disraeli's government. Biggar was not the first Irish politician to understand that if he needed to catch the attention of an indifferent Britain, he needed to make a damned nuisance of himself first. O'Connell had figured that one out sixty years previously and it has been a lesson that every Irish politician of any merit has learned to this day. Remember that matter of distance: Ireland is quite far away from London and in the wrong direction; it is seldom of any real interest to British governments. So there's nothing for it, every now and again when some urgent Irish concern presents itself, than to act the maggot. And at acting the maggot, Joseph Gillis Biggar was world class. Gone was the tame deference of Isaac Butt; in came a you-be-damned assault on British conventions.

Butt has generally been regarded ever since as over-deferential towards long-established parliamentary usages. But why shouldn't he have been? He was, after all, a Tory looking for some sort of devolved arrangement for Ireland, but one decisively within an overall United Kingdom context. Biggar represented an utterly different sensibility, one that disregards the normative elements of British usage and manners as of no account. For Biggar, unlike Butt, these usages were arbitrary and friable and in no sense a universal code. For Butt, they were

indeed a code, representing decency, good manners and legitim-
ated continuity. By disregarding them in so flagrant a manner,
Biggar shifts the ground. His is an elemental cry of *non serviam*.
Biggar was not a Fenian – yet: although he joined late in 1875
and actually sat on the supreme council of the Irish Republican
Brotherhood for a while. But he had a Fenian temperament.
That meant, among other things, not awarding the status of
automatic virtue to codes of British manners. It meant placing
as much distance as possible between British and Irish public
life. This was not explicitly separatist – Biggar was never an
out-and-out separatist republican – but it was implicitly so.

Fenianism was crabbing towards the accommodation it was
to make with the Irish Parliamentary Party, as Butt's home
government MPs came to assume the shape of a properly disciplined electoral and parliamentary grouping under his successor
Parnell. This introduced outright republican separatists into
the heart of mainstream nationalism. Most nationalists did
not regard separatism as remotely practical politics and that
remained the nationalist consensus until the wholly unpredict-
able series of accidents and upheavals tripped off by World
War I and the Easter Rising of 1916. But separatist ambition,
while marginal, was still part of the nationalist mix, one that
no nationalist leader – least of all one as acute as Parnell –
could disregard.

As Parnell's star rose, Biggar's waned. After the first few
heady years of filibustering, he faded more and more into the
background. But his bad manners had broken a taboo, and that
had had the liberating effect that taboo-breaking can sometimes
deliver. To offend against British manners and conventions
in the way he did was a kind of declaration of independence.

What was being challenged was the enormous cultural prestige of England at the very moment of its imperial apogee. It wasn't just pink possessions on the map. It was what we now think of as soft power, where a particular code of manners and mores are projected widely and accepted by invitation. It achieves a kind of cultural cringe in those who thus accept it. There was no cringing from Biggar, or later from Parnell and his acolytes.

The strength and influence of English manners is best summed up in a couple of incidents in James Joyce's *A Portrait of the Artist as a Young Man*. As a six-year-old boy, Stephen Dedalus (Joyce's alter ego) is sent by his father as a boarder to Clongowes Wood College about 40 kilometres south-west of Dublin. It was the most prestigious Jesuit school in Ireland, and was conscious that its social role was to prepare the future Catholic elite for their appropriate positions in society. It played English sports, especially cricket and rugby – games which the newly formed Gaelic Athletic Association, which we shall meet more fully in the next chapter, were to ban their members from playing. Early in the book, one pupil, Nasty Roche, asks Stephen Dedalus his name. When Stephen tells him, Roche says, 'What kind of a name is that?' and then adds, 'What is your father?' to which Stephen replies, 'A gentleman.' Roche rejoins, 'Is he a magistrate?' The assumption that Clongowes boys were all the sons of gentlemen and that their fathers might reasonably be part of the magistracy was something that had percolated down to six-year-olds. This was a little world of provincial mimesis. What was being mimicked, as entirely normative and immutable, was the world of structured British institutions and the codes of good manners and decorum that went with them.

The second incident, told just after the first, recalls Stephen's parents delivering him to Clongowes for the first time. His father, Simon, says to him as he prepares to depart for home that if Stephen wanted anything he was to write home and, whatever he did, never to peach on a fellow. This was pure English public-school slang. The real Simon Dedalus, John Stanislaus Joyce, was from Cork and had been educated at St Colman's College, Fermoy, a good provincial Catholic school with a fine history and one that flourishes to this day. However, you can be certain that nobody in St Colman's would have thought to warn their sons against 'peaching' on a fellow. From the day that John Stanislaus Joyce entered St Colman's, 17 March 1859, to the day in 1888 when Simon Dedalus delivered his son Stephen to Clongowes with that parting advice, the casual adoption of English public-school slang had entered the vocabulary of a certain kind of nationalist Irish person of advancing social ambition. You spoke the prestige lingo, and in this case the adoption was almost certainly the product of the enormous success of popular books of English public-school life, especially *Tom Brown's Schooldays*, first published in 1857. You can be pretty sure that Joyce's father had not picked up a word like 'peach', with the meaning it implied, in Cork or at St Colman's. Thus metropolitan soft power projects itself in little things as well as in big.

And it stuck. Just as Ireland was applauding Biggar for his cheek, its aspiring middle class was busily trying on the glad rags of English popular culture. Right from the start, the operettas of Gilbert & Sullivan were hugely popular in that quarter: the first triumph, *Trial by Jury*, was given in 1875 and a succession of still popular hits followed over the next fifteen years. Along with silly plays like F. Anstey's *Vice-Versa* (adapted from Anstey's novel of the same name) which was one of the staples of drama groups in the better Irish schools (Joyce himself appeared in a production in Belvedere), it was part of that embrace of soft English culture that disgusted intellectuals, yet ran in parallel with the growing rejection of England's hard political power. As late as 1913, there was founded the Rathmines & Rathgar Musical Society, largely devoted to productions of G&S; the eponymous suburbs of Dublin were and are regarded as solidly bourgeois. It is still going strong.

John Stanislaus Joyce wanted to play this game. He may have been a nationalist but he was also socially ambitious – although singularly inept at securing that ambition, being an improvident drunk in later life. And social ambition meant certain accommodations with the dominant culture, even in a small matter like the appropriation of a public-school slang quite foreign to ordinary Irish speech. In this he was marking out his position – and that of his son – *within* the developing world of Irish nationalism. Later, as the fortunes of the real John Stanislaus Joyce declined and his fictional alter ego Simon Dedalus was faced with the possibility of sending young Stephen to a non-fee-paying Christian Brothers' school, he expostulated that the boy had started with the Jesuits and would finish with them because no son of his was going to be educated alongside 'Paddy Stink and Mickey Mud'.*

---

* The Jesuits in Belvedere College, the secondary day school in Dublin that Joyce attended after Clongowes, remitted the fees. They had the measure of the boy – and of his father.

But the game that Simon Dedalus was happy to play was the one that Joe Biggar had implicitly declined to join. And he had signalled his refusal in the most emphatic manner.

THE REST OF what followed is quickly told. Parnell pulled together the three strands in Irish nationalism that mattered: the Parliamentary Party, by the late 1870s decisively under his controlling thumb; the growing land agitation, which was to harrow the Irish countryside in disorder and criminal outrages for the next few years; and the support of the Fenians on both sides of the Atlantic. He had no illusions about the English, whom he disliked and of whom he said on one occasion, '[We] will never gain anything from England unless we tread upon her toes – we will never gain a single sixpenny-worth from her by conciliation.' It might have been Biggar speaking. Or again, writing to his brother John Howard Parnell, he said plainly that 'these English despise us because we are Irish; but we must stand up to them. That's the only way to treat the Englishman – stand up to him.' Biggar's filibustering was treading on English toes with a vengeance and Parnell soon emerged as the principal political beneficiary. Michael Davitt noted his deep dislike of the House of Commons and the consequent pleasure he took in obstruction, quoting him as saying: 'An ounce of parliamentary fear is worth a ton of parliamentary love.'

His radicalism drew him close to other radicals, not least those agitating for tenant rights in the impoverished west. In 1879, he became the inaugural leader of the Land League, a national coalition seeking the establishment of a peasant proprietary. So by uniting the political and the agrarian demand and squaring off the Fenians he effectively united all the potent forces within

Irish nationalism and gave them tremendous momentum. At the head of this mass movement, and its unquestioned leader in parliament, was Parnell.

The land agitation was the most immediate issue, as the post-Famine countryside faced the first agricultural depression in decades, caused in large part by the opening up of European markets to the vast cereal produce of the American prairies and the invention of refrigerated shipping which could deliver Argentinian beef halfway around the world in pristine condition. In response, Gladstone, now back in power since 1880, tried the usual British mix of conciliation and coercion. The conciliation bit was the Land Act of 1881 which established the principle of dual ownership by landlord and tenant and conceded other demands of the Irish Land League, including a Land Commission to adjudicate on fair rents. Still, it wasn't enough for Parnell, who rejected it as inadequate.

Parnell had been arrested in October 1881 on a charge of conspiring with others to prevent the payments of rents and for discouraging the taking over of farms from which tenants had been evicted. He had been lodged in Kilmainham Gaol, from where he issued his rejection of the proposed legislation. In the gaol, Parnell was accommodated in some comfort; many ordinary prisoners were transferred elsewhere to make room for the great man. But with Parnell in Kilmainham, Ireland did not quieten down. To the contrary, agrarian protest threatened to run out of control. 'Captain Moonlight', a generic term for agrarian secret societies, not squeamish about violence or even murder, made his terrifying appearance. It seemed that the only thing worse than having Parnell out and about was having him in prison. So Gladstone proposed a deal.

The deal, known ever after as the Kilmainham Treaty, was the product of six months of secret negotiations between intermediaries acting under Gladstone's instructions and Parnell in Kilmainham. Gladstone was concerned to damp down the fires that blazed in Ireland. Parnell wanted out for personal reasons: he had begun his affair with Mrs Katharine O'Shea, the wife of one of his more useless MPs, and he wished to be with her, not least because their first child together had just died.

He wrote to Gladstone to state that if tenants in arrears were embraced within the terms of the Land Act, he would support it and would use his influence to quell agrarian unrest. In addition, he wanted leaseholders – then excluded from the terms of the act – to be included in its remit.

For each of the principals, it was a gamble. They both needed a deal, but it could not be formalized. It was, in effect, a gentleman's agreement, and therefore based on trust. The deal was done, Parnell and others imprisoned with him were released, and each man kept his side of the bargain. The Land Act was passed; Parnell began to wind up the Land League and now concentrated all his political energies on home rule. The 'treaty' was the whole basis of that trust between Gladstone and Parnell that lasted through the 1880s and foundered only in the shadow of the O'Shea divorce scandal, when Parnell was named as co-respondent.

Three years after the Kilmainham Treaty, there was a general election. Parnell's party won eighty-six seats in the House of Commons, which gave them the balance of power at Westminster. Gladstone's Liberals won most seats but were short of an overall majority. Whereupon, a remarkable thing happened. Herbert Gladstone, the prime minister's son, informed Dawson Rogers of the National Press Agency that his father was now convinced that outright home rule was the solution to Ireland's woes. It may also have been the solution to Gladstone's – whether his decision was based on sincere conviction or electoral calculation has been endlessly debated ever since. But at any rate, the 'Hawarden Kite', named for the Gladstones' country estate, transformed the picture. It committed the Liberals to home rule for Ireland, splitting the party in the process. But Gladstone redeemed his pledge by presenting a Home Rule Bill to parliament in 1886. It was defeated; but it seemed only a matter of time before the whirligig of events would resurrect it. The Irish Question had arrived, a ticking bomb at the centre of British politics. It would remain there, destructively, for the best part of the next forty years and would drive otherwise sensible and level-headed people totally nuts.

It was barely a decade since Joe Biggar had trod on parliamentary toes with his filibustering.

From now on, the impulse towards home rule was not just irresistible. It came to affect all areas of social and cultural life, permeating through the whole of Irish nationalist society. It was grounded in the same rejection of English manners and mores that had its first serious outing with Biggar. This rejection found expression at levels high and low, but few more potent and enduring than at the humble level of sport – to which we turn next.

ELEVEN

THE ASSOCIATION

THERE IS NO understanding nationalist Ireland and its differences without understanding the Gaelic Athletic Association and its hinge position in Irish life, its ubiquity, its multiple virtues and its capacity to attract the sneers of others. It was a critical element in the nationalist adventure; born more or less simultaneously with Parnell's home rule movement, its councils dominated from the beginning by advanced Fenians; resolutely anglophobic; and, most of all, hugely popular and successful after a very shaky start. It was the one Fenian enterprise that commanded genuine mass popular appeal. Other Fenian initiatives were dominated by unrepresentative elites – the 1916 rising was the apotheosis of this tendency – but the GAA was a mass movement. It still is today. It was an indispensable element in nationalist Ireland's drive towards home rule and, beyond that, towards separation.

It was founded in the billiard room of Miss Hayes' Commercial Hotel in Thurles, Co. Tipperary on 1 November 1884. The principal moving spirits were Maurice Davin, a renowned athlete in his youth with many international successes, and Michael Cusack, a native speaker of Irish, a teacher and successful educational entrepreneur.* They became, respectively, the first president and the first secretary of the association. The primary intention was to facilitate the revival of hurling, which had fallen into a state of desuetude since the Famine, and to serve more generally as a medium for native Irish sports and pastimes. Cusack, in particular, was an ardent and radical nationalist, close to if not actually of the Fenians. The choice of early patrons for the GAA was interesting: Archbishop Thomas Croke of Cashel, a nationalist archbishop whose diocesan cathedral was in Thurles; Michael Davitt, the most prominent leader of the Land League apart from Parnell; and Parnell himself.

There was no doubt that the GAA was unapologetically nationalist at a time of radical nationalist sensibility. Not merely radical nationalist, but Fenian: for the Fenians colonized its higher councils from the earliest days and left a permanent imprint of anglophobia in the association. The declared ambition of reviving hurling was fulfilled, but patchily. It was eventually played everywhere, but only played to championship standard south of the Dublin–Galway line which pretty well divides the island north and south. Hurling, as mentioned earlier (p. 136, chapter 7), is predominantly a southern game. No team from

---

* One of the other seven people at that founders' meeting was a stonemason from Co. Tipperary called J.K. Bracken, a Fenian. His fame hardly went beyond being one of the founders of the GAA, but his son's did. This was Brendan Bracken, supporter of Churchill in the latter's wilderness years of the 1930s, Minister of Information in Churchill's cabinet during the war, and founder of the modern version of the *Financial Times*. He died, aged only fifty-seven, as the Right Honourable the Viscount Bracken PC.

north of the line has ever won the Senior Championship, as Kilkenny did in 1904 and many times since.

Instead the big winner for the GAA proved to be Gaelic football, which was basically an invention. Some version of football has been played everywhere in history. The impulse to adopt national codified rules for football – as for most other sports so codified – was largely a product of the coming of the railway. In that sense, every modern form of football is an invention: soccer, rugby (both versions), American football, Australian rules and so on. Some, like soccer, swept the world; others, like rugby union, have an impressive but limited international reach; whereas the American, Australian and Irish versions never travelled.* But Gaelic football, which turned out in time to be the GAA's trump card, was in some respects an afterthought. The very early fixtures organized under its aegis featured athletics and hurling, with football in a minor key. The emphasis on athletics was largely due to Maurice Davin and his earlier international successes in track and field. By organizing athletics meetings under its umbrella the GAA helped to democratize these activities, as the existing Irish Amateur Athletic Association – an offshoot of its British equivalent – was socially exclusive. The GAA, for all its faults, was hyper-democratic from day one. The encouragement of hurling was the very *raison d'être* of the association. Some historians of the game reckon that the GAA saved hurling from extinction, which I think may be exaggerated, but at a

---

* That needs a modest qualification in the sense that Gaelic football, and hurling to a lesser degree, have travelled with the Irish diaspora. There are 64 clubs affiliated to the GAA in Australia; 22 scattered across East Asia, 111 in North America and 71 across Europe.

minimum it restored the great old game to a central position in Irish social and sporting life.

As for football, it was at a double disadvantage when the GAA was formed in 1884. Rugby was already well established, especially in the towns. It was codified and played to an agreed and uniform set of rules. The same was true of association football – soccer – which had been codified for more than twenty years before the GAA was formed. Soccer had made early headway in Ulster, where the Irish Football Association had been formed in 1880, although its adoption in the other three provinces was slower. However, we know that from the mid-1880s new clubs forming in provincial towns like Tuam, Co. Galway, faced a choice between adopting association rules or Gaelic rules. These latter appear to have originated with the Commercials club in Limerick and quickly became the basis of a national codification. At any rate, the rules of the game were sufficiently established to enable the inaugural national championship to be played on a county-by-county basis in 1887.

From the very start, there was a desire to distance the Gaelic code from soccer. Even at this early stage, proponents of adopting Gaelic rules were referring to soccer as alien and English, an indicator that the mindset that later resulted in the notorious ban on 'foreign games' was already germinating. The differences were sufficient to make the point: a different scoring system, with points as well as goals; ability to handle the ball; and no offside rule. All this difference was encouraged by the Fenian element which saw the GAA as a potentially fertile recruiting ground. After many twists and turns, not least the trauma of the Parnell split in 1890, it was the Fenian faction that gained a decisive hold on the young association and ensured that its anglophobia remained a prominent feature of the GAA until deep into the twentieth century.

Thus sport followed other developments already tracked in this book. Nationalist Ireland refused to accept the purity of English property law and repeatedly succeeded in compromising it in favour of tenant rights; it watched delighted as the Church of Ireland was disestablished, thus loosening a brick in the Union settlement; it refused to conduct itself in the House of Commons according to the ordinary usages of English manners; now, it was declaring a sort of sporting independence by refusing to play football by 'English' rules and instead developing its own. Just as the revival of hurling displaced cricket – in the 1880s one of the best-organized of all games in Ireland, and very popular – Gaelic football helped to slow the adoption of soccer and became itself the most popular participation and spectator sport in Ireland.

The population of the island of Ireland, including Northern Ireland, is about 6.5 million people. The GAA estimates that the number of people who either play the games or coach or manage or administrate is more than five hundred thousand, an astonishing proportion of the total population, all the more so when you exclude Northern Ireland Protestants – say, the best part of a million people – most of whom avoid the association as being far too nationalist.* The GAA is based on its 1,600 affiliated clubs, each of which contests its county championships

---

* All games played under the aegis of the GAA in Northern Ireland fly the tricolour flag of the Republic and play the national anthem of the Republic. You would no more expect to hear 'God Save the Queen' at a GAA game in Northern Ireland or see the Union flag on a flagpole than you would expect to see the Jolly Roger flying over Lord's on a test match day or an Irish rebel ballad sung at the Last Night of the Proms.

at different levels of skill. The best from all the county clubs form themselves into a county team which contests the national championship. There is no transfer policy: unless you qualify elsewhere by residence, you play only for the county of your birth. This obviously suits the bigger and more populous counties. You could be the best Gaelic footballer in Ireland: just don't be born in Fermanagh or Longford or Carlow.

When the GAA was founded, the sports scene in Ireland was fluid. As noted above, rugby union was already established but it was exclusive: it was, as it was to remain in many other countries for so long, a preserve of the private schools and the well-to-do middle class. The same was true of field athletics. Cricket still had a well-organized presence, including in areas from which it has since disappeared almost completely. In Tuam, for example, a market town about 35 kilometres north of Galway, the cricket club was the best-established sports body. It had been formed in the 1850s. There was a second cricket club in the town, called significantly the Tuam Democratic Cricket Club, reflecting the fact that class, rather than religion, was the mark of exclusivity. Surprisingly in view of the later strong association between cricket and Protestantism in Ireland, there appears to have been no such difficulty in Tuam in the 1880s. Difference of class did tell, however, in this as in so much else in small provincial towns. And the Tuam cricket clubs had no shortage of opponents all around the county. Today, not one of these survives except for an occasional team that styles itself Co. Galway. Yet the local Gaelic football team that emerged in the town, the Tuam Stars, was founded by members many of whom were also keen cricketers. The later hostility between Gaelic and 'English' sports was not spontaneous: it was manufactured by political hardliners, although it did have a fertile soil in which to grow. Hostility to England and alienation from its institutions were the salient feature of the 1880s and 1890s – the decades that, in many respects, were even more transformative in their long-term consequences than the revolutionary years after 1916.

None of this would be of any interest to most people except for the fact that the very fluidity of the sports scene in Ireland in the 1880s facilitated the arrival of the GAA and its early development was very often embraced and encouraged by people who were keen and enthusiastic cricketers. Michael Cusack himself had played both rugby and cricket, but he recoiled from both because of their social exclusiveness, a feature that seemed more pronounced in Dublin than in provincial Tuam. Cusack was without doubt a peppery anglophobe and a difficult man: he was extruded from his secretaryship of the GAA as early as 1886 on the grounds of neglecting his administrative duties. But the more general point stands: the GAA did not spring to life as a fully formed body viscerally hostile to everything English. *That* required the sedulous efforts of the Fenians, as they conquered the commanding heights of the fledgling association.

This is not to say that the non-Fenian nationalists, of whom there were many in the GAA right from the start, were in some manner anglophile. To the contrary, what is at issue here are questions of degree rather than of kind. There was an exclusionist, anti-English undertow to all in the GAA, including non-Fenians, reflected in the early rule excluding members of the Royal Irish Constabulary and the Dublin Metropolitan Police – the eyes and ears of British rule – from membership of the association. In the circumstances, the initial ascendancy of the Fenians in the GAA, which happened in 1887, saw the departure of the very few

Protestant and unionist members who had joined, repelled by the overt hostility towards their source of political allegiance.

This hostility found its clearest expression in 1905 when Rule 27 of the GAA was introduced. It stated that members were forbidden to play, watch or in any way participate in the activities of 'foreign sports', which in practice meant soccer, rugby, hockey and cricket. This was part of a growing autarkic, exclusionist sensibility that mirrored the protectionist economic policies of the young Sinn Féin party; it also reflected the influence of the cultural revival, especially of the Irish language, which had an implicitly exclusionist impulse. This was the time when the spirit of Irish-Ireland was abroad, shrill in its dislike of England: its most celebrated votary, D.P. Moran, was the editor/proprietor of *The Leader*, a journal whose dyspepsia and anglophobia were matched only by its shrill advocacy of Irish manufactured goods and its Catholic sectarianism. So the GAA ban was not *sui generis*. It survived, honoured as much in the breach as in the observance and a frequent object of ridicule, until 1971. In other words, it faithfully tracked nationalist ideology both before and after independence. Just as independent Ireland finally abandoned economic protection and embraced free trade in the 1960s, the attendant cultural and generational change saw The Ban swept away.

WHAT ALL THIS amounted to was the development of a nationalist Irish lower middle class. In the countryside, the bigger tenant farmers – soon to be owner-proprietors – were the big winners from the cataclysm of the Famine. Much of the ferocity of the land war in the 1880s turned on a determination not to surrender what had been gained. The professional middle class remained small, even in Dublin which was the commercial as well as the political capital (the industrial capital was, by now, Belfast – by a mile). In Dublin, the number of men employed in manufacturing enterprises actually declined during the nineteenth century but the number employed in clerical service jobs such as in transport offices or in legal practices – cost drawers and such like – increased fourfold in forty years. This was the social group politicized by the Fenians, who thus drew this modest class into an awareness of public life for the first time. Prior to the 1860s and 1870s, all nationalist agitations depended on the leadership of top lawyers such as Daniel O'Connell and his associates such as Denys Scully, each of whom had a house in Merrion Square, the best address in Dublin. Scully had studied at Cambridge. Later, the leading figure in the pitiful little rebellion of 1848 was the patrician William Smith O'Brien.

With the Fenians, that changed, as the clerks and scriveners were drawn into the web of public engagement. The Fenians were capable of criminal acts – Clerkenwell was terrorism pure and simple and the later dynamite campaign in England in the 1880s was their doing, anticipating the modern IRA – but it was also a profoundly democratizing force. The people it politicized were a new class in the public square, many of whom were to be enfranchised under Gladstone's Third Reform Act of 1884. And how their new votes counted the very next year! It was the first election fought on the new post-reform register that delivered Parnell his position of parliamentary advantage at Westminster and prompted Gladstone to announce his conversion to home rule for Ireland.

But the Fenian mobilization had its most visible and lasting effect in the GAA. The fact that the association became such a success – and relatively quickly, after suffering a near-death experience in the 1890s in the wake of the Parnell split – is evidence of that. In all the years from 1870 to 1916, it looked as if Fenianism was finished. On the face of it, that was so, for the genius of Parnell had smothered it in an embrace for a while and it seemed that the future lay in advancing the nationalist cause through Westminster. The Fenian attempt at a rising in 1867 receded ever more in the public memory. The dynamite campaign in the 1880s received no public support in Ireland. The whole sub-tradition seemed exhausted and out of time. But it was not so. The new class that Fenianism had enabled imbibed some of its visceral hostility to England and English ways, attitudes that stuck and found expressions that were not themselves overtly Fenian but were culturally so: the embrace of Gaelic football; opposition to the Boer War; the Irish-language revival movement and the cultural revival more generally from the 1890s on.

It was no accident that the character of the citizen in Joyce's *Ulysses* has been said to be based on Michael Cusack. It is certainly plausible, and Joyce was capable of the most savage character assassination in support of his artistic purpose. Just consider the foul-mouthed and smutty-minded Malachi 'Buck' Mulligan, based on the poet, surgeon and wit Oliver St John Gogarty. *Ulysses* itself is a hymn to the whole class that the Fenians politicized: petit bourgeois, precariously respectable, shabby genteel and reflexively ill-disposed to England. Indeed, that class's rural iteration, the virtuous tenant farmer, had had its own literary hymn of praise published back in 1869. This was *Knocknagow*, by Charles Kickham, a Fenian. As a work of literature, it hardly merits mention in the same breath as Joyce's masterpiece. It is overwrought, sentimental and clumsily written. But at its climactic point, it features a hammer-throwing contest – of the sort that Maurice Davin might have won in real life – between a tenant farmer, Matt the Thresher, and the local landlord. The landlord is no villain; to the contrary, he is a decent man. Matt would have been perfectly happy to let the landlord win. But as he lines up his final throw, he sees in the distance the houses and cabins of his home place and he resolves to win 'for the honour of the little village'. This he duly does with a record throw.

The subtlety is about that of a soap opera. But like soap operas, it proved extraordinarily popular. Matt the Thresher and his like came to stand for decency and honour, no longer the representatives of a defeated people but the incarnation of their manly virtue. *Knocknagow* was by far the best-selling book in Ireland in the last third of the nineteenth century. It is still commercially available.

This world of Fenian sensibility, devoid of cultural cringe, enabling the politicization of a class hitherto silent, found its greatest reach and most enduring success in the GAA. The sheer ubiquity of the association, with clubs in every 'little village' – basically in every Catholic parish – in Ireland is testimony to that.* I set the present-day figure out earlier in this chapter: it speaks for itself (p. 199). What is equally worthy of note is the early growth of the association. After the traumas of the 1890s,

---

* As an example, the southern Dublin suburb of Dalkey is middle class, and sometimes upper middle class, in composition. This has not been thought of historically as promising territory for the GAA. Yet in 2017 and 2018, its local club Cuala won the All-Ireland Senior Hurling Club Championship. Dublin has not traditionally been a strong hurling county – although a titan in Gaelic football – which makes Cuala's achievements even more remarkable.

when it nearly died altogether, it recovered steadily from the turn of the new century. In 1908, there were 26 clubs affiliated in Kilkenny, 30 in Meath, 36 in Galway, 18 in Antrim, 77 in Cork and 56 in Tipperary. The equivalent numbers for 1945, barely half a lifetime later, were 75, 84, 129, 77, 182 and 105.

The GAA was considered one of three pillars of the post-independence settlement in nationalist Ireland: there was the Catholic Church with its moral monopoly and its grip on education; the Fianna Fáil party of Éamon de Valera which was in power, usually alone although latterly in coalition, for sixty-five out of the seventy-nine years from 1932 to 2011; and the GAA. Of the three, only the association is standing and in reasonably good shape.

The whole transition away from England and towards a definition of Ireland that was distinct from its big neighbour was a gradual work-in-progress from the Famine onwards. It was not all one-way traffic: the soft cultural power of England – and later, of the United States – ensured that. But in critical areas of governance, autonomy, education and popular recreation, the process was unmistakeable. The legitimacy of British rule in nationalist Ireland grew ever more enfeebled. Ireland withdrew the consent to be governed from London. The Gaelic Athletic Association was the loudest expression of this at demotic and popular level. Codifying your own brand of football when a world-beating alternative was on offer to you was a statement of separatist intent, a constitutional convention on the playing fields of Ireland.

The rejection of English codes was not confined to the demos. It also found expression among the intellectual elite. It is to them that we turn next.

Ormonde Manor House, Carrick-on-Suir, Co. Tipperary, dates from 1569 and was the earliest undefended manor house in Ireland. It was built for Black Tom Butler, 10th earl of Ormonde. The ruins of the tower house it replaced can be seen in the background.

Desart Court, the seat of the earls of Desart, was more typical of the great Irish houses of the classical era, dating from the long century of peace after 1700.

Patrick Street, Cork, *c.*1880. It is low lying – almost at sea level. The rising ground in the background is St Patrick's Hill, giving access to the pleasant suburbs of Montenotte and Tivoli to which the Cork merchant princes, their fortunes made, retreated.

O'Connell Street, Dublin, 1909. The principal street of the modern city, seen here before the destruction visited upon it successively by the Easter Rising and the Civil War. It lies about a mile to the north and east of the medieval town shown on Speed's map of 1610.

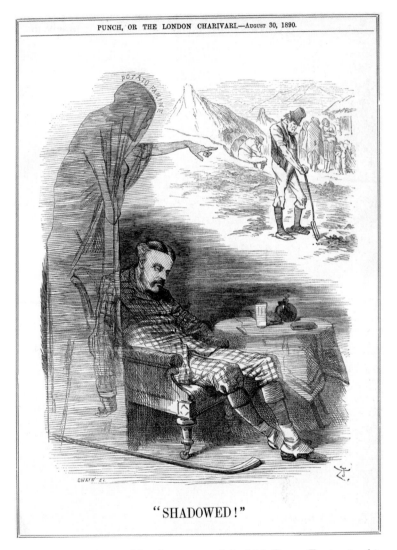

"SHADOWED!"

Arthur Balfour haunted by the spectre of the Irish Potato Famine in this *Punch* cartoon from 1890. The Famine was the spectre that simply would not go away. An equally destructive famine had affected Ireland in 1740–1 but left no legacy in the collective memory. What had changed in a century was the development of a public opinion and a national consciousness.

George Wyndham, *c.*1905. It was he, more than anyone, who unravelled the Cromwellian land settlement and created the social conditions for twentieth-century rural Ireland.

Queen Victoria parades through Dublin with her royal entourage, 1900. It was the last of her four visits to Ireland and the only one to attract significant organized protests.

James Joyce (*right*) with friends George Clancy (*left*) and John Francis Byrne while at University College, Dublin, *c*.1900. There were only twelve graduates in their graduation year, showing how ill-developed was higher education for Catholics. George Clancy went on to become mayor of Limerick and was shot dead by the Auxiliaries during the War of Independence in 1921.

W.B. Yeats, 1904.

Lady Isabella Augusta
Gregory, 1911.

Douglas Hyde.

On Ulster Day, Lord Charles Beresford, F.E. Smith, Sir Edward Carson and other leaders of the Ulster Unionists are among the crowd marching to City Hall to sign a Covenant against Irish Home Rule, 28 Sept 1912.

Anti-conscription rally, County Roscommon, May 1918. The threat of wartime conscription was what finally united all shades of Irish nationalist opinion. After that, British rule in nationalist Ireland was rendered fatally illegitimate. It could only have been sustained by outright military repression.

The reception meal on board the *Saturnia* for guests attending the Eucharistic Congress of 1932 in Dublin.

More than a million Catholics from all over the world attended the 1932 Eucharistic Congress in Dublin. The closing ceremony was held on O'Connell Bridge in the city centre, chief celebrant Cardinal Lauri, the papal legate. This was the apogee of Catholic triumphalism, the culmination of a long historical process.

—><—

TWELVE

THE NECESSITY FOR DE-ANGLICISING THE IRISH PEOPLE

THE IRISH LANGUAGE – Gaelic – survived as the vernacular of the Irish majority until the nineteenth century. Yet all Irish nationalist agitation, from the 1790s onward, has been conducted in English. It was already the language of the elite, of the law, of commerce and of higher education. Modern Ireland is wholly anglophone, with ritual nods paid to the Grand Old Tongue through such totems as bilingual signage (good) and compulsory Irish in schools to the end of second level when students are aged sixteen and seventeen (perhaps not so good).

The declared twin aims of de Valera's Fianna Fáil party, which dominated the political life of the Republic of Ireland for most of the twentieth century, had been the reunification of the island and the revival of the Irish language. In these twin ambitions, it failed. People knew that both ambitions were fantasy: partition incorporates many evils, but it also reflects an intractable reality, which people in the Republic realize cannot just be wished away. As for the Irish language, people have been remarkably relaxed about it: it is held, quite properly, in sentimental regard, but no one seriously believes that it can ever be revived as a vernacular.

Part of the revival campaign was grounded in an assertion that a nation needed its own language as a primary marker of difference. This is tricky. For most of European history, language has hardly mattered at all: in imperial arrangements, such as dominated the continent until 1918, the territories were perforce multi-lingual. The Austro-Hungarian *Kaiserlied* had its lyrics available in seventeen languages – including Yiddish.* But as empires collapsed into nation states, some organizing principle of communal loyalty was needed to replace dynastic loyalty.

Language was an obvious one; thus Poland was where Polish was spoken, for instance. But Poland was also those Roman Catholic lands to the east of German Lutheranism and to the west of Russian Orthodoxy. So which was the primary emotional marker of independence, language or religion? Whatever about Poland, a similar question could be asked of Ireland and receive a much easier answer: religion mattered – and in the end language did not. The Proclamation of the Republic, read out by Patrick Pearse at the GPO in Dublin on Easter Monday 1916, is in English. Its claims to distinct

---

* There is no authoritative source for this number. I have seen estimates ranging from fourteen to seventeen. Anyway there were a lot, which is the point.

nationhood are uncompromising, and not at all compromised by being uttered in the language of the conqueror.

In that sense, Ireland is more like the Americas or Australasia. In the Americas, post-imperial states were formed – from the United States to Uruguay – in which the dominant colonial language was retained as the vernacular lingua franca. But the retention of language did not dilute the sense of difference. Indeed, in all these countries, the running was made by dominant colonial elites who still retained a cultural connection to the imperial metropole – while treating their own indigenes murderously – but wished to be rid of metropolitan political control.

Ireland was closer to this model than to the purely ethnic states that sprang up in Europe after World War I. The traditional colonial elite – the ascendancy – had tried and briefly secured a kind of colonial home rule in the late eighteenth century. A hundred years later, they were in fatal decline. In effect, the slowly developing Catholic middle class replaced them as the vital element in Irish life: it was they who drove the revolution to victory. And their principal external marker was their Roman Catholicism. The more sophisticated among them played this down; the more blatant among them, such as the journalist D.P. Moran, broadcast it loud and clear.

Language did not matter as much as it did elsewhere or as much as revival enthusiasts wanted it to. The attempt to revive Irish came too late, when the emerging new Irish elite had already become thoroughly anglophone. On the other hand, the Reformation and its failure mattered an awful lot. When the dust settled after 1916, the line of partition was drawn where Roman Catholic numbers began to weaken and Protestant numbers began to wax. This was done deliberately and sensibly. Even in 1920, Luther and the Pope were still having it out by the lakes and drumlins of south Ulster.

WHAT WAS HAPPENING at demotic level with the GAA had a parallel expression at elite level. On 9 June 1892, there was founded in Dublin a National Literary Society. It was devoted to the promotion, revival and preservation of Irish literature and higher culture generally and to show resistance to cheap foreign imports. The 1890s were a time when there was a huge explosion in English book, newspaper and magazine publishing, facilitated by the expanding education system and a concomitant increase in literacy. This was reinforced by technology: the mechanization of typesetting by the Linotype and Monotype systems, which increased productive efficiency. The *Daily Mail* first appeared in 1896, the *Daily Express* in 1900 and the *Daily Mirror* in 1903. *Tit Bits*, relentlessly given to down-market gossip and scandal, dated from 1881. British book publishing also grew dramatically in the second half of the nineteenth century. In the first decade of the century, there were 27,000 titles with London imprints. This grew to 83,000 by the 1860s and these numbers continued to accelerate in the latter decades of the century as new printing and composing systems were developed. Most of these new titles were directed at a popular rather than an elite market, taking advantage of the newly literate classes, whose preferences were not always to the stomach of the better educated.

This was the world in which the National Literary Society was formed. It was one, in short, in which English demotic culture was flowing into Ireland through the wholesale distribution operations of companies such as Eason's – formerly the Irish end of the W.H. Smith empire, which had been sold off to its Irish manager when the son of the original W.H. Smith assumed government office under a succession of Conservative administations, specifically when he was briefly appointed chief secretary for Ireland under Salisbury's short-lived government of 1885–6. By selling off his Irish concerns he avoided any conflict of interest.

This growth of the demos was troubling to nearly all of the intellectual elite, a condition that lasted for a long time but was especially shocking when first new. This was the context in which the society was formed. So while what it proposed was a wholly positive purpose – the promotion and encouragement of Irish arts – it also contained a negative charge: the desire to exclude (that word again) English-generated trash, Yeats's 'filthy modern tide'. And sure enough, Yeats, now making a name for himself as a poet and as a figure of ever-growing cultural authority, was one of the founders of the society. The other principal founder was Douglas Hyde.

Hyde was the son of a Church of Ireland rector, born at Frenchpark, Co. Roscommon, in 1860. From an early age, he was a passionate supporter of the Irish language, in which he was fluent. He went to Trinity, where he became a member of the Society for the Preservation of the Irish Language. He went on to become a poet, man of letters and scholar in both Irish and English, but Irish was his first love. When the National Literary Society was formed, Hyde was finishing his compilation subsequently published under the title *Love Songs of Connacht*. He was pressed for time. None the less, he accepted the offer to become the new society's inaugural president and, to that end, he prepared a presidential address to be delivered on the evening of 25 November 1892.

This was entitled 'The Necessity for De-Anglicising the Irish People' and it caused a considerable stir. The pre-publicity had been good; there was an excellent attendance, swelled by the pre-sale of more than a hundred subscription tickets. For an hour and twenty minutes, Hyde spoke to his theme. He held his audience rapt. The press response was positive, summed up by the home rule newspaper *United Ireland*, edited by the influential MP William O'Brien: 'I have no hesitation in saying that it was one of the best, and, what is better, one of the most practical lectures on a national topic that I have heard for a long time.'

So, what did Hyde actually say that evening?

He began by saying that he was not protesting against imitating what is best in the English, 'for that would be absurd', but 'rather to show the folly of neglecting what is Irish, and hastening to adopt, pell-mell, and indiscriminately, everything that is English, simply because it is English'. He then compares contemporary Ireland with the Ireland of old which was once, 'as everyone admits, one of the most classically learned and cultured nations in Europe [and] is now one of the least so'. He charges late Victorian Ireland with being unstudious and unliterary and states that a nation previously highly artistic now produced art objects that 'are... only distinguished for their hideousness'.

What is the source of this decline?

This failure of the Irish people in recent times has been largely brought about by the race diverging during this century from the right path, and ceasing to be Irish without becoming English... With the bulk of the people this change took place quite recently... And is, in fact, still going on. I should like to call attention to the illogical position of men who drop their own language to speak English, of men who translate their euphonious Irish names into English monosyllables,* of men who read English books, and know nothing about Gaelic literature, nevertheless protesting as a matter of sentiment that they hate the country which at every hand's turn they rush to imitate.

Hyde delivered his address to an elite, intellectual audience and its effect was galvanic. Yeats reported one departing member of the audience saying that it was 'the most important utterance of its kind since '48'. Coverage in the nationalist press was positive and even the unionist *Irish Times* allowed reluctantly that it had some merit. The reference to 1848 was astute, for what Hyde had done was to reintroduce cultural nationalism to the public agenda after a silence of a generation. The failure of the Young Ireland movement in 1848 – a nationalist ginger group to the left of Daniel O'Connell – halted the development of this cultural assertion, based as it was on the German Romantic cultural nationalism of Herder, heavily influenced in its turn by Rousseau. It stressed the cultural, linguistic and artistic bonds that brought a people together in nationhood. One of the most obvious integrating forces was a shared language.

The Young Irelanders, back in the 1840s, had accordingly placed an emphasis on these things, not least language, in sharp contrast to O'Connell. Although a native speaker of Irish and

---

* A bit hard, one would have thought, on the language of Shakespeare and Milton.

fluent in the language, O'Connell was wholly utilitarian: as early as 1833, speaking at a St Patrick's Day dinner in London, he noted the advance of English in Ireland, even among the peasantry, and while taking a proper pride in Irish, he laid the emphasis squarely elsewhere by declaring that he was 'sufficiently utilitarian not to regret its gradual abandonment'. The English language was that of law, of commerce, of power, of literary prestige: in short, 'the medium of all modern communication'. By the 1840s, the ageing O'Connell could look back on a series of political triumphs and achievements that had been severely practical and transactional in their means. He never felt comfortable with this new-fangled cultural import from Germany peddled by the Young Irelanders.

For them, however, culture had a further attraction beyond any intrinsic philosophical attractions it possessed. It proposed an integrating force for the Irish nation that transcended Catholicism and – as we have seen – Catholic sectarianism had been the price O'Connell had paid, and had been happy to pay, as the key to mass political mobilization. Cultural nationalism, as proposed by the Young Irelanders, offered a different rallying point, one which could embrace Irish people of all creeds and sects; it was no accident that many of the Young Irelanders, most notably Thomas Davis, were Protestant.

But their enterprise failed in the cataclysm of the Great Famine. After the Famine, Irish political life atrophied for the best part of a generation. Cullen arrived from Rome and consolidated the power and prestige of the institutional church; the Fenians were principally political and military in their ambitions, even if one of their number wrote *Knocknagow*. Parnell was no Catholic (or anything that we know of) but he knew where power lay in nationalist Ireland and he hastened to make deals with the Catholic hierarchy, especially in the area of educational control, such as were needed to secure their support. As with O'Connell, Parnell was strictly business. At no time in his life did he demonstrate the slightest interest in culture or the arts, and he was – in this if in nothing else – the very model of an aloof, philistine Anglo-Irish gent. His great achievement, very material, was to get home rule onto the British political agenda in an irresistible manner. It stayed there, even after Parnell's fall from grace over the O'Shea divorce scandal and his subsequent early death.

Home rule may have been on the agenda, but in the 1890s, with Parnell dead and his party hopelessly and bitterly divided, it seemed a husk of what it had been, a sad, hollowed-out thing. There was a public loss of faith in conventional, deal-making politics; it suddenly seemed shabby and ignoble. The split itself had divided families, sometimes with the greatest possible bitterness, as anyone who has read the heart-stopping Christmas dinner scene in Joyce's *A Portrait of the Artist as a Young Man* can attest. The ground was cleared for the revival of the cultural emphasis of nationhood, and that is what Douglas Hyde was doing when he delivered his address in 1892. It was no accident that Hyde, as with so many of the Young Irelanders nearly fifty years earlier, was himself a Protestant, the son of a west of Ireland rector who in his turn was descended from a long clerical line.

But Hyde was far more than a Protestant looking for an excuse to come in out of the Catholic cold. He was a scholar of some distinction, garlanded with medals and honours from Trinity, and a literary man of growing reputation. He was cool to the point of indifference about religion but he emphasized, both in this lecture and in another address he had given in Canada the previous year which served as a sort of testing of the argument more fully adumbrated at the National Literary Society, that all attempts at cultural revival – especially the restoration of the Irish language to a more honoured place in Irish life – were a cause that could be honourably embraced by Irish people of every religion and background. He was not for the replacement of English by Irish as the natural vernacular; he always allowed that this was absurd and impossible. But he aimed towards, first, a consolidation of the language in those increasingly marginal parts of the west where it was still the vernacular; then, followed by a programme designed to make as much of the Irish population bilingual as was possible.

Hyde's love of Irish was completely sincere. It was not his mother tongue: he had learned it as a teenager from native speakers in his area; his affection for Irish was such that he said in later life that it was the language in which he dreamed. He was also accomplished in a number of modern European languages. But there were negative as well as positive poles to Hyde's project, for his plea in the course of his address to the National Literary Society was not simply the positive one of the revival of a language and literature that had been too long neglected. It was also a defensive rejection of the swelling tide of English cultural vulgarity, in that wave of cheap newspapers and magazines, trashy music-hall entertainments and books that were flooding the country.

This was a fastidious reaction to demotic modernity that was in no sense confined to Ireland. It had echoes – and influential echoes, too – in the upper reaches of English and international cultural life. The horror with which many intellectuals and literary novelists regarded this new mass culture is well attested: T.S. Eliot, D.H. Lawrence and Virginia Woolf were loud in their lamentations on this phenomenon, as was Yeats. The reaction against mass culture produced, among other things, William Morris and the Arts and Crafts movement, stressing the excellence of individual craftsmen and artificers in contrast to the soulless mechanical reproductions of mass culture. This in turn resulted in such things as small hand presses, specializing in beautifully crafted books generally aimed at a limited, elite market. Yeats's sisters Elizabeth and Susan Mary (Lollie and Lily) later started such a press, at first called the Dun Emer Press and later renamed as the Cuala Press. Yeats himself was the presiding editorial presence; indeed, the press's first production was one of the poet's collections, *In the Seven Woods* (1903). Otway Cuffe's preference for Irish tweeds, in the manner of George Bernard Shaw, was part of a similar sensibility.

So Douglas Hyde's plea, when he delivered his address in 1892, was not simply born of Irish circumstances – although all its substance was focused on Irish specifics – but had a wider cultural context that embraced at least an influential part of English intellectual life. Still, it stood as the first coherent statement of a cultural ambition that was soon to be adopted widely throughout Ireland. As others have pointed out many times, the public disgust with politics after the Parnell scandal and the great man's fall from grace and early death repelled people from the grubbiness of public life. In a new cultural revival, there was the promise of something clean and honourable, something that would be ennobling and would invest Irish people with a real sense of pride and of their own worth.

The key movement in all this was the Gaelic League, founded in 1893, largely to give organizational expression to Hyde's analysis. Its primary purpose was language revival: first, to stabilize the number of Irish speakers at a time when successive censuses had demonstrated falling numbers; later, it was hoped, to spread proficiency in Irish to the wider population. Hyde was the first president and Eoin MacNeill, later to be first Professor of Early Irish History at University College Dublin, was the first secretary. From the beginning, it emphasized its cultural remit and declared itself robustly non-political and non-sectarian. This was easier to aspire to than to maintain. Any such project was inherently nationalist to some degree. It stressed things uniquely Irish at the expense of English metropolitan influence, and indeed of outside influence in general. Despite its formal declarations of political neutrality, it drew its principal support from young people, men and women alike, of a broadly nationalist temper.

And it was astonishingly successful. Branches proliferated all over the country, drawing in urban lower middle-class adherents in particular. This was the same social cohort which had been politicized by the Fenians, and their hand, although usually hidden, was never far from the gears and levers of the League. This was amplified by a significant crossover in membership between the League and the GAA, where the Fenian hand was very visible. Indeed, the League provided in the cultural and linguistic sphere what the young GAA was providing on the playing fields: an enterprise proudly and uniquely Irish. It furnished a new focus for social mixing in a country ill-provided with such things: language classes, music and dancing, debates, poetry and other readings. It published its own newspaper, *An*

Claidheamh Soluis (The Sword of Light), initially edited by MacNeill and later, with some distinction, by Patrick Pearse. It established a publishing house, one of its most successful titles being – unsurprisingly – called *Simple Lessons in Irish*. It provided an outlet, hitherto absent, for aspiring writers of fiction in the Irish language and can fairly claim to have created modern Irish-language literature. It first organized a festival of popular Irish culture, the Oireachtas, in 1897. It has renewed itself annually to this day.*

On 8 May 1899, the Irish Literary Theatre, soon to mutate into the Abbey Theatre, put on its inaugural production, the first performance of a play by W.B. Yeats entitled *The Countess Cathleen*. But it was another play, staged by the theatre three years later, that had an electrifying effect on its audience. This was *Cathleen ní Houlihan*, a one-act play co-written by Yeats and Lady Gregory, and set in Co. Mayo in 1798 at the time of the arrival of a small French naval expedition in support of Irish rebels in that year of rebellion. An old woman arrives at a peasant household seeking shelter. She speaks in a manner strange to the peasants but in language that no nationalist in the audience could possibly miss. The symbolism is transparent. She talks of strangers in her house and the theft of her four green fields (the four Irish provinces). Even her name, Cathleen ní Houlihan, was known to all as an allegorical figure standing for Ireland herself. So this is Ireland speaking, calling her sons to self-sacrifice that she may throw the strangers out of her

---

* The 2020 festival was cancelled because of the Covid-19 pandemic. By the time this book appears, it is to be hoped that the Oireachtas, and everything else that is worthwhile in life, is back on track.

house and recover her stolen fields. She then departs, singing the praises of the young men whom she has called to arms:

> *They shall be remembered for ever*
> *They shall be alive for ever*
> *They shall be speaking for ever*
> *The people shall hear them for ever.*

Then, as the play draws to a close, a child of the house is asked if he saw an old lady walking down the road. To which the child replied: 'I did not, but I saw a young girl, and she had the walk of a queen.'

This play caused at least one member of the audience – and it's unlikely he was alone in this opinion – to wonder if such plays should be put on unless people were willing to take up arms in the cause it espoused. In short, was it an incitement to violence? This troubled Yeats in later years, when things that had happened in 1916 and all that had flowed from it, which could not possibly have been anticipated in 1902, had run their course:

> *Did that play of mine send out*
> *Certain men the English shot?*

One can see why the poet's conscience was pricked, but in fact the play, for all its coat-trailing, had no immediate consequences. But it was part of a process. It wasn't just the sudden emergence of the Gaelic League, the GAA and the cultural and theatre revival, although it was no accident that all were born in the same generation. There were other developments in this generally anglophobic milieu. There were enthusiastic centenary celebrations of the 1798 rising, which doubled up as a protest against the Boer War, then just under way, and concerning which there will be more to say in chapter 15. One of the principal organizers of this celebration was a young printer and journalist, Arthur Griffith, just returned from a year in South Africa and a keen pro-Boer, if only on the principle that my enemy's enemy is my friend. In a few more years, he would found a nationalist political ginger group called Sinn Féin, destined to go through many mutations and generally find itself at the radical edge of nationalist life.

Then there was Irish-Ireland. This idea, encouraging the use of Irish manufactures (those tweeds again), had been gradually imported into the cultural sphere: the connections between the GAA and other revival developments is not hard to discern. But it took a journalist of minor genius to give it political focus. This was D.P. Moran, a near-contemporary of Arthur Griffith, who had learned his trade in London and, now back in Dublin, started a newspaper, *The Leader*, in 1900. It was an immediate and continuing success. Moran had a supreme talent for abuse. *The Leader* was a scabrously entertaining cocktail of lower middle-class nationalist prejudice against Protestants, intellectuals, the English, the rich, nationalists like Griffith of whom Moran did not approve, and anything and anyone that prompted the editor's acid ire, of which he had enormous reserves. To be fair to Moran, he was fearless in pointing out the wholly disproportionate Protestant domination of the upper reaches of commercial and professional life in Ireland generally and in Dublin particularly, an awkward reality that many were too fastidious to address. The fullest synthesis of Moran's work was in a book he published in 1905 entitled *The Philosophy of Irish-Ireland*. He had no time for the gentle, scholarly attempt by Douglas Hyde to find an integrating principle of Irish life that could be happily shared by Irish people of all backgrounds, religions and traditions. Moran cut through that with a savage brutality: 'The foundation of Ireland is the Gael, and the Gael must be the element that absorbs.'

Now, by the Gael Moran did not mean people of remote ethnic Gaelic origin, the O's and Macs, but Catholics. For Moran, nationalist Ireland was a Catholic country and that was that. Anyone else wishing to be part of the Irish nation would have to acknowledge, either tacitly or openly – preferably the latter, as far as Moran was concerned – the dominance of Catholic populist democracy. If the language and cultural revivalists were echoes of the Young Irelanders of the 1840s, Moran's was the shrill reprise of the serpent in the Irish garden: the Catholic sectarianism, first harnessed by O'Connell and now recrudescent. Moran was a singular man, in no sense what we would today call a team player, and all in all a nasty piece of goods. But like a kind of holy fool, he saw through wishful cant with a disturbing clarity. For did not his vision of nationalist Ireland come more nearly to pass than any other in the first forty years after independence, that carnival of Catholic triumphalism?

Despite internal differences and mavericks like Moran, all this ferment was going in only one direction. That was towards assertive Irish particularism and a rejection of English culture and mores, insofar as such a thing was possible. (Obviously, there was no question, for example, of replacing English with Irish as the common vernacular, although there were more than a few enthusiasts who dreamed dreams.)

There were, however, internal pressure points within this coalition of nationalist sensibility. The most celebrated were the riots that convulsed the Abbey Theatre, then only in its third year of existence, in 1907. The immediate trigger was a scene in J.M. Synge's masterpiece, *The Playboy of the Western World*, in which it was decided that a slur had been cast on the sanctity of Irish womanhood.

A previous play by Synge, *In the Shadow of the Glen*, had exposed some of the tensions within the cultural-nationalist nexus in a manner that resulted in the final break between Yeats and Maud Gonne, the imperious and beautiful love of his life. The play is set in peasant Co. Wicklow – Synge's home county – and concerns a young woman called Nora (shades of Ibsen's *Doll's House*) who is in a loveless marriage with an old farmer. He pretends to die but doesn't, and his ruse works when Nora befriends a young tramp. Reappearing, the old man disowns her and in the end Nora goes off with the tramp. This set nationalist teeth on edge; Irish women were not supposed to engage in adulterous affairs, least of all with tramps. First, there was the purity angle, then the class one. Most Dublin theatre-goers in the first decade of the twentieth century were newly urbanized, materially precarious but ambitious and very anxious to forget their peasant origins. All this country stuff, and a 'respectable' married woman betraying the most sacred vows in order to go off *with a tramp*: well, that could so easily be represented as a stage-Irish slur on the entire nation.

Which is exactly how Maud Gonne saw it. She wrote to Yeats to say that she thought the play 'horrid' and she broke completely with the poet's aesthetic ideals. 'We are in a life and death struggle with England... and have not time and energy for purely literary and artistic movements unless they can be made to serve directly and immediately the National cause.' She accused him of importing foreign influences, a reference to Ibsen perhaps. Her suspicion of supposed foreign influence echoed the insularity of nationalist desire. (Thus spake Cathleen ní Houlihan.) It was a cry as old as Creon and Antigone: the terrible necessity of public duty against the proper performance of ritual and ceremony. Yeats was having none of it. He wrote in the *United Irishman*, Arthur Griffith's newspaper, that those offended by Synge, or by any controversial play of which they disapproved, were most likely to be 'the most ignorant sort of Gaelic propagandist... the more ignorant sort of priest who... would deny all ideas that might perplex a parish of farmers or artisans or half-educated shopkeepers'. You couldn't but admire Yeats for his sheer chutz-pah. Here was he, a Protestant, defending the sanctity of art as performed in a theatre owned by Lady Gregory, not only another Protestant but the widow of Sir William Gregory, mover of the notorious Quarter-Acre Clause during the Famine. The Abbey audiences may have been anxious to put mental distance between themselves and their peasant forebears but they hadn't forgotten the Quarter-Acre Clause. Yeats was brave.

All this was by way of a taster.

Synge's great work, *The Playboy of the Western World*, opened in the Abbey on 26 January 1907. It is a three-act play and the first two acts passed off without incident. But in the final act, the anti-hero, Christy Mahon, utters the word 'shift' – meaning a lady's slip or undergarment – and this was the proximate reason for an outbreak of protest and rioting that rendered the rest of the play inaudible. The riots continued at each successive performance for the rest of the week.

The rioters were nationalists, offended by what they regarded as a gross caricature of Irish peasant life, representing it as backward, coarse and ignorant. They were D.P. Moran's people, now thrown into violent conflict with Yeats's. Yeats won the public relations battle hands down by his continuing stout defence of the autonomy of art against philistinism. Yet Moran's people had their victory, too. It was their demand that art owed a debt of honour to the wider community that later resulted in the utter indifference of the independent Irish state to high art, made manifest by the ferocious literary censorship that prevailed until the late 1960s. The charge that Synge had caricatured and misrepresented the life of the western peasantry was misplaced: his real crime was to have represented it all too well, with a fidelity to actual speech that was troubling for the audience.

The Abbey rioters were angry because they saw in the characters of the play an embarrassing reflection of themselves, or rather of their antecedents. Most of them had rural roots. They were, for the greater part, relatively new to urban life; the population of Dublin had grown steadily during the nineteenth century, not least by the flight from the countryside in the wake of the Famine. They were, for the most part, lower middle class, conscious of having escaped from peasant backgrounds and unhappy – to put it mildly – to be reminded with such high fidelity of the world they had left behind. It was one thing to sentimentalize country cousins – the myth of the west of Ireland as the *locus classicus* of all that was admirable and virtuous in Irish particularism was central to the success of the Gaelic League – but it was sheer mortification to be reminded of the verbal and sociological reality. That was Synge's crime.

Set in the context of a powerful psychological drama, a truly stirring work of art, the tension proved too great.

That tension was caused by a gap between politics and culture in nationalist Ireland that nothing could bridge in the early twentieth century. Nationalist politics had focused on the material, most obviously on the land question. Its organizational methods were re-imported from Tammany Hall and were not for the squeamish. The cultural revival occurred after O'Connell and Parnell had set the material template for nationalism. It now attempted to overlay a cultural template and to furnish nationalism with myths, symbols and a heroic understanding of itself. In all this, it had considerable success but its sensibility was always at an oblique angle to the utilitarianism of the social and political mainstream. Unlike many other European nationalisms where culture came first and politics second, in Ireland it was the other way round. And it was the other way round for a perfectly good reason: the British provided the necessary context in the shape of the House of Commons. Unlike most of the continent where representative institutions were weak or non-existent, the United Kingdom had a robust law-making parliament to which Irish nationalism had ready access after 1829 and where it learned its trade. In Ireland, as Yeats would discover, the politics would eventually crush the culture, demanding of it exactly that against which Yeats fought with such singular integrity: subservience to the desires and prejudices of the new dominant class. Nationalism cannibalized the cultural revival for those titbits it could digest. It rejected the rest.

The Abbey rioters were not just Moran's people. They were James Joyce's as well. One can almost imagine among them

Bantam Lyons, Alf Bergan, J.J. O'Molloy, Bob Doran, Nosey Flynn (snuffling up the dewdrop from the end of his nose just in time), Corny Kelleher, J.P. Nannetti, Ned Lambert and the sprawling cast of minor characters from whom Joyce made his masterpiece. They were, of course, fictional, but Joyce imbued these characters with a sociological reality that Yeats not only ignored, but missed completely. For Yeats, they were an ignorant, ranting *canaille*, a perfect collective caricature in the service of everything he hated. For Joyce, they were the raw material for the most realistic work of fiction ever written.

What Joyce captured was Moran's world of marginal, urban people, more interested in Samuel Smiles than in high art, or in any kind of art at all. Yeats had a mad vision of an Ireland where a coalition of aristocracy and peasantry would combine to defeat petit bourgeois philistinism, while conveniently leaving the aristos as top dogs.* Joyce, like Moran, knew that the philistine petit bourgeoisie were the present and future of Ireland: they, not the marginal gentry, were the backbone of the cultural revival, especially of the GAA and the Gaelic League. The simple fact was that they had the numbers and Yeats had not, as the poet was soon to find out the hard way. Joyce didn't admire them any more than Yeats did, but he could count.

FOR TWENTY-THREE YEARS until 1915, the Gaelic League maintained its precarious political neutrality, as proposed by Douglas Hyde. Its successes were remarkable and permanent;

---

* When Yeats finally bought a country house, Thoor Ballylee in Co. Galway, Oliver St John Gogarty said cattily that the poet had become so aristocratic that he had started to evict imaginary tenants.

without it, it is doubtful if the Irish language would have survived at all. Once independence came, its influence was seen in
the formal support given by the new state to the old tongue. By
placing the Irish language on an equal footing to English – a
superior one, indeed, according to de Valera's constitution of
1937 which made it the first official language of the state – it
was denying sociological and linguistic reality with an almost
Yeatsian gusto. None the less, who is to say that this positive
discrimination in favour of Irish did not contribute to the sur-
vival of the language?

In 1915, however, the Gaelic League reached a watershed.
Hyde could no longer hold the line. He had had his triumphs,
most notably in 1908 when the long-running controversy over
higher education for Catholics was finally resolved. The Irish
Universities Act of that year consolidated University College
Dublin – formerly the Catholic University and run by the
Jesuits – with the two Queen's Colleges in Cork and Galway
under the new umbrella of the National University of Ireland,
the body which would formally award degrees. Crucially,
control of curricula passed to its senate, which opened the door
for the Irish language to become a required subject for matricu-
lation. (It was interesting that the remaining Queen's College,
deep in Protestant Belfast, was excluded from this arrangement
and became an independent institution.) Hyde became the
first professor of Irish at University College Dublin, a position
he held until 1932. But his control over the fractious Gaelic
League, never easy, finally had to yield to Fenian pressure in
1915. At the League's AGM that year, a motion was carried
which declared the organization to be explicitly nationalist in
purpose. This followed years of pressure. Fenian influence,

always potent, had finally told. The Gaelic League was no longer formally politically neutral, and notionally capable of attracting cross-party support regardless of political or religious affiliation. Hyde immediately resigned the presidency.

It had been successful beyond its founders' wildest dreams. It had created a dedicated cohort of revivalists who provided social leadership and whose influence was to be felt well into the future in the public policies of the independent Irish state. Nearly all the leaders of advanced nationalism had been involved with the Gaelic League at one time or another. Ironically, its greatest failure was in the Gaeltacht, the Irish-speaking redoubts in the west, where the number of native speakers continued to fall. It was an inexorable process which no organization or institution could arrest. In 1851, just as the Famine was ending, most of Ireland west of the Shannon and most of south Munster had Irish-speaking populations that ranged from 25 per cent to over 80 per cent of the whole. A century later, in 1961, only tiny enclaves in the far, far west met this criterion. The Gaelic League, waxing strong halfway through this decline, was impotent in the face of it. Hyde himself acknowledged this as early as 1903 in a letter to a colleague: 'The tide is rising everywhere except in the Irish-speaking districts themselves.'

Eventually, internal tensions in the League took their toll on Hyde, who could no longer maintain the line that the organization was a purely cultural one. The Fenian coup of 1915 that removed Hyde from the presidency of the Gaelic League reflected a certain reality. No organization like the League could remain forever innocent of politics in a country like Ireland. For a movement that many thought moribund, the Fenians were showing that they were very much alive and kicking in bodies like the League and the GAA. What no one could have foreseen was that one year later, in Easter week, they would furnish decisive evidence of just how potent their tradition remained.

Above all, what the Gaelic League achieved was to effect a further distancing from the hegemony of English culture among the anglophone Irish. These were the people so distressed by Synge, a class forming a shared consciousness on the basis of the necessity for a distinctive Irish culture; they were the class that would prove to be the backbone of the future Irish civil service, thus providing Ireland for the first time with a native administrative elite, the essential foundation element of that middle class that had been so conspicuously absent from British-ruled Ireland.

—❊—

THE DEATH OF CROMWELL

I RELAND, AT THE end of the nineteenth century, presented two problems for London. One was obviously that of governance: the demand for home rule, devolution to Dublin of domestic and internal affairs. Very few spoke of anything more than that, and they were for the most part Fenians – and conventional thinking had decided that the Fenians, although their hearts might be in the right place, were yesterday's men worn down by time and fate. This ambition for home rule was fully expected to be fulfilled at some point in the not-too-distant future. For the moment, the Tories were in power, and for as long as they were, home rule was firmly off the political agenda. But surely the ordinary pendular rhythm of British public life would bring the Liberals back at some stage, at which point it would return to the agenda. Of course, an overall Liberal majority would not leave the party dependent on Irish votes in the House of Commons, but surely the party – with its historic commitment to home rule inherited from the great Gladstone – could not endlessly ignore Irish desires. In all this, nationalists were apt to forget that home rule was the very issue that had split the Liberals hopelessly and effectively ushered in twenty years of more or less unbroken Tory rule. As for the opposition to home rule among the unionists of Ulster, that was reckoned to be of no account. What were they but a clamorous regional minority? Irish nationalism's serial failure to acknowledge the seriousness of the Ulster threat already had a past – and sadly it also had a future.

The second major issue was land, and here the Tories had proved to be much better. Gladstone had begun the process of reform with his acts of 1870 and 1881 but the real breakthrough was engineered by a series of Tory reforms, those of Lord Ashbourne in 1885,* Arthur Balfour in 1891 and crucially George Wyndham in 1903. The effect of these measures was the undoing of the Cromwellian land settlement of the 1650s and '60s. It created a new proprietary class and thus placed this social group, principally the former tenants and their successors who had best survived the Famine, in a key position of political and social influence. The consequences of this revolution – for that is what it was, and one arguably every bit as consequential as the political revolution still to come – were not uniformly benign. It did create a society that went in no time from one of the most disturbed in the British Isles to one of the most peaceful. Especially after independence and the ending of the military campaign, nationalist Ireland was one of the least crime-affected places in the world, a situation of

---

* His son was to be president of the Gaelic League for a while.

domestic tranquillity that endured until the development of the criminal drugs trade in the 1970s. But the new class of farmers was instantly transformed from agitating discontents to being very contented indeed. They became a deeply conservative, even reactionary class, determined above all to hold onto their gain. Having subverted some of the central tenets of English property law to make their advance, they now acquired a love of its purest principles as surely as any rock-ribbed old duke. It is no accident that independent Ireland from 1922, with this group as its key electoral demographic, endured a generation of economic sclerosis before gradually coming to its senses and adopting economic policies that had a chance of increasing wealth, rather than hoarding the modest portion already in hand.

The Tory measures of land reform were not acts of charity, or of sudden enlightenment. They had a twin context. One was the great agricultural recession of the late 1870s triggered in large part by the opening up of European markets to American wheat, New Zealand butter and lamb and Argentinian beef, all in consequence not so much of faster ships – although these were coming, too, with steam soon outstripping sail – as of refrigerated ones. These, plus the extension of railway systems capable of delivering the produce at hitherto unthought-of speeds, ensured that the vast resources of these faraway countries now flowed into European markets, with inevitable stress for domestic producers. Thus it was in Ireland.

This crisis provided the context for what followed: the series of land agitations that lasted on and off from the late 1870s to the decisive Land Act passed by George Wyndham in 1903. The response from Liberals and Tories alike was the

usual mixture of coercion and conciliation. Even a Liberal chief
secretary such as the long-remembered W.E. 'Buckshot' Forster
– generally regarded as a man of liberal temper in Britain – was
a strict law-and-order man in Ireland, to the point of resign-
ing over the concessions to Parnell and the Land League in
the 1881 Land Act, concessions which Parnell and the League
affected to find inadequate. He was no less loved than one
of his Tory successors, Arthur 'Bloody' Balfour, who took a
robust and aggressive attitude to prosecutions arising out of the
continuing land agitation of the late 1880s, assisted by a brave
and able prosecution barrister called Edward Carson of whom
more would be heard in later years. Yet it was the Tories who
seemed to realize that law and order was necessary but insufficient. The intellectual breakthrough came with Ashbourne's
act of 1885, because it introduced the principle that underlay
Balfour's act of 1891 and Wyndham's decisive one of 1903: this
was to use Treasury resources to progressively buy out landlords and sell the holdings to the tenants on long-term loans
– rather like mortgages – at advantageous rates. These were
acts of enlightened self-interest: Irish landlords had generally
been ill-regarded by the British governing class, who characterized them, fairly or otherwise, as feckless and shiftless. As the
shadows lengthened for the ascendancy, they had fewer friends
in London, even among the Tories, than they needed.

ASHBOURNE'S ACT OF 1885 was the first to propose the key
principle. Under its provisions, a tenant could borrow the full
purchase cost of his holding, to be repaid over a forty-nine-year
term at 4 per cent. An initial fund of £5 million was provided,
augmented in 1888. In all, the total acreage disposed of was

just under one million, much of it in Ulster. This represented only about 5 per cent of all Irish land. The average holding thus created was slightly less than 40 acres.

The fact that most of the land thus disposed of under the act was in Ulster had, like so much in life, unintended consequences. Ulster tenant purchasers, most of them Protestants, were now themselves no longer interested in any kind of agrarian agitation, their desires having been met. They were therefore able to detach themselves from the wider movement for land reform, with its overwhelmingly southern and Catholic focus. Their new independence meant that they could more comfortably find themselves accommodated inside the big unionist tent, snug with their fellow-Protestants.

In the south, agrarian troubles did not end because of the 1885 act, or indeed because of Balfour's supplementary act of 1891. That act did, however, create the Congested Districts Board, which sponsored public works schemes in the poorer counties of the western seaboard. The funds came in part from the disestablished Church of Ireland. They were applied to such things as building harbours, narrow-gauge railways in remote places, and encouraging cottage industries – domestic piecework being the very opposite of modernization through factory work, a comment on the relative economic backwardness of the south and west. This was part of a more general Tory plan that styled itself Constructive Unionism or, more prosaically, Killing Home Rule with Kindness.

It was nice of them but Ireland was long past being condescended to in this manner. The whole thrust of nationalism had carried Ireland far beyond a desire for mere good government, or the kindness of strangers. The demand was home government, not good government. And when it finally came in 1922, in greater measure than most people could have imagined in the 1890s, there was a price to be paid in economic terms. It is impossible to be certain but the independent Ireland that was poor until the 1960s would almost certainly have been materially better off if some connection to the United Kingdom had been retained.

So various outbreaks of land agitation continued through the 1880s and '90s. Evictions continued: those on the estate of Captain Hector Vandeleur in the town of Kilrush, Co. Clare, in July 1888 becoming particularly notorious. A settlement had existed on this site on the north bank of the Shannon estuary since at least the sixteenth century but was only properly developed as a town with the arrival of one John Ormsby Vandeleur as local bigwig in the eighteenth century. So by the time Captain Hector Vandeleur was the local landlord, Kilrush was very much regarded as a family town. That did not stop them evicting tenants during the Famine, and it did not stop the Captain in 1888. The procedure was simple: a long battering-ram was employed to break into the premises, evict the unfortunate tenants who were in arrears, throw their belongings after them into the street, and as likely as not strip off the roof.

The reason that these particular evictions acquired their notoriety was down to a novel piece of modernization: photojournalism. The photographs of these wretched proceedings were originally taken for a newspaper and soon became familiar images all over Ireland and beyond. Other similar photographs also circulated. So there was no sense that the 1885 act had quelled agrarian agitation throughout the impoverished south and west. What finally settled this great running sore in Irish life was a recognition by the wiser landlords that the game was up, that theirs was a dying world and they needed a deal to usher them to the exit.

Enter George Wyndham. Another Tory of the purest pedigree, he had been to Eton followed by Sandhurst and a commission in the Coldstream Guards. He fought in the Sudan campaign of 1885 – the one that did for General Gordon – before entering parliament in 1889. He was strikingly handsome, a member of the Souls – an aristocratic coterie of persons of superior intellect – and rumoured ever after to be the natural father of Anthony Eden, who did look uncommonly like him. For all his high-born background, he had the common touch withal. He made friends easily, was unstuffy and not overformal. So when he came to Ireland as chief secretary in 1900, he was a breath of fresh air. He had previous experience of Ireland, having been Balfour's private secretary when Balfour himself had been chief secretary in the 1880s and early 1890s. He chose as his under-secretary a successful imperial civil servant, Sir Antony MacDonnell, who in the course of his service in India had acquired the sobriquet of the Bengal Tiger and a reputation for efficient administration. He was an Irish Catholic who drew the suspicion of home rulers on account of his imperial service; his brother was himself a home ruler. Naturally, he also attracted the suspicion of unionists who thought him a closet home ruler. But he was to prove a great strength to Wyndham in what followed.

It was two obscure landlords who began the process that finally settled the Irish land problem. In June and September 1902, two letters appeared in the press from Talbot Crosbie and John Shawe-Taylor. They proposed the establishing of a land conference involving all parties to the land question to see if some resolution could be found which might be a basis for legislation. In this, they had the support of Wyndham and they also attracted mainstream support from John Redmond, now the leader of the reunited Irish Parliamentary Party following the tentative healing of the post-Parnell split in 1900. In addition, their proposal drew the support of William O'Brien MP, who had been leading a group styled the United Irish League; it had begun as the latest vehicle for agrarian protest but soon morphed into the constituency party organization for the IPP. O'Brien welcomed this initiative because he had formed the view that classic techniques of agitation had exhausted their practical possibilities for the moment and that a new path was worth exploring. Interestingly, Shawe-Taylor bypassed the formal body representative of Irish landlords, which had a predictable reputation for inflexibility. This was perhaps the most telling element of the entire démarche; it signalled an attitudinal, and perhaps a generational, change among Irish landlords. In an odd way, it bore a faint echo of those Protestants who were drawn either to nationalism or the cultural revival or both: these were people largely unrepresentative of Irish Protestantism in general, but rather an enlightened minority who knew that the drift of history was not favourable to their traditional position. If the likes of Yeats and Hyde were driven by a mixture of passion and idealism, Shawe-Taylor seems to have been informed by enlightened self-interest.[*]

---

[*] Shawe-Taylor's wife was a daughter of Dudley Persse of Roxborough House, Co. Galway, and elder sister of Lady Gregory.

It was, in short, a mobilization of centralists and moderates, at least disposed to strike a deal, under the benign eye of a chief secretary who took a genuine interest in his job – not a charge that could be laid against all his predecessors. What followed was little short of miraculous. The conference met for the first time on 20 December 1902 and had published a final report on 3 January 1903. Barely two weeks – with Christmas and the New Year interposing – to solve a profound problem of almost three hundred years' standing. By excluding the radicals on both sides, the moderates were able to reach an accommodation.

But without Wyndham, the deal could not have been delivered. What it proposed was a huge extension of Ashbourne's principle from 1885 by which there would be a wholesale transfer of holdings from landlords to tenants, to be financed by British Treasury bonds. The scheme was to be voluntary and landlords were to receive the market value of the lands thus alienated. The tenants, soon to be independent farmers, would repay the loans over a sixty-eight-year period. As a douceur to the landlords, the scheme offered them a top-up bonus on the selling price. They could also retain possession of their demesne lands if they wished. The annuity repayments for the former tenants were generally set at a monetary level lower than the old rents.

This maintained the outer shell of the ascendancy while robbing it of its economic substance and *raison d'être*. As noted above, it delivered not just land but tremendous political influence into the hands of the former tenants; this soon demonstrated itself in the elections for the newly established organs of local government – county councils, urban district councils and so on – under the terms of an 1898 act democratizing local government. These fora proved to be a kind of political kindergarten for the class that would dominate Irish public life deep into the twentieth century and, some might say, into the twenty-first. It was the sitting tenants who profited: excluded were farm labourers and the immiserated poor of the cities, especially Dublin. To these groups, the new beggars-on-horse-back showed the back of their hand and a sustained hostility that has not wholly dissipated to this day.

It was one thing to agree all this, especially in what seemed a trice. It was quite another to frame the necessary legislation and guide it through parliament, which is why – to his eternal credit – the Land Purchase (Ireland) Act (1903) will forever be known as Wyndham's Act. We don't know what horse-trading went on with the Treasury but there must have been some. After all, it was asking the British public purse to make a huge commitment of funds – albeit these funds were raised on the credit of long-term bonds – to a question that was, as with everything to do with Ireland, remote from the most urgent attention of London. In all this, Wyndham certainly benefited from the support of his old boss, Arthur Balfour, now prime minister. But it was done; the legislation was passed, despite the residual grumbling of the more reactionary landlords and the more radical element of land reformers, for whom it didn't go far enough; Michael Davitt, for instance, favoured outright nationalization of Irish land. It was none the less transformative. Within a few years, over 9 million acres had changed hands, ten times more than under Ashbourne's Act. The pattern of life in the Irish countryside was established securely for decades to come.

For most nationalists and people in the series of land agitations, it was a moment of triumph. For all its shortcomings and class exclusions, and for all that it put in the saddle the most conservative and selfish class in Irish life, it solved for good and all a problem of centuries, deemed nigh-insoluble forty years earlier. It was, after all, only forty years from Deasy (p. 161, chapter 8) to Wyndham. It was just over 250 years since Cromwell had come calling. By the time of the creation of the Irish Free State in 1922, the landlord system was a historical curiosity.

The holdings thus established were not just a locus of social reaction. They were, for the greater part, economically unviable. The absence of dynamism and growth in the Irish economy for the first half of the twentieth century meant that the great post-Famine tragedy, that of mass emigration, continued unchecked. Ireland continued to export many of its brightest and best – and most enterprising and go-ahead, as the material advance of Irish-Americans, in particular, was to demonstrate. What remained was a great inertia, superintended by conservative farmers, a barely forming urban middle class of shopkeepers and teachers, and priests. Their little provincial Valhalla depended on the safety valve provided by emigration.

ALL OF THIS carried nationalist Ireland ever farther from the British or English norm. The nature of the land settlement in Ireland was unlike anything on the bigger island. It was the recognition of an exceptional society, one that might be regarded with disdain by English grandees, but whose difference could not be wished away. That difference was now acknowledged in law – and above all, in property law, concerning which the British ruling class had a neurotically protective interest, as proposing principles valuable in themselves in securing a free society but even more valuable in securing the property of those who made the law, property whose origins might not always bear too rigorous a moral scrutiny. It was perhaps no accident that this series of changes to property law was mainly driven by the Conservative Party, for whom one might have thought them anathema, but the Tories are and usually were pragmatists and realists. So, in an odd way, they reversed the pattern of a generation and renewed first principles, by abandoning the landlords in favour of the tenants, thus retaining the integrity of property law. They bypassed the legal compromises necessitated by the various land acts – granting the tenants rights that had previously been thought unbearable – and simply passed on an uncompromised version of property law direct to the former tenants. These former tenants, unsurprisingly, embraced these principles with self-interested enthusiasm.

All this left nationalist Ireland a strange place, socially. It had no native aristocracy since Hugh O'Neill's defeat at Kinsale in 1601 and the defeat of the Old English ninety years later. In this, it was almost unique among Northern and Western European societies. Aristocracies were agents of social cohesion in the long age of deference. Ireland had none of its own, only an ersatz colonial imposition which never folded comfortably into Irish life and always stood apart. Think of Ham Cuffe's remarks about Yeats (p. 145, chapter 7), when he said that 'all country folk tell the same tales and a backward people like the Irish keep theirs longest'. Hamilton Cuffe, thoroughly decent man that he was, was nominally Irish, yet spoke of his tenants as if they were a foreign people. Which they were: the people who needed buttons and teeth, whatever they were, were not English. There was nothing nominal or prevaricating about their allegiance and identity, as there sadly was with Ham Cuffe.

Just as bad, as we have seen, nationalist Ireland had no proper middle class. The reason that poor Thackeray could not raise even pitiful amounts of specie on demand in Cork in 1842 was indicative of a society that lacked the vigorous energy of a mercantile class and the sinews of trade and urgent exchange that such a class furnished. It was all too sleepy and slow. There would have been little point in anyone saying to a Cork trader, as Guizot the French prime minister was able to say to men on the make in contemporary France: 'Enrichissez vous, messieurs!' Sixty years on, at the time of Wyndham's Act, it would scarcely have had more point. The big winners from Wyndham were happy to keep it that way. As I have argued earlier, this essential element of modernization – a functioning bourgeoisie – does not begin to take proper shape until after independence, with the evolving development of its adminis-trative element in the civil service. Its commercial and business arms didn't properly develop until later. But in 1903, what passed for a middle class was exiguous in its economic reach and overall numbers, although capable of providing the social leadership that drove both the land and home rule campaigns and the subsequent republican movement. Such social leader-ship as there was was supplied by the Catholic hierarchy, a poor substitute for the real thing.

In a British Isles context, the contrast with Scotland is glaring. Ever since the Scottish Act of Union in 1707, Scotland had retained its administrative, legal, educational and eccle-siastical particularisms, and its patronage networks, firmly in Scots aristocratic and bourgeois hands. No one ever mistook a Dundas for an Englishman. No one ever mistook those set in governance over Ireland after 1800 for anything else and, tragically, that often included Anglo-Irish families established in Ireland for centuries. Something had to give.

Well, maybe. It's easy to get too far ahead and say that what actually happened was bound to happen. It wasn't. It could have been otherwise. But that is where the Famine is the crucial moment of fracture. After the Famine, which has been the concern of the second half of this book, the tide goes out on whatever legitimacy British rule in nationalist Ireland might have had. You could argue that O'Connell had started the process: it hardly matters. What is evident is that all the major things that did happen after 1850 might not have been inevitable, but they all pointed to a pattern. That pattern was the steady withdrawal of the consent to be governed by England. The longer the process went on, the more that refusnik element seems to dominate. For the nationalist Irish, English rule had accomplished the death of a million people and the forced emigration of another million, while the richest country in the history of the world was mighty relaxed about the whole business.

The sheer bitterness of language directed at British govern-ments and their representatives from at least the 1880s on was impressive, as we'll see more clearly in the next chapter. In 1886, at the height of Parnell's power and influence and with the fledg-ling GAA trying to establish itself, one correspondent wrote to the local paper in north Co. Galway, the *Tuam News*, deploring factionalism and divisions among nationalists: 'I appeal to them to forget their petty differences and join in brotherly love and try to assist the brave men who are fighting Ireland's battle in an alien parliament.' *An alien parliament!* Thirty years before the Easter Rising, an anonymous correspondent in the west of Ireland is declaring what is nominally the national parliament to be alien. There was no bond of affection in that, or pride in a common purpose or a common history – only the alienation of the outsider, answering condescension with verbal acid. Ireland was leaving England long before it actually left.

As we shall see in chapter 15, all this opened the mental ground for the mass refusal of nationalist Ireland to support the British war effort following the 1916 Easter Rising. It was to take an event as unexpected as the rising, coming as it did like a bolt from the proverbial blue, to furnish the proximate cause of this refusal. But it drew on a dormant sensibility, one that had found expression in that humblest of provincial journals, the *Tuam News*, thirty years earlier.

The cultural revival that flourished while politics was undergoing its post-Parnell traumas was imaginatively rooted in the west of Ireland. But it was physically rooted in the city of Dublin, the site of the Abbey Theatre and the setting for Joyce's *Ulysses*. It is to Dublin that we now turn, and specifically to the great book that memorialized it like no other.

FOURTEEN

—✣—

CYCLOPS

J AMES JOYCE'S *Ulysses* is certainly among the greatest urban novels ever written, perhaps even the greatest of all. Many find it intimidating in its various techniques and there is no doubt that this vast arabesque of a book is in places over-wrought, self-indulgent and hugely given to showing off. But it is two other things that are much more important: it is a comic masterpiece, a laugh-out-loud book, and it is the supreme expression of realism in fiction. It is a celebration of the everyday and the ordinary. It gets inside the heads of its central characters with unrivalled fidelity, so that we feel that we actually know what makes Leopold Bloom tick; albeit he never lived, he seems to contain more life than many who did. Moreover, it captures the atmosphere of the city in which it is set with uncanny fidelity. No city – not even Dickens's London – has ever come alive on the page in the way that Dublin does in *Ulysses*.

Dublin is everywhere in this book, like a scent. Even with all the changes in the century and more since the book was set and written, the sense of authenticity, for anyone familiar with Dublin, is uncanny. Its physical descriptions, its capturing of demotic Dublin speech, its miraculous insinuation of the city's atmosphere onto the printed page are such that many people who have never been to Dublin first apprehend the city from the book and then discover a familiar place when they eventually arrive in person.

Roughly two-thirds of the way through the novel, in chapter 12 of 18, the scene moves to a public house in Little Britain Street, just a couple of blocks north of the Liffey. The chapter is narrated by an anonymous figure, speculation about whose identity bothers some scholars but need not bother us. The principal character in the episode is another whose identity is not formally revealed. He is simply known as the citizen, but is generally believed to be based on Michael Cusack, the animating spirit behind the formation of the GAA twenty years earlier (*Ulysses* is set in 1904). The only hint that Joyce gives is when Joe Haines, a journalist who accompanies the narrator to the pub, says of the citizen: 'There's the man that made the Gaelic sports revival. There he is sitting there.' Cusack, who in real life used to address people as 'Citizen', after the French Revolutionary manner, is a plausible model for this character. At one point in the course of his endless anglophobic harangue, the citizen mentions that he had spent time in Paris with one Keven Egan. This Egan, whose name pops up from time to time through the book, was modelled on Joseph Casey, a Fenian printer living in self-imposed exile whom the young Joyce had himself known.

The chapter is a counterpoint between the shabby documentary squalor of Edwardian Dublin and passages of inflated nationalist rodomontade. Joyce contrasts the shabbiness and constrictions of actual Irish life with imagined fantasies about the glories of the Irish past and expectations for its future. Thus the rhetoric of the chapter jerks from the immediate demotic narrative to the fantasy stuff, so that one paragraph may be about ordering a round of drinks and the next few may be about a wholly fantastical lampoon of the language of the Gaelic revival before cutting back to the scene in the pub. That scene, and the others separated by the episodic lampoons, aggregate to a coherent continuous narrative.

The citizen is represented unsympathetically – indeed in a manner outright hostile – as a cadger and a soak. He speaks of England, the English and the royal family in a style almost beyond parody. But it isn't parody: it's exaggeration. If Joyce were not such a scrupulous realist in his documentary passages, you could dismiss this as poetic licence. It is exaggerated for effect, but it is still exaggerated realism. The citizen is hysterically anglophobic. When J.J. O'Molloy, a briefless barrister who is one of the book's myriad minor characters and a member of the company in the pub, speaks of England and its civilization, the citizen lets fly: 'Their syphilisation, you mean. To hell with them! The curse of a good-for-nothing God light sideways on the bloody thick-lugged sons of whores' gets! No music and no art and no literature worthy of the name. Any civilisation they have they stole from us. Tongue-tied sons of bastards' ghosts.'

The citizen is, of course, absurd. But is there any city on the island of Britain where such language could even be imagined, let alone uttered without starting a fight or worse? Or consider this, when the citizen and Joe Haines between them vent about the royal family, remembering the recently deceased Queen Victoria and mentioning the recent visit of Edward

VII – which was a real event, not a fictional invention – to the national Catholic seminary at Maynooth, near Dublin, where he was well received by the Irish bishops.

—And as for the Prooshians and the Hanoverians, says Joe, haven't we had enough of those sausageeating bastards on the throne from George the elector down to the German lad and the flatulent old bitch that's dead?

Jesus, I had to laugh at the way he came out with that about the old one with the winkers on her, blind drunk in her royal palace every night… and her coachman carting her up body and bones to roll into bed and she pulling him by the whiskers and singing him old bits of songs about *Ehren on the Rhine* and come where the boose is cheaper.

—Well, says J.J. We have Edward the Peacemaker now.

—Tell that to a fool, says the citizen. There's a bloody sight more pox than pax about that boyo. Edward Guelph-Wettin!

—And what do you think, says Joe, of the holy boys, the priests and bishops of Ireland, doing up his room in Maynooth in His Satanic Majesty's racing colours and sticking up pictures of all the horses his jockeys rode?…

—They ought to have stuck up all the women he rode himself, says little Alf.

And says J.J.:

—Considerations of space influenced their lordships' decision.

The point hardly needs to be laboured. Joyce, the great realist, has captured a rhetoric so poisonously anglophobic as to be unthinkable on the other side of the water. Yet in Edwardian Dublin, it is a perfectly acceptable, if vulgar, currency. Dublin may be a city ruled from London but its heart is not in it. Earlier in the book, Joyce sums it up with wicked comic accuracy. It's a description of the viceroy processing along the north quays en route to an official function.

William Humble, earl of Dudley, and Lady Dudley, accompanied by lieutenantcolonel Heseltine, drove out after luncheon from the viceregal lodge. In the following carriage were the honourable Mrs Paget, Miss de Courcy and the honourable Gerald Ward A. D. C. in attendance.

The cavalcade passed out by the lower gate of Phoenix park saluted by obsequious policemen and proceeded past Kingsbridge along the northern quays. The viceroy was most cordially greeted on his way through the metropolis. At Bloody bridge Mr Thomas Kernan beyond the river greeted him vainly from afar... From its sluice in Wood Quay wall under Tom Devan's office Poddle river hung out in fealty a tongue of liquid sewage.*

IT HAD NOT been always thus. Dublin had only begun to form as a modern city after 1660. Prior to that, it had been a harbour town of little consequence and modest size. But in the years from 1660 to 1800, it grew to be a city that bore comparison with substantial cities in continental Europe. In a pre-censal era, estimates of population are inevitably imprecise but by 1800 Dublin was

---

* The Poddle was a culverted tributary of the Liffey.

variously thought to be in the top ten European cities by population. According to the most authoritative modern history of the city, the population doubled in the fifty years to 1750 to about 125,000, making Dublin the ninth largest in Europe overall and the fifth largest north of the Alps, 'more populous than Madrid or Berlin, about the same size as Milan, a little smaller than Lisbon'.

It was an English colonial city oriented east, towards Britain. The city's heroic age, very roughly the eighteenth century, marked it as the display space of the new Protestant ascendancy, the grandchildren of the Cromwellian settlement: creoles. The ascendancy, despite occasional outbreaks of creole resentment against the mother country, was in reality tied umbilically to the larger island, whose language they spoke and whose institutions of administration and government they mimicked. All the great literature of the Anglo-Irish tradition, from Congreve and Swift to Wilde and Shaw, was rendered in the English language. Its glorious Georgian architecture, the city's pride to this day, was a provincial variation on a contemporary international style: there are visible echoes of Georgian London, Edinburgh and Bath in ascendancy Dublin, although it was, unlike the latter two, more a city of brick than of stone.

In the 1960s, when a frenzy of new-money development threatened much of the city's architectural fabric, the architectural critic of the *Financial Times*, H.A.N. Brockman, caused grave offence in some Irish quarters by writing: 'The only reason why Dublin remained for so long the beautiful eighteenth-century city the English built is that the Irish were too poor to pull it down. This, unfortunately, is no longer the case.' This teasing denomination of the Irish capital as an English city was resented by many, but the case is fairly stated. Ireland was a country whose social elite was a colonial caste and whose administration was carried on by members of that caste superintended by colonial governors sent over from London. It was they who made the city. Every building of distinction in Dublin – even the College of Science, built as late as 1911 and now remodelled as Government Buildings of the Irish Republic – was built by the English or by their colony. The 'native' Irish – Catholics, in other words – had little or nothing to do with it.

Until around 1800, it was a Protestant city by numbers, although by the time of the first reliable census in 1841, that had been reversed. None the less, the historic fabric of the city was an eighteenth-century creation. The expansion of the city was eastwards, towards the bay and away from the small medieval core upriver. The river Liffey divides the city north and south, giving rise to endless jokes about the north side and the south side.* But the real sociological division, as the city developed, was between east and west; thus it is to this day. East generally good, west not so good.

The beautiful city that the English built is, with only one or two exceptions, all to the east of the medieval core, gazing towards England. This is the charge that provincial Ireland, the neglected hinterland on which the city has historically turned its back, has levelled against Dublin: that it is not properly Irish at all but a colonial implant. This is one of these ignorant charges all the more irritating for containing a considerable grain of truth. The standard provincial slang for a Dubliner is a jackeen: Jack being a diminutive of John, and 'een' being a Gaelic suffix meaning small, thus little John [Bull]. Some of this is just the

---

* On the north side they cut the grass; on the south side we mow the lawn.

normal envy that any capital city attracts from those not of it, but the city which Joyce so memorably recorded had started life as a Viking town, then became the centre of English royal administration from medieval times before its colonial efflorescence in the eighteenth century. There was always something foreign about it, and not so vaguely foreign either.

All that was, of course, history by 1904 when the citizen was venting in Barney Kiernan's but some of that history has always stuck to Dublin. You can't slough off history as a snake sheds its skin. The relationship between Ireland and England underwent a transformation in the course of the nineteenth century, under the influence of Catholic nationalist mobilization in the 1820s and accelerated by the disastrous British response to the Famine. But behind the substance of the new nationalist city lay the shadow of the old colonial one.

IT IS EASY to romance the beautiful city that the English built. It is true that just about every public building of distinction in the modern city constructed before about 1980 was a colonial legacy. At the midpoint of the twentieth century, nothing of significance had been added to the Georgian and Victorian core. Then, in 1953, the young architect Michael Scott built Busaras, the central bus station, just behind the Custom House on the north side. It was defiantly modern and has generally been considered a success, although it could do with a facelift these days.

But the colonial city was far more than splendid public buildings, squares and vistas. Life at the bottom was wretched, as it was in all contemporary cities. The best testimony we have of conditions in the poorer part of Dublin comes from the reports of a heroic clergyman, Rev. James Whitelaw, the first of which he issued in 1805. Based on his many visits to the homes of the poor he ascribed their wretchedness and ill-health to causes that echoed those in any other contemporary city: incredible overcrowding, with sometimes even single rooms being subdivided to provide a minimal and miserable living space. He left graphic and disgusting accounts of the complete absence of any sanitary cleaning system and the consequent concentration of dung heaps – for human and animal waste alike – and rubbish middens in enclosed back yards. Two quotations will suffice: 'Into the back yard of each house, frequently not ten feet deep, is flung from the windows of each apartment the ordure and filth of its numerous inhabitants, from whence that it is so seldom removed that I have seen it on a level with the windows of the first floor; and the moisture that, after heavy rain, oozes from the heap, having frequently no sewer to carry it off, runs into the street by the entry leading to the staircase.' Or, again, writing in 1818 of the Liberties to the south-west outside the line of the old city walls, where Jonathan Swift had been a presence in the eighteenth century: '[There were] many large houses, consisting of a number of rooms; each of these rooms is let to separate tenants, who again re-let them to as many individuals as they can contain, each person paying for that portion of the floor which his extended body can occupy.'

The Act of Union of 1801 did not just begin the long decades of Dublin's decline, it fundamentally altered the city's relationship with England. Hitherto, it had been a colonial capital with a resident aristocracy after the *ancien régime* fashion. After the Union, that aristocracy fled in ever-growing numbers. For a capital city, a colonial aristocracy was better than no aristocracy at all. Their withdrawal left the city to the poor and to a residual social leadership low in numbers and lower in confidence. That social leadership, increasingly bourgeois – bankers, lawyers and such like – then fled in their turn, not to England but to the suburbs being opened up by the railway and by other early forms of public transport. In the suburbs, mainly on the south side, they established themselves as townships, independent of the Dublin Corporation whose jurisdiction only extended to the inner city. In doing this, they could strike a lower municipal rate for themselves, while still taking every advantage of the city to which they still had access and in which they earned their livings.

The net effect was that Dublin, previously a colonial stage set with a secure umbilical link to London, became poorer and more Catholic. With such wealth as there was fled to the suburban townships, the city centre declined inexorably, coming to house some of the worst slum tenements in Europe, many of them fine old Georgian houses now fallen into the hands of rapacious landlords. An increasing number of these landlords were Catholic and nationalist, some of them actually Fenians. It was not entirely accidental that when the great labour leader James Larkin eventually mobilized the tenement poor in 1913, he was opposed not just by the Dublin Castle authorities and the police but by many of the nationalist leadership, clerical and lay, who were more solicitous for the national economy than for the population that sustained it. Few voices were louder in opposition to Larkin than that of Arthur Griffith, the founder of Sinn Féin.

Unlike every big and growing city in England – and, very significantly, unlike Belfast which in the course of the nineteenth century had grown from a medium-sized provincial town to an industrial city greater in population than Dublin – the Irish capital was bypassed by the industrial revolution. It was mainly a commercial city. Its principal industrial output was alcoholic drink. In Guinness, it had one of the largest breweries in the world, plus a plethora of distilleries. It was beer and whiskey money that funded two of the most successful civic restoration projects of the century at the cathedrals of St Patrick (Guinness money) and Christ Church (whiskey money, courtesy of Henry Roe, the proprietor of one of the larger distilleries). But overall, the nineteenth century in the Irish capital was a story of relentless social decline in the city centre, girdled by a series of middle-class suburbs whose denizens made an exiguous contribution to civic life, if even that much.

The historian Peter Gay, writing about the making of middle-class culture in Europe in the nineteenth century, provided examples of contrasting but complementary developments in Manchester and Munich. The first was a booming new industrial city – Cottonopolis – the other the ancient capital of Bavaria under the rule of its Wittelsbach princes. In the course of the century, each city provided itself with a series of civic and artistic institutions that enriched urban life, resulting in much of the modern urban furniture that we can still experience today. In Manchester, typically, this was done by bourgeois enterprise and ambition; in Munich, by royal patronage. Yet the results were remarkably similar. In Manchester, Owens College was founded in 1851 and named for a textile merchant, James Owens. It became the nucleus of the modern University of Manchester. Some years later, three other Manchester merchants invited the German musician and conductor Karl

Hallé to the city and soon the Hallé Orchestra was established as one of the world's most accomplished. There was more: an assertive and splendid mock-Gothic town hall – fit to stand beside other such monuments to civic pride as those in Leeds or Belfast – art galleries, libraries, and all financed from private sources, the pride of a newly wealthy mercantile elite. And then there was the *Manchester Guardian*, founded in 1821 and even in its early days a world-class daily newspaper.

Munich provided itself with similar architectural and cultural infrastructure but in its case directly under royal patronage. King Ludwig may have been mad but he was a supreme patron of the arts. He created Munich University in its modern form, built the two great art galleries, the Alte Pinakothek and the Neue Pinakothek, commissioned churches, widened streets to create pleasing urban vistas, and oversaw the further development of the city's famous English Garden. His successor, Maximilian, continued this tradition while also establishing Wagner in nearby Bayreuth.

Other European cities expanded and developed through some hybrid of these two models, with either royal patronage or bourgeois energy and ambition the principal driving force. Dublin had neither. There were islands of achievement here and there, to be sure: the National Gallery, opened in 1864 and endowed by the railway magnate William Dargan from funds generated by the Dublin Exhibition of 1853. Then there were, towards the end of the century, the National Library and the National Museum, based on the collections of the Royal Dublin Society, a gentlemanly body founded in 1731 to promote practical developments in agriculture, science and the arts. And there was the very substantial civic achievement of providing a supply of clean drinking water to the city in the second half of the century, earlier than many more advanced cities. So, while it would be wrong to propose Dublin as a complete 'centre of paralysis', Joyce's celebrated formula still seems apposite. These benign developments were not part of a grand pattern or a sustained effort carried forward either by royal or aristocratic patronage or by the civic ambition of nouveau bourgeoisie, as in Munich and Manchester – or, indeed, in the most spectacular makeover of all, Haussmann's Paris.

Victorian Dublin had neither a critical mass of aristocratic or royal patronage nor a confident civic-minded and ambitious middle class. The children and grandchildren of the old ascendancy – relics of ould dacency – had largely withdrawn from Irish public life into their own enclosed world. That is why the conspicuous minority like Hyde, Lady Gregory and Otway Cuffe who did so much to drive the cultural revival were themselves unrepresentative of their own class. As for a vigorous bourgeoisie, it was marked absent, skulking in the suburban townships and displaying an indifference to its city's fabric that stood in utter contrast to Manchester and other contemporary boom towns. Victorian Dublin was an anti-boom town. It had the worst of both worlds.

A city that had, at the beginning of the century, been recognizably part of the greater English domain – albeit its creoles had liked to run their own affairs, which they did as best they could until the Act of Union brought them back to the bosom of the mother country – became more and more shabby and impoverished, as whole streets which had been the pride of the Georgian city decayed into the most appalling slums. There was no one to love it or mind it, only lynx-eyed, money-grubbing landlords to profit from maintaining an immiserated proletariat in inhuman living conditions. The city grew more nationalist, and radically nationalist at that. The anglophobia in Barney Kiernan's may have been fiction, but it was fiction from the pen of a supremely realist novelist, with an extraordinary ear for demotic speech. Dublin stayed with Parnell at the time of the split in 1891, very much a minority choice and one which set the city against the countryside. It was, for a little while, Larkin's city. And it was, of course, the centre of the Easter Rising of 1916, the pivotal event in the formation of the modern Irish political imagination. It became the key site of memory for nationalist Ireland's final break with England, by then closer than anyone could have imagined.

The Dublin problem was the Irish problem in miniature: an absence of social leadership for the want of a proper aristocracy or a vigorous industrial/mercantile middle class. So, gradually, something had to fill this vacuum. What filled it were the civic institutions of the new nationalism: the disciplined political party of Parnell; the GAA; the cultural revival, especially the Gaelic League; and the Fenians, who brought a previously excluded lower middle-class cohort into an active engagement in public life. They were not always fashionable, these earnest self-improvers. In his great Easter Rising poem, Yeats first dismisses the rebels of his acquaintance before acknowledging their transformative deed:

> *I have met them at close of day*
> *Coming with vivid faces*
> *From counter or desk among grey*
> *Eighteenth-century houses.*

I have passed with a nod of the head
Or polite meaningless words,
Or have lingered a while and said,
Polite meaningless words,
And thought before I had done
Of a mocking tale or a gibe
To please a companion
Around the fire at the club...

They may not have been fashionable, but they were the indispensable agents of the Irish future.

FIFTEEN

—✂—

WE DON'T WANT TO FIGHT...

THE CENTENARY OF the 1798 rising brought the celebration of that event in Ireland and the eve of another rebellion against British rule, about 10,000 kilometres to the south, in Transvaal and the Orange Free State. These two events were interlinked.

In Ireland, the 1890s were years of disillusion. Parnell was dead. His supporters at the time of the split were a minority in the Irish Party. Many left politics altogether. It is a commonplace to regard the decade as one where the cultural revival pushed politics to the margin. There is much truth in this, but it is not the whole truth. The Fenian tradition was barely visible in the public sphere but it was far from moribund, and it drove the 1798 centenary commemoration. On 2 March 1897, there took place the inaugural meeting of the centenary committee in Dublin. The organizers canvassed a wide swathe of Irish nationalist opinion when issuing invitations to this meeting.

Significantly, no invitations were sent to members of the Irish Party. The old fissure between advanced republicanism and the parliamentarians, patched up by Parnell in 1879, had opened again. Not all who attended were Fenians, but all had the approval of the Fenians.

There was murky politics in all this. A provisional committee had been formed. It was protested by some that no permanent committee be elected until a wider corpus of advanced nationalist opinion in both Britain and Ireland had been canvassed. This view did not, however, prevail at the inaugural meeting. It was resolved instead that the notices and invitations already sent out in Ireland met the case sufficiently and thus backed the position of the existing provisional committee, which now became *de facto* the actual committee. And this committee comprising about a dozen Fenians now dominated most of what followed.

Centenary clubs were established all over nationalist Ireland. Within a few months, there were more than ten thousand members affiliated. There were accusations that elections to local sub-committees around the country were rigged in favour of Fenian elements, charges that were impossible to prove but were at least plausible. The net effect was to copper-fasten Fenian control and to minimize any significant Irish Party influence. But minimizing party influence was as much as the Fenians could do. The party, still split and not due to reunite for another two years, still commanded widespread public allegiance. It was the old story for the Fenians: they seldom had the numbers. The biggest single event of the centenary celebrations took place in Dublin on 15 August, attracting a crowd of over a hundred thousand people to witness the laying of a foundation stone for a statue of Wolfe Tone.* The Fenians were the organizers but the principal speeches were delivered by party MPs, whose standing with the nationalist public ensured that they could not be completely excluded.

Overall, however, the centenary commemoration of the 1798 rising redounded more to the credit of the Fenians and associated advanced nationalists than to the party. It gave advanced nationalism a badly needed shot in the arm and gave energy to a new generation of republican activists. It would be another eighteen years before the fruits of these endeavours would become visible, fruits which, had utterly unforeseen events not interposed, might never have ripened at all. But ripen they did; the 1916 rising had its roots in the centenary commemoration of 1898.

In the autumn of that year, just as the commemoration events were winding down, a young printer called Arthur Griffith returned from South Africa, where he had spent the previous eighteen months, partly for reasons of health. While there, he had edited a short-lived English-language newspaper, worked as a supervisor in a gold mine and become a determined champion of the Boer cause, which aimed at the separation of its two key states, Transvaal and the Orange Free State deep in the interior of the veldt, from British colonial rule. It was this demand that set off the second Boer War in 1899. Prior to going to South Africa, Griffith had embraced forms of radical nationalism. He may even have been a Fenian at one stage, and

---

* The statue was never built in situ; by a great irony, the proposed site at the north-west entrance to the park on St Stephen's Green is occupied by a memorial arch to the members of the Royal Dublin Fusiliers who fought in the second Boer War.

in general he inclined towards the advanced end of the nationalist spectrum.

Now returned to Ireland, he became a journalist and propagandist for the rest of his short life. He was too singular and independent a figure ever to be a party man, although ironically the party he did found in 1905, Sinn Féin, went through many mutations and became the 'brand' for republicanism after the 1916 rising. He set up his own newspaper, the *United Irishman*, in March 1899 and it quickly established itself as an influential voice, publishing contributions from a wide variety of talent, not least Yeats himself.

From the start, and unsurprisingly given his background, Griffith was pro-Boer and anti-war. While in South Africa, he had become friends with John MacBride, who had acquired the military rank of major while leading an Irish Brigade in support of the Boer rebels. The war divided opinion in Britain – Lloyd George made his name by his opposition – although, as usual, majority public opinion supported the troops. Not so in Ireland, where pro-Boer sentiment was easy to tap, and Griffith was in a good position to tap it.

Michael Davitt, who had been second only to Parnell in influence in the heyday of the Land League in the early 1880s, was by now an MP at Westminster, and he resigned his seat in opposition to the war. Griffith had the bright idea of running Major John MacBride as a pro-Boer candidate in the subsequent by-election, sponsored by a hastily assembled Transvaal Committee. MacBride was well beaten by the Irish Party candidate but it was a straw in the wind. Then, in April 1900, the aged Queen Victoria visited Dublin. Although she was generally well received, there was a vociferous advanced nationalist element which deplored her visit. Griffith wrote bitterly in opposition to the visit, seeing it, as so many advanced nationalists did, as a recruiting stunt for the war. Recruitment levels to the British army, previously high, had reduced during the 1890s: another straw in the wind?

The split between advanced and parliamentary nationalism was laid bare by the queen's visit. The party, at last reunited under the leadership of John Redmond, was part of the official welcome. Redmond even went so far as to praise the Irish troops in South Africa, while Griffith came to act as a journalistic focus for pro-Boer, anti-war sentiment. The British eventually won their shabby little war, as they were always bound to do, but it had all been a telling few years in Ireland. First, a rebellion against British rule a century past was celebrated before large and enthusiastic crowds; then, a degree of hostility to the South African war developed which had only a pale echo in Britain itself. That hostility was grounded not in a love of the Boers, about whom most Irish people knew next to nothing – Griffith, of course, being a distinguished exception to that rule – but outright hostility to what was seen as British imperialist bullying of a faraway people who simply wanted to be left alone to manage their own affairs according to their lights and desires.

The queen's visit was her fourth official appearance on Irish soil, the previous three occasions having been in 1849, 1853 and 1861, the last only months before the untimely death of Prince Albert. On the basis of contemporary reports, she had been welcomed enthusiastically on the three previous occasions, with little evidence of protests or rival ceremonies. One historian noted of the 1849 visit that the queen 'visited Ireland amid a display of popular enthusiasm', adding, however, 'this may not have been deep; nor should it be taken as evidence that Ireland was devoid of grievance'. While allowances may be made for an obsequious press and also for the fact that her itinerary was heavily weighted towards loyalist milieux, there is no evidence of any *organized* opposition to the royal visit available for the three visits prior to 1900.* Not so in 1900: the protesters may have been a minority, but they were a clamorous one, and they made their voices heard. By now, sedulous anti-royal propaganda had long since dubbed Victoria 'the Famine Queen', on the wholly false charge that, during that terrible time, she contributed only a nugatory sum – some versions said as little as £5 – from her own pocket towards Famine relief. In fact, she contributed £2,000 – roughly £60,000 in today's money – and she was also patron of a personal appeal for the relief of distress in Ireland and Scotland; this raised £170,000, of which five-sixths went to Ireland. However, it was the £5 story, largely a Fenian fiction, that was widely believed. It was believed because people wanted to believe it. They wanted to believe it because it dovetailed with the declining legitimacy of British rule in Ireland generally. As nationalism waxed, so did people's poor opinion of Britain, and especially of England. It suited the new mood to traduce the British monarch. In short, there was now a critical mass – a market – for sustained and organized protest. Thus the citizen in Barney Kiernan's, heard without objection.

In the same vein, the protests against the second Boer War were also part of this advancing nationalist consciousness.

---

* There is some evidence of protests, but nothing on any organized scale and each visit was subject to very high levels of security.

Britain had fought two other wars since the Great Famine, in the Crimea in 1854–6 and the first Boer War – really little more than a series of skirmishes, albeit it entailed one British military disaster at Majuba in 1881 – without any significant anti-war protests in Ireland and no falling-off in recruiting for the British army.* Again, this had changed by the time of the second Boer War. We have already noted a decline in Irish recruiting in the 1890s, with stories of off-duty soldiers being insulted and even spat at. But something momentous had changed in the course of the 1880s and '90s in Ireland, those most critical of decades. Both the GAA and the Gaelic League, in particular, had been established, with Fenian influence all over the former and never far away in the latter. There was a growing sense that British wars and British royalty had nothing to do with the real Ireland – as decided by ideologues – when we had risings and rebellions of our own to celebrate.

It is important not to exaggerate. This was all the work of a committed and at times fanatical minority. But they had a fertile field in which to sow. The ever-diminishing acceptance of British legitimacy was their fertile soil. By 1900, everyone in nationalist Ireland knew that the British presence in Ireland was going to be diminished or diluted in some manner, through whatever measure of home rule could eventually be agreed.

---

* In the Crimean War, about seven thousand Irish troops died. At the Charge of the Light Brigade, 114 of the 673 men who charged down the wrong valley – the whole thing was a total balls-up – were Irish. Of the 118 killed, 21 were Irish. Of the 127 wounded, 21 were Irish. Of the 45 taken prisoner, 7 were Irish. In 1856, when the troops came back to Dublin, a huge banquet was thrown for them in a tobacco warehouse on the Liffey quays. As they marched down the quays to dinner, they were cheered by an enthusiastic crowd.

Only on the wilder shores of Fenianism was there any serious talk of outright republican separation, but that seed too fell upon the ground, later to germinate. Nor can it be forgotten that when the great European war came in 1914, over two hundred thousand Irishmen enlisted in the British colours and about thirty-five thousand died. The war split the nationalist consensus, with the advanced element – Fenians and all – very much in the minority. But they were the minority who made all the difference in the end.

What they had succeeded in doing was to create in the public mind, or at least a potent fraction of it, the feeling that it was an illegitimate act to support Britain in wartime. Ireland, on this analysis, had no dog in the British fight. That feeling was confined, for the moment, to an advanced minority. But at Easter 1916, their hour struck and nothing was ever the same again, or could be. When the great European war ended in 1918, demobbed Irish veterans returned to an often frosty if not downright hostile welcome. It was a new world, with a new locus of public virtue.

THE SEEDS SOWN in 1898 had taken twenty years to come to harvest. That they did so was a matter of fluke as much as anything else. As usual, what actually happened would have seemed utterly improbable to any observer at the starting point in the process. Nobody in nationalist Ireland took Ulster protests against home rule seriously, but they turned out to be very serious indeed, to the point not only of succeeding but along the way seducing the Conservative Party – that party of throne, altar and tradition – to behaviour that can only be called treasonous. There were far-sighted people, not many but enough, who feared that sooner or later a major war would break out between the European powers. But no one anticipated that the war which eventually came would be as catastrophic as it was, so that it was remembered by contemporaries simply as the Great War. Above all, no one apart from the conspirators who tripped it off could have imagined the Easter Rising of 1916. This conjunction of random events, which were both related and unrelated, provided the crucible in which what actually happened, happened.

While there were accidents and unforeseen hazards along the way, the direction of travel was clear. Nationalist Ireland was loosening its ties to England.

BACK IN 1898, before any of this occurred, what was the state of the Union? The Liberals were formally committed to home rule, but were unlikely to touch that hot potato unless they needed Irish Party support in the House of Commons, as had happened in 1885. This is indeed what happened after 1910 and a home rule act was actually passed at last, but just in time to be suspended for the duration of World War I, by the end of which the transformed situation in Ireland after 1916 and all that had rendered it a dead letter. But at least the Liberals were open to some degree of devolved autonomy. The Tories were not, preferring corporal works of mercy – killing home rule with kindness – as an antidote to any fundamental constitutional change.

So, in a sense, both great British parties were, in their different ways, reconciled to the Irish difference. Whatever else, Ireland could no longer be governed according to standard 'mainland' rules. This much had been implicit in all the shifts of

British position since the Famine, from the state inserting itself into the private property market with the Encumbered Estates Acts and the various land acts down to the special measures designed to kill home rule with kindness in the 1890s. At the same time, Ireland was not just a passive petri dish for British social and economic experimentation. From Parnell's time onwards, organized nationalism – both its political and cultural iterations – was an active factor in the equation.

This active nationalism, comprising different strands and emphases but always tending in the same direction, is what disappointed the Tories' corporal works of mercy. They could build all the harbours they liked in the west of Ireland, or a tangle of hopelessly uneconomic narrow-gauge railways; they could give public support in the form of development grants for farming, fishing or domestic piecework. It made no difference. Nationalism was not going away. It may have seemed so, as political nationalism was utterly demoralized in the 1890s after the trauma of the Parnell split, but there was much that was concealed from the casual gaze. As we have already seen, the cultural revival was shot through with politics, and with Fenian politics at that. Too much had happened in Ireland in twenty years to stuff the genie back in the bottle.

The best proof of this was the Local Government (Ireland) Act 1898. This finally abolished the old system of local grand juries – dominated as they were by ascendancy landowners – and introduced representative local authorities voted in by popular franchise. This democratization of local government was designed to apply the English and Welsh system of local government to Ireland, as a demonstration of both the benignity and efficiency of British rule. It was recognized as neither:

the new local authorities became forcing houses for budding nationalist politicians – the local franchise ensured nationalist majorities – and many of the men who came to rule the Irish Free State after 1922 got their starts on these new local authorities. The increased activity at local level was also a factor in ending the split in the Irish Party in 1900. For the unionist interest in Ireland, it was a further blow, diminishing their local influence even more and providing at least some of the psychological background to the swift settlement of the land issue in 1903. In short, the unionist game was up – and it was a Conservative administration that had accomplished this state of affairs. They had done so for a short-term reason: a Financial Relations Report had discovered that Ireland was over-taxed by £2.75 million a year, something which united Irish nationalists and unionists at Westminster in a rare show of unanimity. The government bought off the nationalists by the Local Government Act, with insufficient safeguards for the old ascendancy interest, and the unionists with a rates subsidy.

FOR THE BEST part of twenty years, the marginal if noisy elements in Irish nationalism that opposed the Boer War, discouraged army recruiting and protested the visit of Queen Victoria, seemed fated to remain marginal. The Irish Party maintained its electoral hegemony and finally got home rule onto the statute books in 1914. It was immediately suspended because of the outbreak of World War I, and the war changed everything. Without the war, no Easter Rising in 1916. Without the rising, we have no idea what would have eventuated.

The rising was a Fenian conspiracy. A nationalist militia, the Irish Volunteers, had been formed in 1913, ostensibly to defend home rule, although against whom was not entirely clear. The Irish Party secured formal control of the Volunteers but a Fenian minority remained hostile to party control. A minority of those Fenians formed a military council and it was they who tripped off the rising. The leaders were executed in short order once it was all over, and this started to swing public sympathy. Sinn Féin, which had nothing to do with the rising, became associated with it in British eyes and the association stuck in the public mind.

The rising has been seen ever after as a foundation moment. Even today, in the nationalist imagination, 1916 is year zero. Irish nationalism – the desire to be shot of English rule – long antedated the days when the leaders of the rising walked out to execution in the Stonebreakers' Yard in Kilmainham Gaol. But those deaths, collectively, represented Ireland's Bastille moment, its Winter Palace moment, its Gettysburg. An old order died and a new world, our world, was born.

Then conscription was introduced in Britain, to compensate for the horrific war losses on the Western Front. It was thought expedient to exclude Ireland from the scheme, a wise reckoning. But the further awful losses at Passchendaele in the autumn of 1917 and in response to the German spring offensive of 1918 caused the government, now headed by Lloyd George, to revisit the issue. In April 1918, the Military Services Act became law. The Irish Party immediately withdrew from Westminster in protest and returned to Ireland. There they made common cause with every element in nationalist civil society. This withdrawal left the party in an awkward position relative to the revived Sinn Féiners, who had already proclaimed their policy of abstention from Westminster. The public might well wonder why it should continue to support a party that had just conceded Sinn Féin's abstentionist point when it could support the real thing, and the process whereby Sinn Féin supplanted the Irish Party as the principal nationalist voice stems from this moment.

The threat of conscription united all shades of nationalist opinion in opposition to it, including – very significantly – the Catholic Church hierarchy, usually hesitant to commit itself to an 'advanced' position. A pledge to oppose conscription was signed by nearly two million people throughout the country on 21 April: it had been drafted by Éamon de Valera, the leader of the revived Sinn Féin. There was a general strike on the 23rd. There were demonstrations. It became clear to the government that any attempt to enforce the conscription law would result in massive civil disobedience and violence. Instead it funked the issue. By the time the war ended in November, conscription in Ireland had been overtaken by events.

Conscription was the issue that, more than any other, united nationalist Ireland. In the general election of 1918, Sinn Féin duly got its reward, sweeping the Irish Party aside. The course was set for the four revolutionary years that followed: the armed rebellion against British rule; the destruction of the British security system; partition of the island because of the intractable Ulster question; and eventually the securing for twenty-six of the thirty-two counties what was effectively independence.

That independence had been declared in 1918 in the most unambiguous manner possible. When a country is engaged in an existential struggle, as Britain was in the war, and a large, identifiable part of its population simply refuses to fight, it is declaring that it no longer considers itself part of that country.

Nationalist Ireland's relationship to the United Kingdom had always been ambiguous – to put it mildly – but the anti-conscription mobilization is the moment when all ambiguity is cast aside. If you won't fight your country's wars, you are no longer of that country. And so it was with Ireland. It took the twists and turns of the next few years to resolve everything, but the spring of 1918 is the moment of *non serviam*, when Ireland declares that whatever it is, it is not British.

CONCLUSION

—⋙⋘—

STILL THE STONE
IN YOUR SHOE

S

O, NATIONALIST IRELAND is not British. It asserted this reality in the most decisive way in the few years following the conscription crisis. Sinn Féin, under the leadership of Éamon de Valera, pushed the old Irish Party to one side in the general election of 1918; it then declined to attend Westminster, instead setting up its own parliament in Dublin, Dáil Éireann. There followed a short but nasty Anglo-Irish war, followed by a peace treaty, followed in turn by a short civil war which the supporters of the treaty – the new Irish government – won. In the meantime, the island had been partitioned. The six north-eastern counties – about two-thirds of the province of Ulster – became Northern Ireland, constitutionally a part of the United Kingdom. The rest of the island gradually mutated into what is now the Republic of Ireland.

Then came the forty-odd years of the big sleep. England did what it had been historically good at and forgot all about Ireland

– both bits of it. Except for a brief trade spat in the 1930s, it forgot all about the south. By a hastily invented convention, it left the north to its own devices, meaning that the local unionist majority could do as they pleased without any vulgar scrutiny from Westminster. This the unionists, believing themselves to be the *echt volk*, did with tribal gusto.

The Republic embraced economic protectionism in the 1930s. It made some sense in the short run but was persisted in for far too long. It was abandoned in the 1960s and Ireland belatedly joined the post-war free-trade boom. It was a time of innocent optimism generally – *les trente glorieuses* to the music of the Beach Boys – and things were materially improving. But then the serpent reappeared in the Irish garden: the troubles revived in the north. It took thirty years of civic misery, all in the service of futile dreams, before a patched-up peace was agreed in 1998.

One thing the troubles underscored was the continuing importance of religion as a marker of allegiance in Ireland. Now confined to Northern Ireland – the south has abandoned the Catholic Church in huge numbers, revolted by serial cases of clerical sexual abuse of minors in its care and other crimes – it none the less remains potent. In the south, few care about confessional affiliation any more. The state behaves far more like a classic civic republic. But in the north, it is still the Prods against the Taigues.

Distance continued to matter, especially where the north was concerned. Remember that distance from Charing Cross to Dungannon (p. 34, chapter 2). So, when Northern Ireland blew up in 1968 and '69, various hapless proconsuls were despatched from London to see if they could quieten the place down, which they could not. One of the early ones, Reginald

Maudling – a Tory politician, then home secretary, remembered afterwards more for corruption and fondness for whisky* than for anything else – spent a day there in 1970. He had his ear thoroughly bashed all day by complainants, supplicants and grievance-mongers of every stripe. Finally boarding his RAF flight to take him back to civilization, he slumped in his seat, barking, 'For God's sake bring me a large Scotch. What a bloody awful country.'

Indeed, it was a faraway country of which they knew little and cared less, yet they were the sovereign power.

In the meantime, the modernization of the Republic proceeded with the expansion of its middle class, especially from the 1960s. Because of a mixture of political incompetence, corruption and economic bad luck, the next two decades were largely a time of retreat. Then, in the 1990s, came the turnaround, with the roar of the Celtic Tiger. Even allowing for the catastrophic crash of 2008, Ireland in the 2020s is as unlike Ireland in the 1950s as it is possible to imagine: social and economic advances previously thought impossible (indeed, thought to be beneath thought itself) have been accomplished.

The so-called 'armed struggle' in the north achieved nothing more than the moral pollution of both communities. When the peace was patched up, the IRA had achieved none of its key strategic objectives: the island was still partitioned and Britain was still the sovereign power. What *had* changed in the north was something utterly unexpected, which had matured during the maelstrom of the troubles. A self-confident, commercially

---

* The political journalist Alan Watkins recalls in his memoir asking Maudling what kind of whisky he liked, only to be told 'a large one'.

and educationally successful Catholic middle class formed itself and now plays a critical part in Northern Ireland's civic and economic life. That's the reversal of an ancient, vicious stereotype. This came first through the extension of free secondary schooling to Catholics under the 1947 Education Act;* second, through the series of British legislative and security reforms prompted by the civil rights campaigns of the late 1960s. So both parts of the island, in their different circumstances, have felt the breath of bourgeois virtue.

Which brings us – *terminus ad quem* – to Brexit.

The Northern Ireland peace agreements were rickety, but enough of them just about held together to stop most of the killings. The paramilitaries did not entirely disappear, merely redeploying their talents as agents of the drugs trade, especially on the loyalist side. There were still 'peace walls' to segregate the more peppery tribal elements. Northern Ireland remained in many respects a place conditioned to mental apartheid.

Formal politics was horribly difficult, with the two tribal extremes now thrown together in a kind of local government. One of the really malign outcomes of the peace deals had been the marginalization of political moderation on both sides, leaving the extremes in charge. How could Ian Paisley's successor party, the Democratic Unionists, God-bothering standard bearers for the *echt volk*, find common ground with Sinn Féin, ventriloquists for the IRA? That they managed even as little as they did for a few years was remarkable.

This was the porcelain-delicate politics into which Brexit

---

* An act opposed, with complete predictability, by the tribunes of the *echt volk*, determined if they could to keep their indigenes ignorant.

threw a large hammer. It was the old story. The Brexiteers were not paying attention to anything beyond their limited, provincial range: not to Scotland; not to the intelligence and youth of their own community; and certainly not to Northern Ireland, or Ireland in general for all that. And yet Ireland was so obviously material in the context of *any* arrangement required to detach the UK from the EU.

It has been a tale long in the telling by now, and depressing. The Brexit enthusiasts will say that it does not really matter, just a little collateral damage below the horizon. Well, there is no inherent harm in Ireland being below the English mental horizon – we hardly expect them to be fussing over us morning, noon and night. But it is reasonable to expect expertise and a sharp eye for what matters when there are adult concerns in play, concerns that can get people killed. There was none of that expert eye, or not enough of it. Everything, including careless forgetting, is bought at a price. It is rather difficult to put porcelain back together again once it has been shattered.

REFERENCES

Introduction

p. 1   'Still, the bigger island has hung together through thick and thin': The standard analysis of this phenomenon, broadly accepted by scholars, is Linda Colley, *Britons*.

p. 4–5   'But the earliest Irish-language version of the New Testament did not appear until 1603': Entry by Nicholas J.A. Williams in Lalor, ed., *Encyclopaedia of Ireland*, pp. 91–2.

p. 5   'anything printed in Ireland before 1700 can be classed as "rare"': Craig, *Dublin 1660–1860*, p. 81.

p. 5   'Contrast this with the continental core... the first Italian press': Hale, *The Civilization of Europe in the Renaissance*, p. 6.

p. 5   'By the mid-eighteenth century': Darnton, *George Washington's False Teeth*, p. 83.

p. 8   'As late as 1690, nearly a hundred years after O'Neill's rebellion': Bardon, *A History of Ireland in 250 Episodes*, p. 225.

1: Faith and Fatherland

p. 16   'the most dangerous nuclear situation': Dick Kerr, CIA officer, quoted in Hersh, *Reporter: A Memoir*, p. 275.

p. 17   'Estimates of fatalities are problematic': Wilson, *Europe's Tragedy: A History of the Thirty Years War*, p. 787.

p. 18   'In Elizabethan Ireland... the Protestant Reformation became fatally identified': MacCulloch, *A History of Christianity: The First Three Thousand Years*, p. 670. A similar point is emphasized in his *Reformation*, p. 394.

2: It's a Long Way to Tipperary

p. 36   'In extenuation, it's worth noting': Bardon, *A Narrow Sea*, p. 108.

p. 42   'as remote and inaccessible to the English as "the kingdom of China"': Bardon, op. cit., p. 105.

3: Half In and Half Out

p. 52   'In 1500 the taming of the physical environment': Colm Lennon, *Sixteenth-Century Ireland: The Incomplete Conquest*, Dublin: Gill & Macmillan, 1994, p. 1.

p. 53   'What shall we do for timber? / The last of the woods is down': 'Lament for Kilcash' by Frank O'Connor, in Michael Steinman, ed., *A Frank O'Connor Reader*, Syracuse: Syracuse University Press, 1994, pp. 235–6.

p. 57   'Moreover, there was *mal de mer* to cope with': Ó Siochrú, *God's Executioner*, p. 79.

p. 57   'the cost of defeating O'Neill': Bardon, *The Plantation of Ulster*, p. 53.

p. 62   'God bless the king': Quoted in Chenevix Trench, *Grace's Card*, p. 34.

p. 63   'A crucial element in this project': Colin Jones, *The Great Nation: France from Louis XV to Napoleon, 1715–99*, London: Allen Lane, 2002, pp. 92–3.

p. 63   'There were other, less formal, connections': McBride, *Eighteenth-Century Ireland*, pp. 228, 246.

4: Jackie Goes to Ballybay

p. 66   'Theobald Wolfe Tone was one of the most remarkable': Barrington, *Personal Sketches*, pp. 110–11.

p. 67–8 'The result of the rebellions of 1798': The best account of the Wexford rising is Gahan, *The People's Rising*; that of the Ulster rising, Stewart, *The Summer Soldiers*.

p. 69   'It is a churlish soil': Letters from Drennan to Samuel McTier and William Bruce, quoted in an essay by Ian McBride in Dickson, Keogh and Whelan, eds, *The United Irishmen*, pp. 60–61.

p. 79   'He represented himself to the electors of Clare': The best modern biography of O'Connell is Patrick Geoghegan's two-volume work, which deals with the events of the Clare election in vol. 1, titled *King Dan*, p. 248ff.

p. 79   'energies [were] directed... You have heard the tones': Oliver MacDonagh, *The Hereditary Bondsman: Daniel O'Connell 1771–1829*, London: Weidenfeld & Nicolson, 1988, pp. 250, 254.

p. 83   'I cannot say that Lawless ever': O'Connell to a correspondent in 1830, quoted in the entry on Lawless in *Dictionary of Irish Biography*.

5: Gallant Allies in Europe?

p. 89–90 'were a constant reminder': James Hawes, *The Shortest History of Germany*, London: Old Street Publishing, 2017, p. 49.

p. 103   'Foremost among these Romans': McBride, op. cit., p. 229.

6: The Empty Centre

p. 105   'In 1842, William Makepeace Thackeray was in Cork.' All references to Thackeray in this chapter are from his *Irish Sketchbook*, in particular pp. 79–85.

p. 108   'Seven years before Thackeray was in Ireland, Alexis de Tocqueville was here': All references to de Tocqueville are taken from Larkin, ed., *Alexis de Tocqueville in Ireland*, in particular pp. 87–8.

p. 110   'The population started to grow around 1780': The best summary of pre-Famine population growth is in Ó Gráda, *Ireland: A New Economic History 1780–1939*, p. 67.

p. 111   'The cause was simple: diet': Mokyr, *Why Ireland Starved*, p. 6ff.

p. 111   'A statistical estimate of male heights': Ó Gráda, op. cit., pp. 21–2.

p. 112   'That growing population was a net growth': Ó Gráda, op. cit., p. 74.

p. 113   'Masses of refuse, offal and sickening filth': Quoted in Francis Wheen, *Karl Marx*, pp. 81–2.

p. 117   'A survey of industrial capacity in the British Isles in 1871': Ó Gráda, op. cit., p. 352.

p. 118   'By the time of independence, in 1922, Ireland had pretty much universal literacy': Tobin, *The Best of Decades*, 169–70, based on a summary of 'Investment in Education', a government-sponsored review of secondary-level education in the Republic of Ireland, supported by the OECD (1966).

p. 122   'Between 1955 and 1957': Tobin, op. cit., pp. 4–5.

p. 127   'No Irish farmer appreciates his young strapping son': Kevin O'Nolan, ed., *The Best of Myles: A Selection From 'Cruiskeen Lawn'*, London: Picador, 1977, p. 39.

7: Looking Down on Inistioge

p. 134   'I have lived for most of my life on the Nore': Butler, *Escape from the Anthill*, p. 88.

p. 138   'troops of slatternly, ruffian-looking fellows': Thackeray, *Irish Sketchbook*, pp. 38–9.

p. 138 'most picturesquely situated': Ibid., p. 43.

p. 139 'Imagine four walls of dried mud': De Beaumont, *Ireland*, pp. 128–9.

p. 140 'And that's why the pitch at The Rower-Inistioge': The fullest account of the decline of hurling in Co. Kilkenny, only summarized here, is given in Siggins and Lewis, eds, *100 Not Out: The History of Cricket in Leinster*, Dublin: Cricket Leinster, 2019, p. 383, which in turn acknowledges its source as M. O'Dwyer, *The History of Cricket in Co. Kilkenny*, n.p., 2006.

p. 141 'This account is based on his granddaughter's memoir': Iris Origo, *Images and Shadows: Part of a Life*, p. 40ff.

p. 142 'Otway Cuffe was Ham's younger brother': Much of this material is based on the essay 'Anglo-Irish Twilight' in Butler, op. cit., p. 83ff.

8: Encumbered Estates

p. 155 'There are Catholic inns': Thackeray, op. cit., p. 34.

p. 156 'I am not, nor ever have been': David Herbert Donald, *Lincoln*, New York: Simon & Schuster, 1995, p. 221.

9: Disestablishment

p. 165 'Article 5 of the act stated': O'Day and Stevenson, *Irish Historical Documents Since 1800*, pp. 6–10.

p. 165–6 'a holy man, whom God has not overwhelmed with work': De Tocqueville, *Journey in Ireland*, p. 11.

p. 168 'In all, over 43,000 decrees were issued': Hickey and Doherty, *A New Dictionary of Irish History from 1800*, p. 469. Other statistics concerning the Tithe War from the same source.

10: Of Man's First Disobedience

p. 182 'In opposing it, Biggar droned': Bardon, *History of Ulster*, p. 360.

p. 184 'He was barely a year in parliament before he made his mark': Lyons, *Parnell*, p. 54.

p. 188 'What kind of a name is that?': James Joyce, *Portrait of the Artist as a Young Man*, first published 1916, London: Vintage, 2005, p. 5.

p. 191 '[We] will never gain anything from England': Lyons, op. cit., pp. 32, 63, 105–6.

11: The Association

p. 195   'It was founded in the billiard room': The standard history of the
          GAA is de Búrca, *The GAA*. A useful book tracing the influence of
          the young association is W.F. Mandle, *The Gaelic Athletic Association
          and Irish Nationalist Politics*.

p. 200   'In Tuam, for example': All references to Tuam, Co. Galway, in
          connection with the GAA are taken from a remarkable book by
          the late Noel O'Donoghue, *Proud and Upright Men*, privately
          published. To the best of my knowledge, no commercial edition
          was ever published – a shameful omission – although it appears
          that copies are occasionally available from the ubiquitous
          Amazon, although not at the time of this writing.

p. 203   'In Dublin, the number of men employed in manufacturing':
          Dickson, *Dublin*, pp. 344–5.

p. 206   'In 1908, there were 26 clubs affiliated in Kilkenny': de Búrca,
          GAA, pp. 73, 161.

12: The Necessity for De-Anglicising the Irish People

p. 210   'In the first decade of the century, there were 27,000 titles with
          London imprints': Feather, *A History of British Publishing*, p. 98.

p. 212   'This failure of the Irish people': The full text of Hyde's address is
          available at https://www.thefuture.ie/wp-content/uploads/1892/11/
          1892-11-25-The-Necessity-for-De-Anglicising-Ireland.pdf and is
          discussed in Dunleavy and Dunleavy, *Hyde*, p. 183ff.

p. 213–14 'Although a native speaker of Irish': Geoghegan, *Liberator*, p. 9.

p. 214   'Parnell was no Catholic': In his preface to *Enigma*, Paul Bew
          mentions that most people thought Parnell veered from
          agnosticism to mainstream Anglicanism with a soft spot for
          Catholicism, but adds intriguingly that Tim Healy believed that
          there was a streak of Plymouth Brethren in him, that sect enjoying
          some purchase among contemporary gentry in Co. Wicklow.
          Bew, *Enigma*, p. xii.

p. 217   'The horror with which many intellectuals and literary novelists
          regarded this new mass culture': This phenomenon is given its
          fullest analysis in John Carey, *The Intellectuals and the Masses: Pride
          and Prejudice Among the Literary Intelligentsia 1880–1939*,
          London: Faber & Faber, 1992.

p. 223–4 'We are in a life and death struggle with England': Anna MacBride
          White and A. Norman Jeffares, eds, *The Gonne–Yeats Letters
          1893–1938*, New York: W.W. Norton & Co., 1994, p. 178.

p. 229   'The tide is rising': Letter from Hyde to Colonel Maurice Moore, October 1903, quoted in Dunleavy and Dunleavy, *Hyde*, p. 298.

13: The Death of Cromwell

p. 241   'By the time of the creation of the Irish Free State in 1922': Bull, *Land, Politics and Nationalism*, p. 177; Lee, *Ireland 1912–85*, p. 71.

p. 244   'In 1886, at the height of Parnell's power and influence': O'Donoghue, op. cit., p. 36.

14: Cyclops

p. 252   'According to the most authoritative modern history of the city': Dickson, op. cit., p. 152.

p. 252   'In the 1960s, when a frenzy of new-money development': Quoted in Frank McDonald, *The Destruction of Dublin*, Dublin: Gill & Macmillan, 1985, p. 17.

p. 255   'Into the back yard of each house': Reports of Rev. James Whitelaw (1805) quoted in Richard Killeen, *Historic Atlas of Dublin*, Dublin: Gill & Macmillan, 2009, pp. 114–15.

p. 257   'The historian Peter Gay': Peter Gay, *Schnitzler's Century: The Making of Middle-Class Culture 1815–1914*, London: Allen Lane, 2001, p. 9ff.

15: We Don't Want to Fight…

p. 267   'One historian noted of the 1849 visit': Boyce, *Nineteenth-Century Ireland*, p. 130.

SELECT BIBLIOGRAPHY

Reference Works

Connolly, S.J., *Oxford Companion to Irish History*, Oxford: Oxford University
Press, 1998

Hickey, D.J. and Doherty, J.E., *A New Dictionary of Irish History from 1800*,
Dublin: Gill & Macmillan, 2003

Lalor, Brian, ed., *Encyclopaedia of Ireland*, Dublin: Gill & Macmillan, 2003

McGuire, James and Quinn, James, eds, *Dictionary of Irish Biography*, 9 vols
and 2 supplements, Cambridge: Cambridge University Press, 2009,
2018

O'Day, Alan and Stevenson, John, eds, *Irish Historical Documents since 1800*,
Dublin: Gill & Macmillan, 1992

Other Works Consulted

Bardon, Jonathan, *A History of Ireland in 250 Episodes*, Dublin: Gill &
Macmillan, 2008

_____, *A History of Ulster*, Belfast: Blackstaff Press, 1992

_____, *The Plantation of Ulster*, Dublin: Gill & Macmillan, 2011

_____, *A Narrow Sea*, Dublin: Gill, 2018

Barrington, Jonah, *Personal Sketches and Recollections of His Own Time*, first
published 1872, Dublin: Ashfield Press, 1997

Bartlett, Thomas, *Ireland: A History*, Cambridge: Cambridge University
Press, 2010

Bew, Paul, *Ireland: The Politics of Enmity 1789–2006*, Oxford: Oxford
University Press, 2007

_____, *Enigma: A New Life of Charles Stewart Parnell*, Dublin: Gill &
Macmillan, 2011

Boyce, George, *Nineteenth-Century Ireland*, Dublin: Gill & Macmillan,
2005

Bull, Philip, *Land, Politics & Nationalism*, Dublin: Gill & Macmillan, 1996

Bourke, Richard and McBride, Ian, eds, *The Princeton History of Modern
Ireland*, Princeton: Princeton University Press, 2016

Butler, Hubert, *Escape from the Anthill*, Dublin: Lilliput Press, 1986

Chenevix Trench, Charles, *Grace's Card: Irish Catholic Landlords 1690–1800*, Cork: Mercier Press, 1977

Colley, Linda, *Britons: Forging the Nation 1707–1837*, New Haven: Yale University Press, 1992

Comerford, R.V., *Ireland: Inventing the Nation*, London: Hodder Arnold, 2003

Craig, Maurice, *Dublin 1660–1860*, Dublin: Allen Figgis, 1969

Darnton, Robert, *George Washington's False Teeth*, New York: W.W. Norton & Co., 2003

De Beaumont, Gustave, *Ireland: Social, Political and Religious*, first published 1839, Cambridge, MA: Belknap Press, 2006

De Búrca, Marcus, *The GAA: A History*, 2nd ed., Dublin: Gill & Macmillan, 1999

Dickson, David, *Dublin: The Making of a Capital City*, London: Profile, 2014

Dickson, David, Keogh, Dáire and Whelan, Kevin, eds, *The United Irishmen*, Dublin: Lilliput Press, 1993

Dunleavy, J.E. and Dunleavy, G.W., *Douglas Hyde: A Maker of Modern Ireland*, Berkeley/Los Angeles/Oxford: University of California Press, 1991

Feather, John, *A History of British Publishing*, 2nd ed., London: Routledge, 2006

Ferriter, Diarmaid, *The Transformation of Ireland*, London: Profile Books, 2004

Foster, Roy, *Modern Ireland 1600–1972*, London: Allen Lane, 1988

———, *Vivid Faces: The Revolutionary Generation in Ireland 1890–1923*, London: Allen Lane, 2014

Gahan, Daniel, *The People's Rising: Wexford 1798*, Dublin: Gill & Macmillan, 1995

Garvin, Tom, *Nationalist Revolutionaries in Ireland*, Oxford: Clarendon Press, 1987

Geoghegan, Patrick, *King Dan: The Rise of Daniel O'Connell*, Dublin: Gill & Macmillan, 2008

———, *Liberator: The Life and Death of Daniel O'Connell*, Dublin: Gill & Macmillan, 2010

Hale, John, *The Civilization of Europe in the Renaissance*, London: HarperCollins, 1993

Hersh, Seymour, *Reporter: A Memoir*, London: Allen Lane, 2018

Hoppen, K. Theodore, *Elections, Politics and Society in Ireland 1832–1885*, Oxford, Clarendon Press, 1984

Howe, Stephen, *Ireland and Empire*, Oxford: Oxford University Press, 2000

Jackson, Alvin, *Ireland 1798–1998*, Oxford: Blackwell, 1999

_____, *Home Rule: An Irish History 1800–2000*, London: Weidenfeld & Nicolson, 2003

Larkin, Emmet, ed. and trans., *Alexis de Tocqueville's Journey in Ireland*, Dublin: Wolfhound Press, 1990

Lee, Joseph, *The Modernisation of Irish Society 1849–1918*, rev. ed., Dublin: Gill & Macmillan, 2008

Lydon, James, *The Making of Ireland*, London: Routledge, 1998

Lyons, F.S.L., *Charles Stewart Parnell*, New York: Oxford University Press, 1977

_____, *Ireland Since the Famine*, London: Weidenfeld & Nicolson, 1971

McBride, Ian, *Eighteenth-Century Ireland*, Dublin: Gill & Macmillan, 2009

MacCulloch, Diarmaid, *Reformation: Europe's House Divided 1479–1700*, London: Allen Lane, 2003

MacDonagh, Oliver, *States of Mind*, London: Allen & Unwin, 1983

McGee, Owen, *The IRB*, Dublin: Four Courts Press, 2005

Mandle, W.F., *The Gaelic Athletic Association & Irish Nationalist Politics 1884–1924*, Bromley: Helm, 1987

Mansergh, Nicholas, *The Irish Question 1840–1921*, London: Allen & Unwin, 1965

Mokyr, Joel, *Why Ireland Starved*, London: Allen & Unwin, 1985

Moody, T.M., ed., *The Fenian Movement*, Cork: Mercier Press, 1968

O'Brien, Conor Cruise, *States of Ireland*, London: Hutchinson, 1972

_____, *Passion and Cunning*, London: Weidenfeld & Nicolson, 1988

O'Donoghue, Noel, *Proud and Upright Men*, n.p., n.d.

Ó Gráda, Cormac, *Ireland: A New Economic History 1780–1939*, Oxford: Clarendon Press, 1994

Origo, Iris, *Images and Shadows: Part of a Life*, London: John Murray, 1970

Ó Siochrú, Micheál, *God's Executioner: Oliver Cromwell and the Conquest of Ireland*, London: Faber & Faber, 2008

Pearce, Edward, *Lines of Most Resistance*, London: Little, Brown, 1999

Stewart, A.T.Q., *The Summer Soldiers: The 1798 Rebellion in Antrim and Down*, Belfast: Blackstaff Press, 1995

Thackeray, W.M., *The Irish Sketchbook*, first published 1843, Dublin: Gill & Macmillan, 1990

Tobin, Fergal, *The Best of Decades: Ireland in the 1960s*, Dublin: Gill & Macmillan, 1984

Townshend, Charles, *Easter 1916: The Irish Rebellion*, London: Allen Lane, 2005

Wheen, Francis, *Karl Marx*, London: Fourth Estate, 1999

Wilson, Peter, *Europe's Tragedy: A History of the Thirty Years War*, London: Allen Lane, 2009

PICTURE CREDITS

INDEX